S0-BOE-771

KNOWLEDGE MOBILIZATION IN THE SOCIAL SCIENCES AND HUMANITIES
MOVING FROM RESEARCH TO ACTION

By Alex Bennet and David Bennet
Mountain Quest Institute

With
Katherine Fafard, Marc Fonda, Ted Lomond,
Laurent Messier and Nicole Vaugeois

Foreward by Francisco Javier Carrillo

In cooperation with
The Social Sciences and Humanities
Research Council of Canada (SSHRC)

MQI PRESS
Knowledge Series

Copyright © 2007 **MQI PRESS**. All rights reserved.
In the spirit of collaborative advantage, with attribution,
any part of this book may be copied and distributed freely.
To keep **MQI PRESS** publishing, donations are welcome.

MQI PRESS
Knowledge Series

Frost, West Virginia
RR 2, Box 109, Marlinton, WV 24954
United States of America
Telephone: 304-799-7267
Fax: 304-799-0861
Email: dbennet@mountainquestinstitute.com
www.mountainquestinstitute.com

ISBN: 9780979845901
Graphic design: www.inkfish-design.com
Print: Gráfica Maiadouro S.A., Portugal

CONTENTS

FIGURES

*"A little knowledge that acts
is worth infinitely more
than much knowledge that is idle."*

Kahlil Gibran (1883-1931)

FOREWARD

by Francisco Javier Carrillo [1]

While Evolutionism as a scientific theory has contributed to making humans aware that we share biological roots with the rest of Nature, Globalism as a world perspective has contributed to making us conscious that we share a planetary future with all life on Earth. That future looks increasingly grim, as evidence on biosphere disruptions, climate changes and ecosystem imbalances resulting from human action, as well as on the associated environmental and social impacts, becomes substantial. Particularly on the social front, we are far from foreseeing and being prepared for the challenges posed by today's global dynamics.

What sort of changes, what kind of knowledge is required to confront this unprecedented challenge to mankind? It is evident enough that both changes in individual behavior that have environmental impacts as well as changes in cultural and political frameworks that breed them are required. It may be less evident that in order to accomplish those changes our understanding of collective human behavior and our capacity to manage it are key factors. Knowledge about ourselves and the ability to innovate social organization at local and global scales are at the core of human destiny.

Enter Knowledge Mobilization as a powerful methodological framework and action program, and the relevance and timing of this book becomes evident. Alex and David Bennet shed new light on the social knowledge cycle, recognizing all significant agents and processes of a knowledge value system. While doing so, they show awareness of the complex interweaving of both highly institutional (e.g., universities and government) and highly self-organizing (e.g., communities and networks) agents and processes. But the conceptual sophistication required to incorporate advanced contemporary theories does not prevent them from focusing into what is primordial: social improvement. While it is arguable whether knowledge is or is not necessarily action-laden, when it is it leads directly to what Peter Drucker wisely saw as the core of management: committing current actions with future value outcomes. In the end, this connection between knowledge and social value is what matters from the perspective of collective well-being.

Under this perspective, an evolutionary path for Knowledge Management emerges. Such a path moves along the capacity to fully incorporate advancements from the Social Sciences into the theoretical, methodological and technical frameworks of social value delivery. Conversely, since KM is dealing primordially with the "intangible" or "intellectual" dimensions of social value, it belongs naturally into the explanatory and technical realm of the social sciences. KMb is a leading example of capitalizing social science theory and methods into KM practice. This is an impressive collection and innovative array of concepts, methods and tools that is

---

1 Professor of Knowledge Systems at the *Tecnologico de Monterrey*, México, and Chairman, *The World Capital Institute*

at the same time sensible and pragmatic to serve the purpose of putting the best of existing and emerging human knowledge at the service of creating social value.

A knowledge society basically means one conceived, designed and evolving according to the value dynamics of represented or knowledge entities (ideas, emotions, foresights), which is by far an uncharted territory. Therefore, knowledge societies are to a large extent still utopic, though not improbable. They are possible to the extent that the task of understanding and managing their subject matter advances. There is enough circumstantial evidence that the perceived principles that account for micro and macroeconomic behavior have reached their limits when dealing with knowledge-based value. Knowledge Economics and Knowledge Management will benefit significantly when they fully incorporate the explanatory and technological resources that have been developed to unravel the represented realities of human behavior and social structure. Such powerful resources should leverage the capacity to understand and manage social knowledge-based processes such as value production and distribution, collective decision-making and participation, social identity and belongness, cohesion and innovation, etc. Such understanding, in turn, should help overcome the decaying walls of industrial civilization corroded by unsustainable consumerism, mediatized democracy, unbalanced world institutions and self-centered ethos.

The transition from industrial to knowledge societies is not a mere ideal, for societal and human development is an ongoing process, and even major disruptions start from existing conditions. Incremental moves in that direction are already taking place in emerging knowledge societies—cities, regions, countries—deliberately and systematically applying knowledge-based development policies. These policies often include imaginative and bold changes in social organization and role definitions; for example, in the way in which public information, collective knowledge construction and community participation are improved through both conversational and ICTs-based methods. These qualitative changes will more often and more deeply be required to transform the archaic institutions of the industrial civilization into the purposeful design of knowledge societies.

The knowledge-based perspective founding KMb is as advanced as it is pertinent. While a large proportion of what is done in the name of KM is still resource-based (i.e., content transactions subordinated to a prevailing and often tacit value structure), the KMb approach subverts and makes explicit the value base against which all knowledge assets and processes are to be weighted. This move reveals the true meaning of Knowledge Economy as an understanding and management of the whole of collective human preferences—not only those with a material or monetary base—and Knowledge Society as a civil order in which dynamic community balance (including continued self-sustenance) and not just financial growth become central.

Hence, KMb can be identified as a k-based value system. In that sense, it incorporates the meta-knowledge platform required to feed back practice into awareness. Increasing local and global social consciousness and capacity to take effective action might be the only path to the medium-term survival of life on Earth. Even more transcendental, it might be the path to overcome the entanglement of the human condition so clearly pointed out by biologist Jeremy Griffith: the flagrant contradiction between human moral ideals and human behavior drives.

In the decisive quest for global environmental and social balance, ignorance—in the form of intolerance, superstition, dogmatism and self-denial patterns—is the worst liability, and knowledge mobilization—in the form of transparency, public awareness, community action, social innovation and international reorganization— the best asset. Major landmarks in human history may well be described as transcendent knowledge mobilizations. Perhaps the most transcendent knowledge mobilization so far, and the first of a global scale, is required right now.

PREFACE

The leadership shown by the government of Canada in creating and implementing the Knowledge Impact on Society program designed to move knowledge from the researcher to the citizens has stimulated the preparation and research forwarded in this book. As we move into the future the importance of optimizing the applications of research for the welfare of all citizens grows exponentially. The Canadian approach to knowledge mobilization serves as a model for future research, where knowledge mobilization complements—and becomes as important as—the research itself. This book lays the groundwork for that movement forward.

As used throughout this book, the term community denotes the target audience in the knowledge mobilization (KMb) process, that group of people who are the beneficiaries of implementation of research findings. That group may be a community of preschoolers, or a community of small business owners, or a geographically dispersed community of immigrants or single parents. The term community leaders denotes those individuals who—though not necessarily formal partners in the KMb process—understand, are involved in, and have passion around helping their community and its citizens. They are part of the larger stakeholder group, and may be considered advocates within the community.

Representative of the KMb approach itself, relying on pragmatic language and actions with theoretical grounding, this book presents KMb in a way that makes sense and is accessible to researchers, practitioners, change agents, community leaders and other invested stakeholders. The goal is for the stakeholder community itself to become a community of learners as they implement research findings, moving from awareness, to understanding, to belief, to feeling good about it, to ownership, to being empowered and knowing what to do, and finally to taking action and changing behaviors.

This book is intended as an idea-generator and resource. It is not prescriptive. Just as knowledge is situation dependent and context sensitive, so too is the KMb approach for implementation of new knowledge. As the study of society, and the human relationships within and with society, the social sciences disciplines include a wide array of fields such as sociology, psychology, economics, anthropology, history and political science. Each of these fields has a unique focus and approach to exploring human society and human relationships, with as many differences in research areas as there are people within each field! Therefore, any KMb approach must be as robust and flexible as needed—both proactive and adaptive—to support the area of research, the target audience, and the larger stakeholder community.

As we continue to explore the exciting potential offered through knowledge mobilization, we simultaneously begin to realize that knowledge mobilization is on the cutting edge of knowledge management, moving new ideas and shared understanding into the hands of the people at the point of action. This is where the day-to-day decisions are made that will improve our communities, our businesses, and our nations.

ACKNOWLEDGEMENTS

First and foremost our deep appreciation to The Social Sciences and Humanities Research Foundation of Canada, who are walking, and sometimes running, down the path of knowledge mobilization. This book started out as a white paper, became a treatise, then grew into a draft of the book which was used as an event intermediation in concert with the Knowledge Impact on Society research awards. Katherine Fafard, Marc Fonda, Ted Lomond, Laurent Messier and Nicole Vaugeois chose to actively participate in bringing this final book into existence. Our thanks also to those KIS awardees and other members of the SSHRC team who contributed to this effort in a variety of ways from the sidelines. This was truly a collaborative effort. And our gratitude to Francisco Javier Carrillo, who so well captures our hopes and intent in the Foreward.

Our thanks to the team at the Mountain Quest Institute including, but not limited to, Andrew Dean, Ginny Ramos, Mark Turner, Dawn Buchanan, Susie Price-Weber, Cindy Taylor, and Cathy Fulk, all of whom helped keep the retreat center, farm and animals on track while we wrote and rewrote this book. A special thanks to Barbara Bennet, who provided editing insights, and Erica Engquist, who took a lead administrative role in the production process. See *www.mountainquestinstitute.com*

Our gratitude to our to our graphic artist, editor and friend, Fleur Flohil, and our printer, Gráfica Maiadouro, for their rich contributions to making this book a reality.

Finally, our deep gratitude and best wishes to those researchers, practitioners, community leaders, and stakeholders who are mobilizing knowledge to frame a new world. May you achieve great successes.

Alex and David Bennet
July 15, 2007

CHAPTER 1

EXPLORING KNOWLEDGE MOBILIZATION

THIS SECTION INCLUDES: 1.0 INTRODUCTION; 1.1 SOME DEFINITIONS; 1.2 KMb AND KNOWLEDGE MANAGEMENT; 1.3 GUIDING PRINCIPLES; 1.4 KMb AS A TRANSFORMATIVE APPROACH; 1.5 THE POWER OF DIVERSITY; 1.6 EMPOWERING PEOPLE.
FIGURE: 1-1 THE FOCUS AREAS OF KNOWLEDGE DEVELOPMENT AND MOBILIZATION.

1.0 INTRODUCTION

Knowledge mobilization (KMb) brings knowledge, people and action together to create value. KMb goes far beyond the dissemination of knowledge from source to beneficiary, researchers to community. It is not just knowledge transfer, and while dynamic knowledge brokering is essential in terms of identifying stakeholders, building networks and relationships, and designing activities to nurture knowledge sharing, this is still not enough. KMb embeds knowledge generation (creation) and knowledge use within the core structure of community and organizations (Clark & Kelly, 2005).

For purposes of this book, knowledge is considered the capacity (potential or actual) to take effective action in varied and uncertain situations (Bennet & Bennet, 2004). Extended descriptions of data and knowledge and the distinction between them are introduced below and further explicated in chapter 2. Knowledge mobilization is the process of creating value or a value stream through the creation, assimilation, leveraging, sharing and application of focused knowledge to a bounded community. In terms of the social sciences, this would entail the effective creation, movement and tailoring of knowledge from its source (researcher or expert) to its application (practitioner, community leader, community) such that consequent actions are effective and sustainable. This can best result if a resonance exists or has been developed such that there is a living flow of shared understanding among all stakeholders and the means and opportunities to move community-based knowledge to enhance subsequent research-based knowledge development. (A discussion of process and knowledge flows is provided in chapter 6).

Knowledge mobilization is a process—or it may be a program comprised of a number of specific processes. The KMb approach taken depends on the timing, application, situation and needs of the community and stakeholders it touches. For a simple problem, the KMb process may end when the problem is solved, but for a more complex problem the process may continue as long as the action sequence is needed to achieve the objective. In a social setting new thoughts and behaviors (proposed by

> *Knowledge mobilization is the process of creating value or a value stream through the creation, assimilation, leveraging, sharing and application of focused knowledge to a bounded community.*

researchers) emerge and then build on other thoughts and behaviors (from change agents) and then become mixed with yet another set of thoughts and behaviors (from within the community). As this happens, the KMb process may continue well beyond the end of the KMb project. We call such mixing, entwining and unpredictable associations the process of entanglement, with the end result being impossible to trace retrospectively.

Entanglement is the mixing, entwining and random associations of ideas and concepts.

The need and challenge for knowledge mobilization processes arise from the increasing change, rising uncertainty and growing complexity of local and global environments. The present surprise-prone world creates demands and pressures at all levels of society, making it essential to react quickly and effectively. In short, we live in a CUCA world (increasing Change, rising Uncertainty, growing Complexity, and an exorbitant amount of Anxiety as people become entangled within this environment) (Bennet & Bennet, 2004). Simultaneously, much of the human race is moving toward an economy of abundance where the continuous emergence of knowledge is unfolding concepts that would have been classified as science fiction ten years ago.

In the area of social sciences and humanities, whether a need has been around for a long time or has recently emerged the solutions are similar: identify and create or locate the best knowledge and efficiently and effectively apply it at the point of need. This process of knowledge mobilization is situated within the paradigms of theory, praxis and action. It combines knowledge gained from research, the accumulated knowledge and experience of researchers, the specialty knowledge of change agents and organizational or community development specialists, and the knowledge acquired from the lived experience of community leaders and citizens.

Consider the increasing national and global potential for catastrophic social, political, and economic failures and the potential health impacts of epidemics and pandemics. These provide a compelling need for KMb. For example, in considering the prevention and intervention of catastrophes it would be reasonable to assume that the most promising practices would emerge from those parts of the world that have experienced similar challenges. However, continuing research and technological developments could also yield significant breakthroughs in mitigating major disasters. Since before the best decision can occur both of these knowledge sources—experiential findings and new research—must be considered, understood and connected in the context of an identified need, collaboration and learning are fundamental to KMb. This process of collaboration and learning is consistent with, and supportive of, the relevance and importance of collaborative advantage in the global economy (see chapter 2 for a discussion on collaborative advantage). This process is also consistent with the world-wide need to raise the level of human thinking and understanding to protect and sustain humanity during pandemics, large disasters and terrorism. Knowledge mobilization can serve as a vital link between the research communities, those who have learned from past experiences, and local practitioner and larger stakeholder groups. Both content knowledge and pragmatic insights can

The need and challenge for knowledge mobilization processes arise from the increasing change, rising uncertainty and growing complexity of local and global environments.

be of great value to local communities throughout the world as they face significant uncertain and surprise-ridden issues and threats.

In Figure 1-1, knowledge development and knowledge mobilization are depicted as separate focuses, with both supported by knowledge, information management and information technology systems. The creation of knowledge occurs wherever people are thinking, feeling, learning and interacting. In this model, knowledge development is the deliberate creation of knowledge through research, study, experimentation and analysis in a specific domain of inquiry to enhance human understanding. For example, university research focuses on specific, well-bounded questions and areas to create new knowledge. The knowledge created is generally theoretical and may be abstract, covering fundamental theories, laws, guidelines, principles, etc.

While knowledge creation occurs wherever people are thinking, feeling, learning and interacting, knowledge development is the deliberate creation of knowledge through research, study, experimentation and analysis in a specific domain to enhance human understanding.

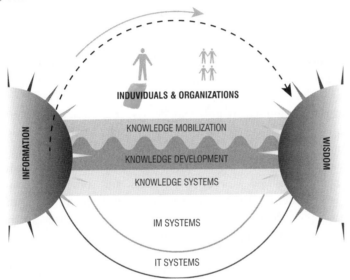

FIGURE 1-1: The focus areas of knowledge development and mobilization.

While knowledge mobilization also leads to the creation of new knowledge through the growth of shared understanding and learning from feedback, its focus is on learning and behavioral change through the application of developed knowledge, i.e. research findings. KMb may begin with the creation of deep knowledge from research organizations or world-class experts (knowledge development). This expert knowledge is created through effortful experience, years of reflection and learning, and having lived with the subject (Ross, 2006; Ericsson, et al., 2006). Through chunking, iterative assimilation, questioning, problem solving and dialogue, researchers and experts create within their minds the capacity to address a situation from a conceptual, theoretical, analytical and systemic perspective. While they may—or may not—have a great deal of pragmatic application experience, the deep understanding and insights they possess in their domain of expertise is an invaluable resource for helping resolve a multitude of social challenges.

Since academic researchers are under ever-increasing pressure to produce articles to acquire tenure, promotion and research grants, their research often remains inaccessible, locked into the academic world of cloisters and libraries, known only to the authors and a small number of professionally-related colleagues. Simultaneously, since their research may be specifically focused on a small segment of reality and simplified and cleansed to enable valid data to be taken, it may lack a connection to the deep and vital knowing and social knowledge developed in practice and in communities.

As stakeholders move through awareness, understanding, belief, and acceptance of new ideas and approaches that take knowledge from research to local actions, the decisions made in the day-after-day life of their communities change. Providing research information in isolation is not likely to change someone's behavior since users need to understand and adapt research results to their local situation and context. Knowledge mobilization does, however, provide the process for decision-makers (community leaders or social workers, for example) to take an evidence-based approach, i.e., decision-making based on the best use of available, validated research and emerging practices that moves well beyond a simple linear model of research application.

For example, the immediate goal may be to create value through actions taken by practitioners, who are frequently community leaders acting as change agents to help communities solve local problems. Practitioners might include teachers, social workers, medical personnel, counselors, or other specialists, depending on the knowledge being mobilized. Community leaders, and some practitioners, are the individuals who understand the local situation as well as the community's needs, culture and people. Their experience and knowledge are central to the decision-making and implementation processes needed for local communities to understand and resolve problems. However, these practitioners typically will not know or understand the theoretical and conceptual aspects underlying a problem, and the community they support may have difficulty even defining the problem in a manner that can lead to solution. In fact, many community problems could be considered as "wicked problems" or (to use Russel Ackoff's term) "messes." Messes are situations in which it is clear that something is not right but it is difficult or impossible to identify the problem (Ackoff, 1978). These are the gaps that KMb seeks to close—the gaps between the theoretical knowledge of understanding, the pragmatic action of change, and the experiential and intuitive knowledge of the community members. In other words, KMb is an approach to *weave the flow of knowledge* (the capacity to take effective action) among researchers, practitioners, advocates, policy-makers, communities and other stakeholders, weaving a whole cloth that wraps around a messy problem and—through leadership, resonance, collaboration and energy—dissolves it.

> *As stakeholders move through awareness, understanding, belief, and acceptance of new ideas and approaches, the decisions made in the day-after-day life of their communities change.*

While it may seem that these gaps can easily be closed by transferring the deep knowledge of the researcher to the practitioner who, in turn, can transfer their knowledge to stakeholders, this is an oversimplified and dangerous assumption. The knowledge of the researcher in not necessarily *consciously known* by the researcher; much of that expertise is unconscious and intuitive and is at best difficult to put into words. It is also chunked and composed of patterns related to the scale and foci of the researcher's interests. At the same time, practitioners have their own tacit, pragmatic knowledge that they act upon, but are unable to explain the reasons for their actions. Similarly, practitioners may know the local needs, context, people and history of a situation, but have difficulty transferring this awareness and comprehension to researchers. Therefore, the contribution of all parties becomes essential for effective decision-making, and collaborative implementation is embedded in a continuous cycle of learning and action.

> *The KMb approach seeks to facilitate the learning and sharing of knowledge through the conscious development of connections, relationships and the flow of information.*

Implementation of social sciences research is difficult at best through a piecemeal approach; it is most successful when undertaken with a coherent and integrated plan of action. The KMb approach seeks to facilitate the learning and sharing of knowledge through the *conscious development* of connections, relationships and the flow of information among all KMb stakeholders. Events and processes are put in place to facilitate the creation, sharing, and understanding of as much information (and knowledge) in a specific domain as possible to ensure that the most effective decisions are made through cooperative and collaborative approaches.

In the social sciences, mobilization of knowledge both influences and is influenced by the public and its environment. Knowledge has the ability to mobilize people, that is, by creating an atmosphere of collaboration, identifying a worthwhile goal, and leveraging shared understanding, *people can self-mobilize* to make decisions and take action. When knowledge in the hands of committed decision-makers is connected to a clear, worthy need, that knowledge moves beyond the capacity to take effective action to the role of focusing and energizing action. Such relationships can lead to self-organization which fosters the emergence of an autopoietic system adjusting to—and coevolving with—its environment. As von Krogh and Roos claim:

Knowledge has the ability to mobilize people by creating an atmosphere of collaboration, producing a common vision, and leveraging shared understanding.

A process of self-organization may happen in two ways. Either the development of a self-organizing system's autonomy is a process of integrating various components that can be controlled by the needs of the system to maintain its organization; or it is a process of rejecting various components at the system's boundary. (von Krogh & Roos, 1995, p. 38)

Since by definition and practice part of the KMb system is embedded within its community, the latter option is neither feasible, nor desirable. Thus the desired option is for the KMb process to self-organize and simultaneously interact with—and become a natural part of—the community. Since learning is essential for the behavior changes necessary to resolve a community's issues, it is expected that KMb implementation will occur most effectively when all participants are operating within an atmosphere somewhere between order and chaos. For example, a cooperative, yet spirited dialogue between policy decision-makers and their constituents facilitates informed judgment that when coupled with individual motivation empowers the creation and diffusion of ideas—what Dorothy Leonard calls creative abrasion (Leonard-Barton, 1995). This can also be referred to as the edge of chaos, a state that permits creative ideas to emerge and participants to readjust their mental models (Battram, 1996; Marion, 1999; Bennet, 1996).

Because social problems are almost always complex and their solutions unpredictable, learning with feedback and flexible implementation becomes essential for successful outcomes. KMb results can be assessed in several ways. The first is the level of value they provide to their recipients, both short-term and long-term: what changes have occurred within the community, and have the issues been resolved or removed. For example, for a county-wide substance abuse problem, the number of substance abuse cases can be tracked over time and classified to connect specific actions with specific problems. A second outcome is the amount of learning fed back to improve the effectiveness of the KMb process itself. This information can then be used across other KMb processes for overall program improvement. Finally, where double-loop learning (Argyris and Schön, 1978) or transformational learning (Mezirow, 2000) has occurred, special inquiry would be helpful to better understand the local conditions and actions that created the identified shift in perspective.

> *When knowledge in the hands of committed decision-makers is connected to a clear, worthy need, it takes on the role of focusing and energizing action.*

Responsibility is the willingness, capability and courage to act.

In the exchange model forwarded by Lavis and others, researchers and decision-makers are jointly responsible for the uptake of research knowledge (Lavis, et al., 2003). This concept of responsibility moves beyond issues of guilt and fault to the ability to act, whether responding to a situation or issue or taking advantage of an opportunity. There is an iterative, cumulative feedback loop between idea generation and idea use, between research and the beneficiaries of research, between innovation and the use of innovation (Castells, 1996), between developing solutions and implementing solutions. This is a feedback loop that should be continuously questioned and tested, one that requires critical thinking by all parties. The feedback part of the process also spawns new ideas, perspectives and a commonality of thinking and acting that can streamline and accelerate KMb effectiveness. There is the danger, of course, that the loop degenerates into noise through misunderstandings and distrust, or that the loop gets locked into a second rate interpretation and outcome. Noise reduction often requires a system shock or failure of some type to wake participants up to the importance of their relationship, interdependency and inter-commitments to each other. This opens the door for double loop learning, critical thinking, rethinking positions, and moving the frame of reference from a personal to a systems level. Such perturbations can then allow the loop to restart and rebuild itself to achieve higher-level performance. Noise creeps in when people quit listening, become antagonistic, or develop private agendas at odds with the intended objective. Each of these elements (and there are others as well) is situation and personality-dependent, and must be handled locally and professionally. However, a continuous reminder to all concerned of the importance and goal of their common purpose, and such interventions as coaching in effective dialogue, can help keep the noise level low. In addition, clarifying language differences and respecting cultural and background idiosyncrasies may be needed to keep knowledge sharing moving. Open discussions on what information and knowledge are, people's characteristics, limitations and sensitivities to mental models (Senge, 1990), or exploring meaning perspectives (Mezirow, 2000) will provide stabilizing mechanisms that give the process a baseline for listening and creating meaning.

1.1 SOME DEFINITIONS

Some ideas and conclusions of the theoretical biologist Tom Stonier may help put data, information and knowledge on a firm basis. In 1992 Stonier asserted "that information has physical reality (and is not related merely to human information activities)…" (Stonier, 1992, p. 8). Five years later he came to the conclusion that information is any non-random pattern or set of patterns (Stonier, 1997). Data would then be single patterns, and data and information would have organization but no meaning until some organism recognized and interpreted the patterns. In other words, meaning comes from the combination of non-random patterns and an observer who can interpret these patterns to create recognition or understanding. It is only when the incoming patterns are integrated with the internal neural patterns within the brain that they take on meaning to an individual (see the discussion of context in chapter 2). These units of understanding are referred to by Stonier as "semantic complexes." He says,

From the biological viewpoint, information is any non-random pattern or set of patterns.

> …a semantic complex may be further information-processed as if it were a new message in its own right. By repeating this process, the original message becomes more and more meaningful as, at each recursive step, new semantic complexes are created. As these impinge on ever larger areas provided by the internal information environment, whole new and elaborate knowledge structures may be built up–a process which leads to understanding. (Stonier, 1997, p. 157)

Thus knowledge exists in the human brain in the form of stored or expressed neural patterns that may be activated and reflected upon through conscious thought. This is a high-level description of the creation of knowledge that is consistent with the neural operation of the brain and, according to Stonier, is applicable in varying degrees to all living organisms. In other words, knowledge is created within the brain by consciously, or unconsciously associating internal neural patterns from memory with incoming patterns from the environment (sensing), and then iteratively complexing/mixing the result with other internal patterns of the mind (reflection) (Stonier, 1997). From this process new patterns are created that may represent understanding, meaning and the capacity to correctly anticipate (to various degrees) the results of potential actions. This recognition of the existence and importance of thought and thinking as *patterns of the mind (in the brain)* has recently been reinforced by research into world-class competency (Ross, 2006). Similarly, Hawkins argues that the purpose of the brain is to make predictions and anticipate the future:

Our brains use stored memories to constantly make predictions about everything we see, feel, and hear…Prediction is so pervasive that what we "perceive"—that is, how the world appears to us—does not come solely from our senses. What we perceive is a combination of what we sense and of our brains' memory-derived predictions. (Hawkins & Blakeslee, 2004, p. 86-87)

Hawkins then goes on to explain how the cortex works to be able to constantly predict the immediate future. For example, when we walk down a flight of stairs our brain is automatically anticipating the next step as it controls the legs. This is why it can be so dangerous to "miss" a step—our body has anticipated a normal step and is not prepared for the surprise, potentially leading to a fall. Given this predilection to anticipate, and the fact that knowledge in someone's brain is useless to all but that individual unless it is acted upon, it seems wise to tie knowledge to action.

A broad, operational definition of knowledge then becomes: *knowledge is the capacity (potential or actual) to take effective action* (Bennet & Bennet, 2004). Although perhaps not universally accepted, a large number of thought leaders in the field of knowledge management (and others) have tied knowledge to action (Argryis, 1993; Sveiby, 1997; Wiig, 2004; Huseman and Goodman, 1999; Devlin, 1999; Bennet, 2005). Tying knowledge to action allows it to have varying levels of quality depending on how well a specific action achieves, or is expected to achieve, its anticipated consequences. Since the future can never be known with certainty,

Knowledge without action is wasted; action without knowledge is dangerous.

tying knowledge to the results of actions also makes it clear that it is not absolute: knowledge cannot be considered as either true or false, but rather is taken as having a probability less than one, and hence always open to some degree of uncertainty. If this were understood by decision-makers, double-loop learning and critical thinking might come easier, and the rigid thinking that sometimes blinds decision-making might be avoidable. (See chapter 2 for a further discussion of knowledge.)

Another consequence from this description of information and knowledge is that each of us, by developing a history of emotional and memory patterns within our unconscious (tacit information and knowledge) also builds a perspective of "who" and "what" we are. This would include how we see ourselves as well as a set of beliefs, opinions and assumptions that represent powerful and invisible constraints, limitations and biases that can significantly hinder our perceptions, interpretations and understanding of external reality. As noted earlier, Senge calls this universal human frame of reference a *mental model* (Senge, 1990); Mezirow, in a much more in-depth analysis, uses the term *meaning perspectives* (Mezirow, 2000). The phenomenon surfaces when competent, intelligent people are unable to become aware of their limited perspectives, thus making bad decisions due to their blindness to things seen by others. This can easily destroy communication and knowledge sharing between two competent, well-meaning people; for example, researchers and community leaders. This is why it is critical to recognize that adequate knowledge to ensure the best decision is rarely available to a single individual such that decision-makers at all levels must be willing to listen to others and question their own mental models or ways of seeing the world.

Wisdom is a desired but not necessarily obtainable outcome of the knowledge mobilization process. In this application, *wisdom is considered the ability to apply knowledge for the balanced benefit of the individual, the community and humanity*. It is especially important that community leaders have a forward-looking perspective that includes their responsibility to be fair as they meet the needs of all members of their communities. In meeting these responsibilities there will often be conflicts of interest, value issues and questions of equity. Everyone in the KMb process will need to take a broad and high-road view of the objectives and the people served. Decisions and actions have to be made with long-term consequences and the greater good in mind.

Wisdom is the capacity to apply knowledge for the balanced and longterm benefits of Life.

1.2 KMB AND KNOWLEDGE MANAGEMENT

KMb has both subtle and structural differences from *knowledge management* (KM), which can be considered as a systematic management approach for optimizing the effective application of intellectual capital to achieve organizational (or community) objectives. Intellectual capital covers the broad spectrum from tacit to explicit knowledge loosely framed through a discussion of human capital, social capital and corporate capital (Bennet & Bennet, 2004). Human capital, a company's or community's greatest resource, is made up of every individual's past and present knowledge and competency, and their future potential. Each person brings a unique set of characteristics and values from the past, including expertise, education and experience. Built on these characteristics and values are a set of capabilities and ways of seeing and living in the world (such as creativity and adaptability). Just as important is a person's future potential which is highly dependent on an ability to learn and quickly respond to emerging challenges.

Knowledge management is a systematic approach to optimizing intellectual capital to achieve objectives.

Social capital includes human and virtual networks, relationships, and the interactions across these networks built on those relationships. It also takes into account all the aspects of language, including context and culture, formal and informal, and verbal and nonverbal communication. Added to this is an element of patterning that deals with timing and sequencing of exchange, as well as the density and diversity of the content. Social capital also includes the number of interactions between individuals in a relationship network, the length and depth of those interactions, and the frequency of those interactions; in short, how much, how often, and how intense. From this short discussion it is clear that social capital is the life blood of the knowledge mobilization process. *Corporate capital*, sometimes called organizational capital or structural capital, includes all the content in databases and information that employees (or stakeholders) can visibly get their hands around, everything that has been made explicit.

The KM focus is largely tied to organizational mission needs. KMb, as envisioned by the authors, is focused on new knowledge that has emerged (and is in the process of emerging) through research, with implementation driven by the content of that research and the identified stakeholder groups that are perceived as "needing" the application of that knowledge. In other words, the end goal in the social sciences and humanities is focused on altruistic support to bounded citizen groups or local communities. This introduces a difference in perspective, with KM being a *broad field* (not a discipline) that is intended to improve organizations through the effective creation, sharing, leveraging and application of knowledge, and KMb (bounded activity) being a *process* (or group of inter-related processes) for moving specific knowledge to action to value. KMb moves knowledge either from identified need to research discovery to research implementation to action, or from research to practitioner (change agent) to community, all working together in continuous loops. On the other hand, KM considers intellectual, social and human capital and how these capitals can be created and managed to improve organizational performance.

The primary beneficiaries for KMb are the local communities. The movement of knowledge involves all phases of the KMb process, and where learning loops are established all KMb participants become beneficiaries. In contrast, KM moves from the mission or specific objective to identification of knowledge needs, to location of needed knowledge and/or purposeful creation of new knowledge. KM may also deal with implementation and the sharing of knowledge through teams, communities of interest and practice and cultural development. Team and community members will, in turn, either: (1) use these ideas in their current work, (2) store this information away for future use, or (3) build on these new ideas. Although teams are also used in the KMb process, the focus is on specific bounded knowledge; in KM the focus often starts with the organization and may or may not get involved with specific knowledge, learning or professional growth of individuals. For example, the concept of personal knowledge management (PKM) has more recently come into focus, it has yet to be broadly included in the KM arena.

KMb, with its focus on specific knowledge, considers the nature of the knowledge involved and the learning and development of process participants, as well as the value (or value stream) created. *Value streams* connote the challenge of developing solutions to community issues that are sustainable and effective. This may require longer-term KMb involvement as well as developing solutions that become embedded within the culture and structure of the community.

1.3 GUIDING PRINCIPLES

Guiding Principles help frame the boundaries, strengths, weaknesses and expectations of KMb implementation.

While knowledge mobilization is far too young to have developed strong rules, these guiding principles represent relevant tendencies. They also suggest a flavor of the nature of knowledge mobilization. Since knowledge is situation-dependent and context sensitive, each principle is a rule of thumb that may or may not provide insight into a specific application. With time and experience, researchers, practitioners and community leaders and citizens will undoubtedly contribute their own insights as they push the edge of knowledge mobilization advancement.

Due to the human mind/brain tendency to make sense of the world (Edelman & Tononi, 2000), **knowledge has a mind of its own.** Knowledge can and will organize itself if it is allowed to. Learning, understanding and the use of knowledge create new levels of understanding that tend to propel and guide the knower toward new horizons. Thus, in addition to asking what KMb can do for participants, ask what the participants can do with knowledge.

Knowledge has the inherent capacity to mobilize. Knowledge is not a tool; it is the source and energy of performance. Performance may be considered the capacity to achieve objectives with the highest quality of results. Knowledge builds and releases: ideas, energy, understanding, awareness, possibilities, options, self-efficacy, growth, wisdom, balance, and learning. The deeper the knowledge and the more categories it encompasses, the greater the potential for understanding and meaning creation, and the better the predictive capability of action results.

Knowledge mobilizes people and provides the energy and direction for high performance.

Execution at the point of action is the challenge and the payoff. As the capacity (potential or actual) to take effective action, knowledge is *directly tied* to action. (Bennet, 2005) The capacity for effective execution through people interacting within a robust dialogue is a source of high performance. As Bossidy and Charon proclaim, "The intellectual challenge of execution is in getting to the heart of an issue through persistent and constructive probing." (Bossidy & Charon, 2002, p. 32) This can only be done well by the person on the scene of the action.

A KMb program creates the capacity for an organization to mobilize knowledge that produces value or a value stream. In the implementation of social sciences and humanities research, the KMb program is composed of a set of KMb processes designed to move knowledge out into the sectors where it can be used to improve society. A KMb process moves a specific area of knowledge to a specific recipient (community) to create value. As discussed in chapter 2, value is considered worth in terms of usefulness or importance to the recipient, with the knowledge being mobilized *in resonance* with the needs of the community. By resonance is meant a close relationship, chemistry, exchange of energy or compatibility between the knowledge and the users and among community members. When resonance occurs there is "…an interactive dynamic and order that naturally emerges from spontaneously behavioral resonance." (Marion, 1999, p. 232)

Value streams come from effective and sustainable KMb processes.

Collaboration and participation transcend paradigm limitations. Systems constrain, people explore. Everyone can learn, be creative, grow and contribute. Since no one has all the answers, everyone benefits via collaborative work experiences. Since individuals have their own paradigm, collaboration and knowledge exchange can break open limiting paradigms and thereby create more options for the effective use of knowledge.

Knowledge carries with it the responsibility of its application. Knowledge has no inherent value in terms of goodness. It is *how it is used* that conveys value. Therefore, in the social sciences and humanities it falls to the researcher, practitioner and community leaders and citizens to ensure that the knowledge created through the KMb process is used in a way that supports the betterment of society.

Communities as complex adaptive systems contain many semi-autonomous people that interact with each other with varying levels of self-organization.

The benefits of KMb are not always immediate or easily recognizable. A community is a complex adaptive system, and as such will almost always contain non-linearities, sources, sinks and delays. Feedback loops may be self-reinforcing or damping, improving a situation or making it worse. While improvements may be noted, there may be a non-linear cause and effect relationship between implementation actions and those improvements. Conversely, there may be no visible improvement for a period of time, and then all of a sudden dramatic visible change, what is called a tipping point in complexity theory. Unpredictability is a natural part of the world of complexity.

1.4 KMB AS A TRANSFORMATIVE APPROACH

The process of KMb can touch people in personal ways. The potential offered by knowledge—at the core of KMb—simultaneously intersects with the self and humanity, the internal and the external, in such a way as to offer the potential to make a difference for individuals and communities (Bennet, 2005). As connections and relationships build and knowledge is shared, understood and applied, a number of shifts occur. For practitioners, there may be a shift from assimilation to the sharing of best practices and best patterns (those patterns emerging from the collection of best practices). The process of KMb itself encourages universities to expand their role from the dissemination of information to the creation of, and participation in, learning communities and environments. This fosters the readiness, willingness and ability of students and communities to take control of their own learning as they become self-empowered to resolve local issues and problems.

Conversely, "evidence-based" can easily become synonymous with "exclusionary" and "normative" with regard to scientific knowledge (Holmes, et al., 2006). In other words, evidence-based decision-making is good to strive toward as a model, but it is only one model. As change continues and complexity builds upon itself, decisions must be made faster, often without the opportunity or possibility of figuring out cause-and-effect relationships to the situation at hand, nor the opportunity to access and assess the applicability of rigorous evidence. What happened in the past can only serve as a starting point for what will happen in the future, i.e., decisions-makers must move beyond a heavy reliance on historical case studies. Evidence, to be relevant, must be directly related to or repetitive of decision-specific content and context. The more rigors applied to research, the more opportunity to discover solutions with higher significance, but all research by its nature is situation dependent and context sensitive. This is essential for decision-makers to understand; while strong evidence can aid in decision-making, it cannot be a substitute for rigor of thought, reflection at the point of action, and the intuitive understanding that results from the patterns of past experience.

Transformational learning begins with a disorienting experience and ends with the creation of a new frame of reference that better matches reality.

Depending upon its application, KMb can result in a transformation program, that is, it can create a marked change—a change of character, culture, or structure—that results in a better community. Transformations can occur in individuals, groups, organizations, cities, or even nations. In general, a transformation indicates a significant change (or shift) within the entity being transformed. For example, an organization can be transformed through a significant change in its culture, or through a merger or a near collapse that results in a large change in perception of its own identity, purpose or mission. Transformational learning occurs when an individual, recognizing that their past perception of reality and understanding of the world and themselves may no longer be appropriate, identifies with a new set of beliefs and assumptions that guide future actions (Mezirow, et al., 1990; Mezirow, 2000). The process of lifelong learning or formal education frequently results in some degree of long-term transformation for an individual.

While transformation can be initiated by an external event or circumstance, outside pressure or force is rarely able to effect permanent change. Long-term change almost always begins within the individual or the community. In other words, the actual transformation comes from within—some internal change in structure, belief set or behavior patterns—perhaps engaging a new operating philosophy (Lennick & Kiel, 2005). For example, long-term change in communities can come from the continuous support of the major stakeholders coupled with the feedback learning loops that provide the opportunity and knowledge for community members to reconsider beliefs and behaviors, and to gradually move toward more effective actions.

To be effective, the KMb process should model (mirror) the types of shifts desired. For example, to move stakeholders from passive dissemination and assimilation of information to active, participatory construction and applications of knowledge, the KMb process itself should create and reflect these transformations. Since knowledge is primarily socially constructed, involved stakeholders may have a shift in frame of reference, a change of thinking and behavior modification, thereby putting knowledge, experience, observation and feelings together in new ways. To move communities to action, the KMb process may need to shift practitioner paradigms from unquestioned trust to the insistence on demonstrated trust built upon the availability of, access to, and scrutiny of evidence. The insistence on, and understanding of, research-based knowledge and its application to decision-making and implementation can go a long way toward improving local community problems.

> *To be effective, the KMb process should model (mirror) the types of shifts desired. A person who believes they are empowered and can accomplish some task or worthwhile goal will have a much higher probability of success than one who does not.*

For a change agent to facilitate change, it is not enough to know that people need to change, or what they need to change to, or how they need to change—these are necessary but not sufficient to create real change. One must also understand the world from the viewpoint of the individual and from this knowledge find ways to get the individual to want to change, to know how to change, to believe that they can change, and to know where they can find and get help if they need it. Thus, where KMb is concerned, the initial goal is to provide the information and knowledge that enables other individuals to understand their own need for change while encouraging and nurturing feelings, ownership, empowerment and self-efficacy. (This approach to individual change is a core theme running throughout this book, see chapter 3 for an extended discussion.) This is no small task. However, trust, conversation, mentoring, expressed and understood opportunities and possibilities, compassion, empathy and patience will help, as will honoring diversity and building empowerment through knowledge.

1.5 THE POWER OF DIVERSITY

KMB requires an inclusive—not exclusive—approach, all voices heard, representative of diverse points of view and open minds. As developed and developing countries alike move toward knowledge-based economies, technology and media have become interfaces across diversity, whether diversity of thought, learning, age, functional focus, economic status, health, geographic location, etc. For purposes of this book, diversity is considered the quality of being diverse (difference or variety). (American Heritage Dictionary, 1996).

Diversity is the source of friction, learning and creativity.

The power of diversity can be understood from several perspectives. In one sense, diversity can lead to disagreement, misunderstanding, or the inability to communicate or relate to others, perhaps eventually ending up in chaos. From an organization's perspective, diversity may either be extremely productive and useful or very harmful. Teams or groups are often selected on the basis of the diversity of individual membership. This diversity may result from expertise among differing disciplines, or perhaps from individuals with different modes of thinking and perceiving problems. When differing perspectives are combined with ongoing learning and understanding created by communication and dialogue among the members of a team or community, such diversity frequently leads to improvements in problem solving and decision-making capability. In other words, a team of diverse but competent members can leverage their knowledge to achieve far more then the individuals could achieve working separately. A significant byproduct of this process is the increased learning that all the members achieve through dialogue.

Another aspect of diversity in organizations is the capacity to provide diverse products and services. When this occurs organizations are no longer dependent on one particular market or customer base, providing a statistical safety margin for survival and growth. Even the willingness to try different products and services provides a significant learning experience in a dynamic and uncertain market place, thereby again increasing the chances of sustainability. Of course, this use of diversity must be coupled with effective feedback and learning from mistakes as well as successes. It also requires that an organization (or community) be flexible and adaptable, and willing to try new ideas and actions. Thus, although diversity brings with it additional responsibilities and difficulties in getting individuals to work effectively together and communicate, when effectively implemented its overall benefits far outweigh the additional costs. This same pattern occurs when implementing KMb in a community.

A third benefit of diversity relates to action. When a group or a team takes action to implement a decision, a set of individuals who see the world differently and yet understand the intent and objective of the decision can offer a wider variety of potential implementation paths. This portfolio of possibilities can provide a wider scope of activity with a higher probability of success. As above, it also offers a learning experience to each team or community member who is implementing the actions. As individual experiences are fed back to the group or team as a whole, both the individuals in the group and the collective capability of the group will grow over time, producing higher effectiveness in execution.

A fourth benefit of diversity occurs when individuals are exposed to a diversity of views and opinions from others. Such exposure has a tendency to broaden an individual's perspective, with that individual opening up to more new ideas. This process also helps an individual to become more critical of their own thinking, assumptions and beliefs, which in turn lead to the development and use of multiple mental models.

The bottom line is that diversity needs to be orchestrated. The benefits that accrue are much like brainstorming, not only are different viewpoints advanced, but different reactions are solicited. Social capital influences human capital, i.e., people build on and learn from each other.

1.6 EMPOWERING PEOPLE

Knowledge empowers people. For purposes of this book, empowerment is considered the investment of power, or to supply an ability, to enable. (American Heritage Dictionary, 1996). From learning theory, we know that individuals who *believe* they can learn, *can* learn. Extrapolating this concept to empowerment, a person who believes they are empowered and can accomplish some task or worthwhile goal will have a much higher probability of success than an individual who does not believe they are empowered to do so. The value of empowerment lies simultaneously in the freedom and responsibility given individuals to accomplish something, and in the internal recognition of the personal capacity and capability to do so.

Empowerment is the greatest lever in the Universe.

Empowerment is both a formal doctrine and policy as well as an informal expectation, trust and attitude. With empowerment must come sufficient context knowledge, experience, and recognition of the scope within which empowerment applies. Where knowledge workers are concerned, empowerment is extremely important, because it gives them the self respect, trust, and opportunity to make maximum use of their knowledge and competencies. Thus, empowerment among and between researchers, practitioners, community leaders and citizens, and the larger stakeholder community is embedded in the process of KMb.

As discussed throughout this book, there are a great many theories, relationships, tools and meta-tools that come into play as the KMb process unfolds. Knowledge mobilization has a broad scope of applicability. KMb is focused on connecting universities and institutes doing research in the social sciences and humanities with communities and other groups throughout a city, a nation or the world that can benefit from their work. But this relationship is not a simple connection. As will become increasingly clear, KMb encompasses a set of sustainable processes that includes knowledge, relationships, and learning to help ensure adding real value that meets the needs of a specified population. We proceed.

REFLECTIVE QUESTIONS CHAPTER 1

> What changes have you noticed in your workplace or community life that might reflect rising societal complexity?

> How might bounding the focus of research knowledge in support of a desired change, and identifying the specific target community in need of this change, help facilitate development of a knowledge mobilization process?

> How would you go about empowering your own local community relative to some specific need of the community?

> Have you ever taken action based on the best knowledge available to you and later discovered extensive research in the area of your decision that would have helped you achieve better results?

> What do you perceive as the value of your relationships (social capital) in your everyday work?

CHAPTER 2
THEORY AND APPROACHES

THIS SECTION INCLUDES: 2.0 INTRODUCTION; 2.1 DEVELOPING SOME KNOWLEDGE ABOUT KNOWLEDGE, 2.1.1 Levels of Comprehensibility, 2.1.2 A Knowledge Taxonomy, 2.1.3 Context; 2.2 TAKING ACTION IN A COMPLEX SITUATION; 2.3 COLLABORATIVE ENTANGLEMENT; 2.4 ACTIN LEARNING; 2.5 COMPARING KMb AND ACTION LEARNING; 2.6 RELATED APPROACHES, 2.6.1 Action Research, 2.6.2 Appreciative Inquiry, 2.6.3 Community Service-Learning, 2.6.4 Social Marketing.
FIGURES: 2-1 KNOWLEDGE MOBILIZATION: ASSIMILATING AND APPLYING THE RIGHT KNOWLEDGE TO SOLVE PROBLEMS, MAKE DECISIONS, AND TAKE EFFECTIVE ACTIONS; 2-2 SEVEN CATEGORIES OF KNOWLEDGE; 2-3 THE CONTEXT AVENUES; 2-4 DEVELOPING COLLABORATIVE ADVANTAGE: AS AN ORGANIZATION, AS A NATION, AS A CONNECTED WORLD.

2.0 INTRODUCTION

Knowledge mobilization (KMb) is an action journey within an identified action space. KMb seeks to create and implement actions based on new research that increase the chances of achieving a desired outcome. Typically, an identified problem or situation represents a discrepancy between what exists and what is desired. For explication purposes consider that KMb is being used to change a problem or situation within a community that is complex, encompasses several disciplines, has no easy solution, is dynamic, and can only be influenced—not controlled—by KMb team actions. This is what Russell Ackoff calls a "mess" (Ackoff, 1999). Figure 2-1 below represents the knowledge mobilization process.

At the top of Figure 2-1, the triangle and the related words and arrows around the triangle represent the generic flow of information that occurs within the KMb process. The three concepts of people, knowledge, and action are the fundamental factors in determining KMb efficacy. These concepts, while perhaps appearing to be simple, are in fact extraordinarily complex. This can be seen by recognizing the large number of their potential states, the range of their variability and the difficulty of anticipating the outcome of transitions from one state to another. For example, knowledge can be theoretical, practical, broadly descriptive or narrowly focused. It may be based on any of a large number of frames of reference. A social scientist would express her knowledge of cultural traits very differently than an anthropologist or an evolutionary psychologist. As introduced in chapter 1, to be understood by others knowledge usually requires situational information and a common or reasonably close mental model. Later in this chapter we will discuss a knowledge taxonomy with seven categories, each category having its own special semantics, categories of thought and expression. There are always many ways to take actions in the same situation and rarely is there only one "right" action to take. Considering the great variety among people, the taxonomy of knowledge and spectrum of possibly correct actions,

Messes often require multi-perspectives and several knowledge fields of inquiry for their resolution.

33

*KMb uses
knowledge within
the mess to help
resolve the mess.*

the difficulty of predicting or anticipating the outcomes is often insurmountable. What can be done is to identify a cone of desirable possibilities (see Figure 2-1) and monitor the KMb process and its feedback loops to ensure the program is kept within the cone, with interim decisions and actions made to guide the results and keep the outcome within the cone?

Starting at the top of the triangle from information and following the flow, we see that people—through their experience, competency, and observations—take information in, and as they learn more about a particular area, create knowledge, that is, theories, laws, understanding, meaning and expectations related to the behavior of a specific situation. This knowledge may have been created by experience, study, reflection, conversations, or all of these—and more.

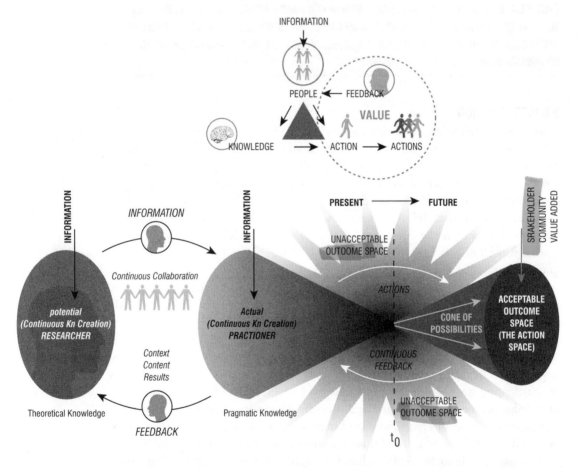

FIGURE 2-1: Knowledge mobilization. Assimilating and applying the right knowledge to solve problems, make decisions, and take effective actions.

The figure shows information flowing into the knowledge mobilization team. While representative of stakeholder groups, the potential makeup of this team is highly dependent on what is trying to be achieved. (See chapter 6 for a discussion of potential KMb team member roles.) The KMb team works together to develop a strong, highly focused and shared understanding of the situation to be resolved. In this sense-making and analysis process several knowledge areas will most likely be needed and combined to develop a sound and objective understanding of the situation, creating a melding of researcher, practitioner and stakeholder community knowledge. Analyzing and learning about the situation would typically require considerable dialogue among the different knowledge area experts. As each team member learns from the others, a systems level perspective emerges that provides an objective understanding of the properties and context of the situation. This dialogue and team learning process lays the groundwork for independent yet collaborative thinking and open communication, just the characteristics needed for double-loop learning, critical thinking and mental model shifting. Community leaders on the KMb team will take the lead in providing other team members with insights and in-depth understanding of the community's formal and informal processes. They will also be very useful in advising on culture, potential participation issues and expectations of the larger community stakeholder group.

In the sense-making and analysis process several knowledge areas will most likely be needed and combined to develop a sound and objective understanding of the situation, creating a melding of researcher, practitioner and stakeholder community knowledge.

Through continuous collaboration among all KMb team members there will develop a mutual understanding of the roles that each of the knowledge categories (see section 2.1 below) plays in developing and implementing a KMb program. Due to the situation's complexity, a single decision and action will probably not suffice because the situation, being complex and adaptive, may well adjust temporarily and then return to its original condition if left alone. A series of actions that "pushes and nudges" the community toward a new emergent stability may be the best approach. Also, the KMb team may decide to start with small steps, planning to observe and adjust their actions as the situation responds to their implementation strategy. The heart of knowledge mobilization is the process of bringing the right knowledge together with the right stakeholder group, and building a KMb team that can mold, share and apply this knowledge to problem solving, decision-making and implementation. Closely related are the challenges of creativity, innovation and learning from implementation feedback.

A complex adaptive system may have to be over stressed to move it towards a new stability.

Returning to Figure 2-1, an acceptable outcome space, shown in the figure by the cone on the right, can be developed that anticipates the need for flexibility of implementation. This is particularly important when working with a complex system where single cause and effect control is not possible. Under these conditions it will probably be necessary to initiate several parallel actions to seed the system and nudge it toward the desired outcome. KMb team-members will also need to remain open to learning and adjusting their tactics as the situation unfolds. This means that they should constantly monitor both their own performance and their impact on the situation. When KMb is thoughtfully and intelligently executed, the situation will move in the desired direction, although the path that the situation takes in response to KMb actions is not likely to follow the original plan. Figure 2-1 indicates this uncertainty by the cone shown on the right, called the *cone of possibilities*. When implementing a KMb process, this cone represents the acceptable outcome space as estimated by the KMb team prior to initiation of actions. The arrows on the right in the figure represent feedback from actions taken by the organization. This feedback, when taken and analyzed through action research and action learning, is then used to upgrade the KMb team's knowledge and understanding of their actions and effectiveness. This feedback may also enhance understanding in any of the seven knowledge categories discussed below. How well they can achieve shared understanding and mobilize their knowledge to solve problems and make effective decisions, and their efficacy of execution, will largely depend on the passion, knowledge and abilities (and relationships among) KMb team members. These factors, together with their capacity to deal with complex adaptive situations, represent the source of KMb power and value.

2.1 DEVELOPING SOME KNOWLEDGE ABOUT KNOWLEDGE

Each knowledge mobilization approach will have to mobilize different levels of knowledge (in terms of level of comprehensibility) and different types of knowledge (in terms of the areas of knowledge needed to develop and implement solutions). In addition, the recognition that knowledge is situation-dependent and context-sensitive can shift the way knowledge is shared based on the intent of that sharing. The discussions below on these three areas (Levels of Comprehensibility, A Knowledge Taxonomy, and Context) builds on the introduction to knowledge provided in chapter 1.

For purpose of this discussion, data is taken to be sequences of numbers and letters, spoken words, pictures, even physical objects when presented without context. Information is data with some level of context and is usually descriptive, answering questions such as who, what, when and where. Information can be stored in computers and sent over communications lines. Knowledge—built on information—often addresses the how and why questions. Knowledge is created within the individual's mind by selecting and organizing information in such a way as to create the *capacity (potential or actual) to take effective action.*

2.1.1 Levels Of Comprehensibility

It is useful to consider knowledge as having a number of levels of comprehensibility ranging from data to *information, sense-making, understanding, meaning, intelligence* to

Comprehensibility— existing only in the mind of the individual—depends upon the individual and the context and the content of the situation.

wisdom. This is not to say that data is knowledge (see the definitions above). Considering levels of knowledge in terms of comprehensibility from simple to the most complex helps bring out the different attributes of knowledge and provides some measure to understand the level of knowledge an individual has (or needs to have) relative to a particular domain of reality or situation of interest. As with all models, these levels should be considered as potentially useful guides rather than absolutes. Note that this is a model dealing with *comprehensibility,* the levels of knowledge needed in a specific context to support the ability to take a specific effective action. Data and information are provided in context, therefore contributing to the creation of knowledge at the point of action. A detailed discussion of context is at 2.1.3 below.

All knowledge is composed of information arranged in a certain manner such that the new patterns represent knowledge with its insight, understanding, meaning, etc. However, all information is not knowledge. The brain creates thoughts via patterns of neuron firings and the strengths of their connections. Considered individually, these patterns represent information. When mixed with other patterns to create new patterns, these new patterns may form knowledge (provided they represent insight, meaning, understanding, etc. that agrees with the external reality).

As patterns of the material world, the mind is to the brain as waves are to the ocean.

From a systems perspective, something that makes sense appears consistent with your own experience relative to that situation. *Understanding* means a more detailed awareness and insight into the causal relationships in addition to the elements and boundaries of the situation. Understanding applied to a complex system could include recognition of the emergent phenomena of the situation. The next level, *meaning*, considers the context of a situation in terms of its relationships to, or impact on, the environment or individuals, and other significant factors. Hawkins forwards that a major function of the brain is to anticipate the future. "Prediction is not just one of the things your brain does. It is the primary function of the neocortex, and the foundation of intelligence. The cortex is an organ of prediction.... even behavior is best understood as a byproduct of prediction." (Hawkins & Blakeslee, 2004, p.89) *Anticipation* is the capacity to estimate the effect of a perturbation on a situation.

A useful and widespread interpretation of *intelligence* is a capacity to set and achieve goals. There are a large number of interpretations and descriptions of wisdom, many of which might be considered outdated for modern times. For convenience, we choose Sternberg's pragmatic approach to wisdom, which he defines as,

> The application of successful intelligence and creativity as mediated by values toward the achievement of a common good through a balance among (a) interpersonal, (b) intrapersonal, and (c) extrapersonal interests, over (a) short and (b) long term, in order to achieve a balance among (a) adaptation to existing environments, (b) the shaping of existing environments, and (c) selection of new environments. (Sternberg, 2003, p. 152)

2.1.2 A Knowledge Taxonomy

In any specific KMb application there will be several areas of knowledge needed to develop and implement solutions. A knowledge taxonomy would be the grouping (naming and classifying) of types of knowledge by similarities and differences. As a framework for recognizing and working with knowledge, the following taxonomy offers the following groupings for understanding different types of knowledge looked at from the viewpoint of what knowledge is needed to do a particular type of work or take a particular action:

A taxonomy provides a structure for comprehension and interpretation.

Kmeta: Meta-knowledge or knowledge about knowledge, its creation, attributes, flows and integration.

Kresearch: Theoretical and evidence based knowledge composed of theories, laws, principles, and observations that provide guidance for understanding phenomena and the relationships among variables, attributes, processes etc. Why things happen.

Kpraxis: Pragmatic knowledge that relates to rules, heuristics, change management, dynamic processes and an understanding of how systems behave, change and adapt.

Kaction: Knowledge in action, often tacit. Local knowledge that guides the hands-on activities and implementation of knowledge.

Kdescription: Knowledge composed of descriptive information-who, what when, where.

Kstrategic: Strategic knowledge that considers the action, activity or task in terms of its role in overall strategy and long-term impact on the community.

Klearn: Knowledge related to individual, group and organizational learning that considers the learning of the KMb team, the learning capacity of the solution as the future unfolds, and the impact of the task solution on the learning capacity of the community.

Taken together, these categories of knowledge play different roles in the KMb process. Meta-knowledge, **Kmeta**, represents the capacity to understand, create, assimilate, leverage, sculpt and apply various types of information and knowledge. Since most complex situations contain several disciplines and categories of knowledge, our use of Kmeta (knowledge about knowledge) also includes the ability to bring knowledge together. William Whewell, in his 1840 synthesis, *The Philosophy of the Inductive Sciences*, spoke of consilience as "…a 'jumping together' of knowledge by the linking of facts and fact-based theory across disciplines to create a common groundwork of explanation," (Wilson, 1998, p. 8). E. O. Wilson also uses consilience to mean, "The explanations of different phenomena most likely to survive … those that can be connected and proved consistent with one another," (Wilson, 1998, p. 53). In making sense of complex situations, the consilience of different frames of references and knowledge categories may provide the best understanding for developing a solution.

KMb puts the concept of consilience into practice.

Evidence based knowledge, **Kresearch**, includes theoretical as well as empirical knowledge and represents the fundamental concepts that explain *why* things happen and those validated by the repeatability of empirical results. Such knowledge serves as a guide for setting expectations and possibilities and provides the user a level of confidence. Pragmatic knowledge, **Kpraxis**, represents the practical understanding of situations and *how* they change or *can* be changed. Much pragmatic knowledge is tacit, experiential and intuitive. Knowledge in action, **Kaction**, represents the ability to take specific actions that achieve the desired result. It includes understanding the *local* context and situation within which the action is taken.

Descriptive knowledge, **Kdescription**, is information that informs the *what*, *who, when* and *where* of a situation. As can be understood from the discussion of knowledge offered by Stonier (see section 1.1), all knowledge is composed of information, but all information is *not* knowledge. Knowledge is information that, when combined in the mind (associated or *complexed*), creates understanding, meaning and, where action is involved, the anticipation of its outcome. The role of **Kstrategic** is to ensure that the actions taken are in consideration of their long-term impact and are consistent with the strategy, identity, and values of the organization. The role of **Klearning** is to ensure that as the process unfolds, KMb group members learn from each other and, when appropriate, build organizational learning into the task outcome to ensure that the organization is capable of adapting to future changes in the environment.

The above seven categories should be considered as a useful spectrum of knowledge areas, sometimes overlapping and often having gaps between them. They are selected for their usefulness in the problem solving, decision making, execution and feedback learning processes, particularly when dealing with complex situations. Members of the KMb team may have expertise in one, several, or none of these categories and the knowledge needed will depend on the content, context and desired outcome of the situation/problem. The more complex the situation, the more categories of knowledge may be needed for the team to be successful. Another challenge is communicating when the knowledge may be tacit or implicit. For example, organizational team members may have a good intuitive feel for their co-workers reaction to the KMb effort but may have difficulty translating this tacit knowledge to their non-organization team members. While there are techniques for making this transfer easier, at times it can be very difficult. As Leonard and Swap note,

Spectrums highlight diversity which can lead to heightened creativity.

> Knowledge varies in terms of its 'stickiness', that is, how difficult it is to transfer from one situation to another, it may not be easy to transfer complex content knowledge, or 'know-what,' but process knowledge ('know-how') is particularly difficult to transfer because it relies even more upon pattern recognition, which in turn depends on experience and deliberate practice. (Leonard & Swap, 2004, p. 231)

Figure 2-2 below provides an overview of these categories of knowledge for easy reference.

2.1.3 Context

Knowledge is dependent on context. In fact, it represents an understanding of situations and their context, insights into the relationships within a system, and the ability to identify leverage points and weaknesses to recognize the meaning in a specific situation and to anticipate future implications of actions taken to resolve problems. (See Bennet & Bennet, 2007a, for a more detailed discussion of context.)

A popular KM adage is "context is king!"

Shared understanding, the underlying purpose of most communication and a primary goal of knowledge mobilization, is taken to mean the movement of knowledge from one person to the other, recognizing that what passes in the air when two people are having a conversation is information in the form of changes in air pressure. These patterns of change may be understood by the perceiver (if they know the language and its nuances), but the changes in air pressure do not represent understanding, meaning or the capacity to anticipate the consequences of actions. The perceiver must be able to take these patterns (information) and—interpreting them through context—re-create the knowledge that the source intended. This same phenomena occurs when information is passed through writing or other communications vehicles. In other words, content and context (information) originating at the source resonate with the perceiver such that the intended knowledge can be re-created by the perceiver. If the subject is simple and familiar to both participants, knowledge sharing (re-creation) may be easy. However, if the subject is complex and the parties do not have common contexts, sharing may be very challenging.

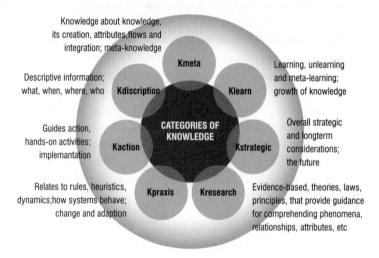

FIGURE 2-2: Seven categories of knowledge.

While at some level all knowledge is context-sensitive, pragmatic knowledge draws directly on the lessons of past experiences within specific circumstances to determine how things actually work. Pragmatic knowledge is knowledge focused toward action because it is continuously customized and improved by close observation of the action effectiveness in meeting expected results. This is earned knowledge, a "knowing" that individuals—and by extension the organizations within which they work—have built through experience, and understanding how to interpret situations

> *The innate ability to evoke meaning through understanding—to evaluate, judge and decide—is what distinguishes the human mind from other life forms.*

and what actions to take to achieve desired outcomes. This pragmatic way of knowing helps interpret relationships not easily recognizable, that is, the relationships that exist between how a situation is seen (the individual frame of reference), what rules individuals use to determine their actions, the types of actions that are taken, and how well these actions achieve the desired results. It can be closely linked to the capacity of community groups to learn from their own experiences. From this perspective, knowledge arises through citizens from their efforts in reflecting, experimenting, and identifying new ways of how things work in their jobs, and through community members from their lived day-to-day experiences. Pragmatic knowledge creation then becomes primarily a matter of learning through actions and day-to-day conversations with others, and secondarily through internal discovery and inquiry.

The innate ability to evoke meaning through understanding—to evaluate, judge and decide—is what distinguishes the human mind from other life forms. This ability enables people to discriminate and discern—to see similarities and differences, form patterns from particulars, and create and store knowledge purposefully. In this human process to create meaning and understanding from external stimuli, *context shapes content*. Though often repeated, this phrase still captures the imagination. While the content of the external stimuli may be constant, when you change the context the meaning can be entirely different! For example, the simple statement "Let's get together" could *mean* "sometime," or some specific time set earlier or later in a conversation or assumed because of the subject of the conversation, or could possibly be a nice thing to say without any real intent behind it. Given that context supports a specific meaning, the more relevant clues added to the content the higher the resonance of shared understanding.

Further, it might be said that context shapes and re-shapes content every minute of every day as individuals refresh their thoughts.

In order to understand the significance of context in KMb, eight primary avenues of context that may directly impact the content of a message are discussed briefly below. While one part of a conversation between two individuals is used to explore these avenues, each context could be considered from the viewpoints of the source (S) and the perceiver (P) based on their perceptions of the interaction that is occurring. It is recognized that feedback of some nature is always present (the perceiver cannot be completely passive), that conversations are social experiences, and that in a participative relationship an immediate reversal of roles will occur when the perceiver responds. It is also recognized that in a face-to-face example there are the physical characteristics related to sound that influence what humans perceive as they listen. These might include loudness or amplitude, pitch or frequency and tonal quality or wave-form. These layers of context could also be extrapolated across to written and virtual text. For example, the choice of words and sentence structure in a virtual resource, the tone of the writing, the impact of visual approaches in support of text, or the feelings present from past interactions

The higher the number of related context patterns, the higher the possibility of resonance between the source and perceiver and the greater the level of shared understanding.

with the originator of the text. Further, as represented by the well-known McLuhan-originated meme (*the medium is the message*) (McLuhan, 1964), the specific medium of communication directly affects the content, and each context will potentially relate differently to the various mediums of exchange. The key word here is "affect." McLuhan did not seek to "isolate the concepts behind the words but to integrate them as perceptions." (Gordon, 1997, p. 305) In other words, understanding the medium and the perceiver's interaction with the medium provides a greater opportunity to interpret and integrate the intent of the message with the perceptions of the receiver (the perceiver). This understanding brings new weight on the approaches and vehicles chosen for a knowledge mobilization process or program.

Figure 2-3 provides a brief description of the avenues which are further explicated below (Bennet & Bennet, 2007a).

THE CONTENT

Context 1 focuses on the content itself: the specific nouns and verbs selected, the adjectives and adverbs used in the primary expression, and the structure of the sentence that support this expression.

THE SETTING

Context 2 is the setting or situation surrounding the content of information; that is, the words and structure of the words expressed before and after the primary expression that provide further explication of the intent of content.

Contexts 1 and 2 are informational in nature and directly tied to the use and rules of language. Syntax is the body of rules used by/in sources when combining words into sentences. Syntax is often taken for granted in those who have grown up with a native language (residing in the unconscious), but syntax will be different from region to region and must be learned by those coming from a different native language. There are also morphological rules (regulating the formation of words); semantic rules (determining interpretations of words and sentences); phonological rules (dealing with allowable patterns of sounds); and phonetic rules (determining pronunciation of words and sentences) (Baker, 1989). These rules facilitate the ability of the perceiver to understand the words and structure of the words use by the source. They are also sensitive to region and must be learned when acquiring the language in use (in our case English) as a second language. For native speakers these rules reside primarily in the unconscious.

Taking another perspective on structure—and noting that the most commonly used symbol in the written English language is the space between words—Stonier contends that "the absence of structure within a structure may carry information as real as the structure itself." (Stonier, 1997, p. 23) He provides the following insight:

> Holes and spaces within an organized structure may comprise a significant part of the organization of that structure, and hence contain information ... The information content of such holes or spaces is entirely dependent upon the organization and behavior of the structures or systems which surround them. This demands that there exists information which can exist only as long a there exists a context or structure—a form of information which appears to disappear the moment the structure disappears. (Stonier, 1997, p. 23)

This observation leads us to consideration of the absence of content.

Context 3 is that which is not expressed, not available, what we call *silent attention/presence*. Attention represents awareness and focus. Presence represents immediate proximity in terms of time or space. Recall the Post-Modernist query:

Does a tree really fall if no one is around to hear it? In Context 3, someone is there—present and aware—but no tree is falling. There is silence.

Presence without interaction objectifies, what has historically been defined (in a negative sense) as treating people like things. But even this objectification cannot be separated from language. In the presence of another, even in silence the perceiver is embedded in an unseen dialogue based on past and perceived future interactions. In fact, Hanks states that, "In the production of meaning, silence and the tacit dimension play as great a role as—if not an even greater role than—does articulate speech (Hanks, 1996, p. 3). Silence can pull feelings and memories into conscious awareness. It has language in terms of meaning, i.e., when somebody *does* not answer a question, they are communicating more than their non-words. Sometimes what is not said can have more meaning than what is said. For example, in solving the Mystery of Silver Blaze, Sherlock Holmes says,

> Before deciding that question I had grasped the significance of the silence of the dog, for one true inference invariably suggests others. The Simpson incident has shown me that a dog was kept in the stables, and yet, though some one had been in and had fetched out a horse, he had not barked enough to arouse the two lads in the loft. Obviously the mid-night visitor was some one whom the dog knew well. (Doyle, 1994, p. 26)

Context 1	Information… content (specific nouns and verbs selected, and the adjectives and adverbs used in the primary expression, and structure of sentence that supports content).
Context 2	Information… the setting or situation surrounding the content of information.
Context 3	Silent attention/presence… that of which we are aware but is not expressed, not available.
Context 4	Non-verbal, non-voiced communications patterns… associated information signals (Emphasis and tone). In face-to-face interactions this would include body expressions, attitude and physical appearance, as well as other sensory inputs.
Context 5	System of shared context. Mutually shared common information/patterns with meaning (culture, environment, history, etc.).
Context 6	Personal context. Internal beliefs, values, experiences and feelings that emerge into conscious awareness (6 and 7 work together)
Context 7	Impact of unconscious processes, memories and feelings on context 3, 4, 5 and 6. Can be thought of in terms of (1) the unconscious, (2) experiences and feelings (memories) not in conscious awareness, and (3) empathetic process that can mirror behaviour.
Context 8	Overarching pattern context. Higher levels of patterns of significance that emerge in the mind.
	Higher numbers of related (relevant) patterns equals greater resonance between the source and perceiver and the increased sharing of understanding

FIGURE 2-3: The context avenues.

Context 4 includes the non-verbal, non-voiced communications patterns that inevitably exist in conjunction with the content, whether (in our example) face-to-face interaction, hand written exchanges, or computer supported information. This is what could be termed associated information signals. In the convention used in nonverbal communication literature, this would be encoding (expression) from the source, and decoding (interpretation) of the perceiver. These are, of course, interdependent.

In a face-to-face example, this would include emphasis (stress) and tone as well as body expressions (facial, hand movements, eye activity, posture, etc.), physical appearance, and every way that attitude can be expressed non-verbally. Non-verbal gestures can provide a form of semantic representation in a visual mode. This can affect both integration and inference making (Nisbett & Ross, 1980). Visual cues such as nodding and eye and facial movements have been shown to improve comprehension (Rogers, 1978). In their recent work, Choi, Gray and Ambady (2004) explore non-verbals in terms of *unintended* communication and perception. They focus on the automaticity of communicating emotions, expectancies, social relations and personality from what they term the actor's (source) and perceiver's perspectives. They conclude that although people exert some control over social exchange, a great deal is accomplished automatically as they unknowingly and effortlessly express feelings, beliefs and desires through non-verbal means as they navigate their social worlds (Choi, et al., 2004). Gray and Ambady, 2004). In other words, a great deal of the context provided by the source in a face-to-face encounter through non-verbals is absorbed by the unconscious mind of the perceiver based on feelings, beliefs and desires. Thus, non-verbals are a form of expression, closely linked to context 6 below, which can be viewed as an unconscious expression of internal beliefs, values, feelings and expectations of the source in a face-to-face exchange.

Context 5 is focused on the system within which interaction takes place, the mutually-shared, common information and patterns with meaning *within the system*. The context of the system would include an understanding, either consciously or unconsciously, of the boundaries, elements, relationships and forces within the system.

This is the domain of shared context, generally including factors related to a mutual past or current environment, and potentially including culture, organizational structure, and former and current social relationships. While most of this resides in the unconscious, since it is continuously massaged by day-to-day experiences and thoughts it is near the surface of the mind and readily accessible. For example, if the actors have a past relationship and know each other's personality, background, competency, and way of thinking, knowledge sharing may proceed easily and effectively. On the other hand, if the source is speaking to an audience of 200 practitioners, unless they are all in the same profession or share some other common domain of interest and knowledge (such as living in the same community addressing a similar problem), the style, words and behavior need to be carefully planned to ensure widespread re-creation (sharing) of the speaker's knowledge.

Context 6 is the personal context which includes beliefs, values, experiences and feelings that emerge into conscious awareness. Personal context would also include positions that individual's take that are locked into the conscious mind, unconscious patterns that are made conscious by the emerging content of the message (what might be termed implicit knowledge), and the core values and beliefs that rise to awareness by virtue of "feelings." Contexts 6 and 7 work together, with context 6 being those aspects that surface in an individual's thoughts and feelings and context 7 being those processes occurring of which an individual is unaware, i.e., occurring in the unconscious.

PERSONAL CONTEXT

When an individual hears information, it is immediately compared with what is already known and believed to be true. It is also interpreted from that individual's mental model or personal frame of reference made up of beliefs, values and objectives. It is also connected to recent memories and past experiences. A judgment or feeling about the received information is quickly generated and this feeling—modulated by any personal feelings related to the individual speaking and any reactions to the overall environment—plays a strong (often unconscious, which moves us into context 7) role in how the individual reacts to, interprets and accepts what is said. In fact, the individual may reject and not hear something that the speaker is saying if it conflicts with that individual's beliefs. If the feelings generated are strong, the individual may quit listening entirely while internally preparing a rebuttal. In short, in a threatening or uncomfortable environment, people hear what they want to hear.

Context 7 is the impact of *unconscious processes*. These can be thought of in terms of (1) the unconscious response to external stimuli (environment); (2) experiences and feelings (memories) not in conscious awareness; and (3) empathetic processes that can mirror behavior.

THE UNCONSCIOUS

The selection, interpretation and meaning of incoming patterns are very much a function of pre-existing patterns in the brain (Bennet & Bennet, 2006). In other words, learning and understanding are created in the mind as patterns already in the mind combine with incoming patterns from the external world or current situation. In fact, recent experimental evidence coming out of social psychology (Dijksterhuis & Bargh, 2001), cognitive psychology (Knuf, 2001) (Aschersleber & Prinz, 2001) and neuro-psychology (Frith, 2000) (Blakemore & Wolpert, 2000) have reached the same conclusion that there is a "disassociation between conscious awareness and the mental processes responsible for one's behavior ..." (Bargh, 2004, p. 38). This would purport that an individual's behavior (the behavior of the source in this face-to-face example) would not necessarily be driven by conscious awareness and intentions.

Empathetic processes that mirror other's behavior would indicate a positive, receptive attitude on the part of the perceiver. For example, such mimicking as arms folded while standing and conversing frequently occur without either participant's awareness. These are subliminal connections.

Context 8 is the overarching pattern context, higher levels of patterns of significance that emerge in the mind. These include: (1) the unconscious—and sometimes conscious—connecting of contexts 1 through 7 to develop a pattern of

PATTERN CONTEXT

understanding or behavior; and (2) the development and recognition of patterns of patterns among different interactions (over time). The connecting of multiple contexts would include comparing, manipulating and combining patterns. While generally only a "feeling" or "knowing" will be available in the conscious mind, underneath any interaction or sequence of interactions the unconscious may be busy recognizing, storing and integrating the patterns emerging out of contexts 1 through 7.

As noted above, the development and recognition of higher-level patterns among multiple and different interactions occurs over time. While this generally forms in the conscious mind as a feeling or a sense of knowing (intuition), it may also be accompanied by a mental remembering of an emotional response from previous interactions. In the face-to-face example referenced above, the thought, knowing or feeling that emerges as a result of different or multiple interactions provides a guide or pattern for an individual's response, knowledge that can be applied to the current situation in terms of response to the source. Whether promulgated by the conscious or unconscious mind, the higher the number of related patterns, the higher the possibility of resonance between the source and perceiver and the greater the level of shared understanding that is necessary to mobilize knowledge.

Having built a level of complexity through the exploration of context as relative to knowledge mobilization, a short discussion of complexity is in order.

2.2 TAKING ACTION IN A COMPLEX SITUATION

Complexity is the condition of a system, situation, or organization that has some degree of order, but too many elements, relationships, and causal influences to understand in simple analytic or logical ways. (Bennet & Bennet, 2004). In the extreme, the landscape of a complex situation is one with multiple and diverse connections with dynamic and interdependent relationships, events and processes.

To address complex community issues, the KMb process itself must be complex adaptive. While there are certainly trends and patterns, they may well be entangled in such a way as to make them indiscernible, and compounded by time-delays, non-linearity and a myriad of feedback loops. While sinks (absorbers) and sources (influencers) may be identifiable and aggregate behavior observable, the landscape is wrought with surprises and emergent phenomena, rumbling from perpetual disequilibrium. In this landscape, implementation of research findings will likely be unique, dynamic, difficult to define or bound, and have no clear set of solutions.

The results that are observable will most likely be emergent, the result of a combination of actions interacting with a dynamic environment. Emergence is a global or local property of a complex system that results from the interactions and relationships among its agents (people), and between the agents and their environment. Examples are culture, trust, attitudes and identity. In short, it will probably not be possible to identify a direct cause-and-effect relationship between implementation actions and the results of these actions.

As introduced earlier, other potential properties of a complex adaptive system include nonlinearities, time delays, tipping points, power laws, correlations, unpredictability, and butterfly effects (Battram, 1998; Gladwell, 2000; Gell-Mann, 1994; Buchanan, 2004). Simultaneously, the system has multiple connections, relationships and is surprise prone. For example, a tipping point occurs when a complex system changes slowly until all of a sudden it unpredictably hits a threshold that creates a large-scale change throughout the system. Since large-scale change may be a desired outcome, seeking a tipping point may be part of the implementation strategy; however, since tipping points are typically unpredictable and may significantly deviate from planned outcomes, there is a need for strategic flexibility.

As discussed in the Introduction, since people and communities are complex adaptive systems, implementation of research in the social sciences means making decisions and taking actions in complex situations. This means taking into account boundaries, people, networks, events, trends, cultures and structures, the elements of research implementation, the makeup of the implementation team, their relationships with stakeholders and the interactions among all of these elements. Approaches to understanding complex adaptive systems include observation, reflective thinking, dialogue, intuition, analysis, reasoning, critical thinking, lucid dreaming, synthesis, and effortful learning (Bennet & Bennet, 2007b).

While a depth discussion of complexity is beyond the scope of this book, there are ways for influencing complex adaptive systems. These include boundary management, absorption, optimum complexity, simplification, sense and respond, amplification, and seeding. Boundary management is influencing around the boundary of a situation (or community). Absorption is bringing the complex system into a larger complex system so that the two can intermix, thereby resolving the original issue by dissolving the problem system. Optimum complexity is building the optimum amount of complexity into the implementation strategy to deal with the complexity of the situation. Simplification reduces the uncertainty, but may miss core issues and often creates system backlash, resulting in counter intuitive system behavior. Sense and respond is a testing approach where a situation is first observed, then perturbed in some manner, and the response to that perturbation studied, thereby providing a learning process to understand system behavior. Amplification is an evolutionary approach where a variety of actions are tried to determine which ones succeed, then building upon (amplifying) those that are successful. Seeding is the process of nurturing emergence through a set of simultaneous actions that move the system in a desired direction. (See Bennet & Bennet, 2007b, for a lengthy treatment of decision-making in a complex situation.)

When dealing with complex problems, one size does not fit all.

Understanding the characteristics of complex systems builds an appreciation for the significance of a flexible, adaptive, collaborative approach to the pragmatic implementation of research expertise.

2.3 COLLABORATIVE ENTANGLEMENT

As citizens increasingly recognize that organizational and national boundaries are artificial constructs in a connected global world, the Industrial-age value creation found in individual economic structures is diminishing as the value created through collaborative advantage escalates. For example, a young doctoral student from Portugal comes over to the Mountain Quest Institute in West Virginia to learn about the latest research in applying the Intelligent Complex Adaptive System organizational model that ensures survival and continuing high performance in a changing, uncertain, and increasingly complex environment. Or, a health care advocate in Canada partners with emerging health care associations in the Far East to ensure an understanding of, and up-to-date information on, emergent flu strains. Whatever the situation, context or level of application, successful knowledge mobilization is built on collaborative approaches among the sources and beneficiaries of knowledge, wherever they are located throughout the world.

Collaborative entanglement means to purposely and consistently develop and support approaches and processes that combine the sources of knowledge and the beneficiaries of that knowledge to move toward a common direction such as meeting an identified community need. Collaborative advantage can be described in terms of open communications, shared understanding, and decision-making that collectively moves collaborators in an agreed-upon direction. Collaborative entanglement also includes the execution and actions that build value for all stakeholders, whether for a community, an organization, or a nation. In other words, collaborative entanglement engages social responsibility and in doing so provides a platform for knowledge mobilization.

Building bridges between people creates networks that drive the future.

Figure 2-4 explores the relationship among various approaches—such as action learning, action research, appreciative inquiry, community service-learning, participatory inquiry and social marketing—that contribute to collaborative entanglement. This is an iterative, interaction-based model that promotes social and personal progress through the facilitation of new ideas, increased connectedness and capacity building among research and community stakeholders, and greater mutual access to growth opportunities. This is similar to the model of community development that bridges the social distance between different sectors and social groupings described by Norton, et al., (2002). The collaborative entanglement model is highly participative, with permeable and porous (unclear and continuously reshaping) boundaries between the knowledge researcher and knowledge beneficiary as well as between the research and application of the research, i.e., *the research itself becomes part of the process of implementing research results.* Lee and Garvin contend that to be effective, knowledge exchange depends on multi-directional, participatory communication

Collaborative entanglement includes the execution and actions that build value for all stakeholders, whether for a community, an organization, or a nation.

among stakeholders (Lee & Garvin, 2003). *The collaborative entanglement model moves beyond knowledge exchange to the creation of shared understanding resulting in collaborative advantage and value results.* In addition, collaborative entanglement utilizes but moves beyond the historical push/pull emphasis, consistent with the findings of Beyer and Trice that the push/pull model of knowledge utilization is inadequate (Beyer & Trice, 1982).

In Figure 2-4, action learning, action research, appreciative inquiry, community service-learning, participatory inquiry and social marketing (discussed later in this chapter) are representative approaches that contribute to collaborative entanglement. These approaches all contribute to building social capital. Recall that social capital includes human and virtual networks, relationships, and the interactions across these networks built on those relationships. It also takes into account all aspects of language, and includes context and culture, formal and informal interactions, and verbal and nonverbal communication. Added to this is an element of patterning that deals with timing and sequencing of exchange, as well as the density and diversity of content. This would include the number of interactions between individuals in a relationship network, the length and depth of those interactions, and the frequency of those interactions; in short, how much, how often, and how intense (Bennet & Bennet, 2004). The recognition and awareness and understanding of KMb— and a willingness and commitment to engage in the KMb process—might itself be considered social capital.

Social capital can further be considered in terms of bonding, bridging and linking (Szreter & Woolcock, 2004; Kawachi, et al., 2004). Bonding refers to developing horizontal relationships among those with similar interests or identity; bridging refers to developing horizontal relationships among those with differing interests or identity; and linking refers to developing vertical relationships. The social interaction in which bonding, bridging and linking take place builds relationships, cohesion, trust, and thus social capital (Putnam, 2000).

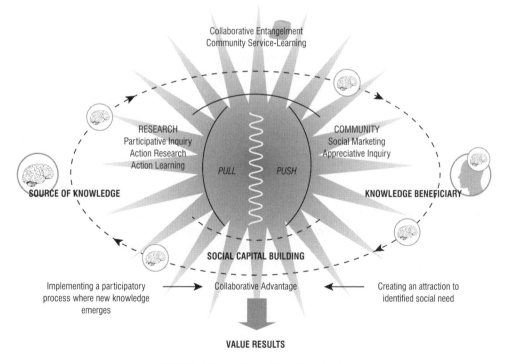

FIGURE 2-4: Developing collaborative advantage:
as an organization, as a nation, as a connected world.

The relationship network is the matrix of people that consists of the sum of the individual's relationships, those people with whom the individual has a connection or significant association, and with whom the individual currently interacts or has interacted with in the past. The relationship network is both horizontal and vertical,

Since day-after-day individuals have the capacity to choose those with whom they interact, by those choices they are laying the groundwork for future decisions.

and therefore managing it includes elements of bonding, bridging and linking. Relationship network management—focused on building, using and increasing social capital—occurs when stakeholders recognize the potential of relationships and use them to share and learn, creating and sustaining a deliberate give and take movement, or flow, across the network.

Basic concepts of successful relationship network management include *interdependency*, trust, common framework, openness, flow and equitability, all of which support a community's ability to successfully take collaborative, cohesive action. (Bennet & Bennet, 2004) Interdependency is a state of mutual reliance, confidence and trust. It connotes a two-way relationship with, in terms of figure 2-4, both researchers and community members taking responsibility for nurturing and sustaining the relationships. *Trust* is based on integrity and consistency over time, saying what you mean and following through on what you say. Respect and reputation also contribute to the perception of trust across teams, communities, and organizations. A *common framework* could include a common language (cultural, functional, or organizational), common stories, shared values (the ground truth), shared moral standards, or a shared vision/mission/direction. *Openness* is directly related to trust and a willingness to share.

> Successful relationship network management builds on interdependency, trust, common framework, openness, flow and equitability.

A relationship cannot exist without interactions, without the flow of information and knowledge. The *flow* of data, information and knowledge is across and among networks of technology systems and people; shared through teams, communities and events; and facilitated through knowledge repositories, portals and systems. This free flow is mutually dependent on both the researcher and the community. It becomes each decision-maker's responsibility to assure that they have what they need when they need it to make the best decisions in alignment with an agreed-upon direction, what is called a connectedness of choices. *Equitability* in a relationship is characterized by fairness and reasonableness. When used in law, the concept includes the application of the dictates of conscience or the principles of natural justice. The intent of an equitable relationship is that both sides get something out of the relationship, consistent with what they have given to the relationship. In reality, both sides often gain more than either contributes, since relationships often produce synergy and ideas shared beget new ideas. (This is further discussed in chapter 6.)

None of these six concepts can be created by directing or controlling. They all arise from the nature and sequence of interactions among the individuals involved and depend upon each person's perception and feelings about the other. Effective relationships evolve over time and are created by interacting, testing, questioning, listening, respecting and carefully building a positive image of, and belief about, the other person. Good relationships emerge from a history of interactions, and as such must be nurtured and protected to be sustained.

We have discussed collaborative entanglement in order to bring out the importance of the relationships and communication among all process participants. While this creates the framework and foundation for KMb success, there are several specific areas of practice that play important roles in support of KMb high performance. These supporting efforts are briefly described below. They are: action learning, action research, appreciative inquiry, community service-learning and social marketing.

2.4 ACTION LEARNING

According to Marquardt, "One of the most valuable tools for organizational learning is action learning." (Marquardt & Reynolds, 1994, p. 39) He describes it as "…both a process and a powerful program that involves a small group of people solving real problems while at the same time focusing on what they are learning and how their learning can benefit each group member and the organization as a whole." (Marquardt, 1999, p. 4) Action learning takes a systems approach to the learning process. It is based on the premise that people learn by doing. Such learning is usually done by small groups of 5-8 individuals who share common goals and learning desires. Using dialogue, brainstorming and other knowledge leveraging techniques they focus on a specific task or project with clear deliverables. There may or may not be a facilitator, depending on the nature and experience of the group members.

Many action learning projects start with an introductory workshop to bring the participants up to speed on what action learning is and how the process works. The intent of this workshop is to psychologically and socially prepare participants for a group process where individuals come together to work on real issues through sharing—and learning from—their experiences (learning by doing). It combines learning through social interaction, individual reflection, making choices, taking action on those choices, and carefully studying and learning from the results. The intent of using groups can range from working on and through individual issues and problems to a focus on meta-learning in terms of group processes, or both. For example, while an action learning group may get together to focus on an organizational issue, they may simultaneously be working out personal relationship or communication issues as well. As with any team formation, the team-members will also work out their own individual roles and responsibilities in the group and in the organization. The process moves from a presentation of the issue or problem to a clarification and unification of what the problem really is. This process is grounded by an emphasis on questions that constructively challenge team member assumptions and mental models. The result is often followed by the emergence of new insights that when acted upon create new questions that stimulate learning from the experience. This is similar to the U. S. Army's after action review approach in which a great deal of learning takes place after the action is completed.

$L = P + Q$ is even more important today as we move into a CUCA world.

The originator of action learning, Reg Revans, was a scientist working at the Cavendish Laboratories at Cambridge University, who asked what he called "silly questions." During his work with the National Health Authority he coined the expression $L = P + Q$ [(Learning = Programmed Instruction (knowledge in current use) + Questioning (insights into that which is not known)]. This summarizes the foundational idea behind action learning (Marquardt, 1999, p. 29). Since answers tend to collapse thinking and questions lead to more questions and to more thinking, his approach greatly facilitates learning. In his review of Marquardt's book, Revans noted that, "The wisdom inherent in action learning is even more important in dealing with the rapid changes in today's world." (Revans, 1998)

Although the concept originated many years ago, action learning has now come to the forefront as an effective way to meet the demands of the new world. There are recognized successes throughout the current literature. As individuals experience action learning their domain of experience and sources of knowledge expand as a result of solving real-world problems. Not only have they made useful contacts and learned from those contacts, they see the enterprise in a new light and understand their own work within a broader context (Marquardt, 1999).

According to Marquardt there are five ways in which action learning can be applied: problem solving, creating a learning organization, team building, leadership development, and personal and career growth (Marquadt, 1999). Each of these areas has their own knowledge domains with accompanying paradigms. Although they have been studied by researchers and organizational development specialists for the past several decades, much work remains to be done. Their importance continues to increase rapidly as the world becomes more turbulent, unpredictable and complex (Senge, et al., 2004; Leonard & Swap, 2004; Katzenbach & Smith, 1993; Marion, 1999).

Action learning teams can initiate and spread organizational learning.

The changing world zeitgeist ensures that challenges and demands are continuously being placed on these critical aspects of organizational performance. Because of the changing environment they must continuously adjust and sometimes reinvent themselves. For example, organizational learning can be facilitated by creating a program of numerous action learning groups within the firm. As they learn and complete tasks, the diffusion of group members throughout the organization will spread their learning while creating seeds of recognition that can move the culture toward acceptance of organizational-wide learning. At the same time, problems get solved, team members observe and participate in leadership events and participants learn how to learn in a social environment. This use of groups emphasizes learning in addition to results, opening the door to critical thinking and double-loop learning via dialogue and the questioning of old beliefs and assumptions that block or limit individual perspectives.

2.5 COMPARING KMB AND ACTION LEARNING

From the above descriptions, several similarities between KMb and action learning stand out. Both emphasize learning, both use feedback as a source of learning, and both seek to learn from the task so that team/group members grow professionally as they accomplish work objectives. KMb places the emphasis on task outcome embedded learning, whereas action learning seems to be silent on this issue. KMb is designed more for difficult tasks that require a range of competencies and deal with uncertainty and change, although there is insufficient experience with its implementation to fully anticipate its efficacy and range of applications.

According to Marquardt, "Within the next ten years, only the learning organizations will survive" (Marquardt, 1999, p. 76). From this, Marquardt proposes 20 action learning characteristics that contribute to organizational learning. (Marquardt, 1999, p. 90) Examples include:

- Outcome orientation
- Designed to systematically transfer knowledge throughout the organization
- Done on the job, rather than in the job
- Breaks down barriers between people and across traditional organizational boundaries
- A mechanism for developing learning skills and behavior
- Systems based
- Problem focused rather than hierarchically bound
- Active rather than a passive approach
- Allows for mistakes and experimentation

Action Learning reinforces organizational learning by setting examples and demonstrating results. It suggests many activities that foster organizational learning through the interactions of team members with other organizational employees. These details of implementation are useful and effective ways to influence local parts of an organization and should be easily adaptable to KMb implementation. One might say that action learning is the action and learning arm, with KMb providing the knowledge, strategy and guidance for outcome success.

Action learning and KMb may complement each other, one for the action and two for the knowledge and strategy.

KMb should also bring the latest research theories and evidence-based knowledge to the process, allowing new ideas and techniques to be applied in organizations and communities that may not be aware of the latest developments in a field. New research findings from areas such as decision-making, learning, strategic thinking, and complexity are being reported frequently in the professional literature, and even in the popular press. KMb can provide a test bed for validation of some of these new ideas. Action learning, on the other hand, uses employees and generally does not bring outside experts in, and is therefore limited to internal knowledge for problem solving. The reason given is that experience with the problem is more important than experience with the answer (Marquardt, 1999). While in a steady state situation and environment this approach might be satisfactory, in a turbulent, unpredictable situation and environment this approach is likely to be solving new problems by old anecdotes, and employees may have more difficulty seeing and understanding the problem than would experienced outsiders. For example, employees within the organization would likely have difficulty recognizing the need for a paradigm shift in thinking, that is, the need for expanding the knowledge paradigm to include an organic framework of thinking in terms of emergence, non-linearity and energy flows. Such a change would also include the awareness, understanding and need for flexibility and adaptation in most problem solutions (Bennet, 2006).

Other areas in which KMb and action learning may be compared include team development, facilitation, creativity, problem solving, decision-making and execution. If we assume that KMb teams are composed of "outsiders" and employees, whereas action learning teams are composed of employees only, we begin to see some differences in how they would operate. KMb team development might take longer to get up to speed, but would be more objective than action learning teams. Action learning teams would understand their organization better and should be able to make good use of their established relationships to gain needed information and cooperation. However, KMb teams would likely be more creative due to diversity and independence of members. This diversity would also allow more objectivity and bring more potential solutions to the table. All of these comparisons are general and highly dependent on specific team makeup and the nature of the situation/problem.

In summary, it appears that there is a strong synergism between KMb and Action Learning that could benefit both approaches. Having been around since World War II where it began in the coal mines, action learning has gathered significant experience as exemplified by Marquardt's discussions of specific ways of implementation (Marquardt, 1999). KMb is in the development stage and is open to some of the latest research findings in areas such as the creation and leveraging of knowledge, new techniques for learning, and ideas for dealing with Ackoff's complex messes (Bennet & Bennet, 2007b).

2.6 RELATED APPROACHES

Four additional approaches that are representative of those that can be used in the implementation of research to help build social capital are explicated below. These are: Action Research, Appreciative Inquiry, Community Service-Learning, and Social Marketing (see Figure 2-3 above).

2.6.1 Action Research

The term action research has a wide variety of interpretations. It is a social movement in terms of a research approach built on the premise that stakeholders are most knowledgeable concerning their own needs, bringing in the involvement of those most affected in order to facilitate change from within. Much like knowledge itself, this approach is situation dependent and context sensitive, relying on multidisciplinary approaches, theories, models and research methods (White, et al., 2004). It promotes ownership, shared decision-making and action.

Action research builds understanding and energy around a problem or issue.

While the protocol for action research is loose, it must begin with building trusting relationships (see the discussion of relationship network management in 2.3 above) among all stakeholders, and building understanding and energy around a problem or issue. Newman makes a case for the use of five tools: narrative inquiry (reflections made to determine the importance of values in specific situations as they arise); critical inquiry (insights pulled from external influencers such as political pressures, newspaper articles, etc.); case studies (used to explain phenomena and shape understanding of related events); reflective practice (realigning past performance); and the practice of critical incidents (recognizing situations as they arise over time) (Newman, 2000). The National Health Service Scotland (NHSS) found that action research methods fostered closer ties between the production and use of research. Key elements of their approach included putting greater evidence on local context specific research, integrating tacit knowledge and building the capacity to use research evidence through knowledge brokering (Sharp, 2005).

Related approaches include action science, action inquiry, co-operative inquiry, participatory inquiry and participatory action research. While emerging from differing ideological perspectives and intellectual traditions, what all of these have in common is a movement from a self-contained approach to research to more participatory, collaborative approaches. As forwarded by Freire, the ontological position of all participative approaches to inquiry is "the connection between subjectivity and objectivity, never objectivity isolated from subjectivity." (Freire, 1982, p. 30) Participative approaches also express the fundamental importance of experiential knowing.

As described by Reason, participative inquiry is more of a philosophy based on the need to empower the beneficiaries of knowledge by connecting them to the source of knowledge. Reason presents three models of participative inquiry: co-operative inquiry, participatory actions research and action inquiry. Co-operative inquiry has four phases: (1) deciding on the problem and agreeing on procedures for observation; (2) carrying out those procedures in detail; (3) testing ideas and strategies and recording the results; and (4) developing declarations and assumptions, reflecting on the process and results, adopting new hypotheses and moving forward based on these new hypotheses (Reason, 2000). Participatory inquiry is participative action research, similar to the process described above.

Action inquiry is based on Argyris' double-loop learning, similar to the notion of reciprocal learning growing out of relationships between researchers and non-academics (SSHRC, 2005). Double-loop learning occurs when existing underlying assumptions, beliefs, norms, procedures, policies and objectives are considered in addition to detection and correction of problems (Argyris & Schön, 1978). Reason has developed two theories of action based on double-loop learning. As described by Karadimos,

> Model I has governing variables that are based on independent motivators, winning as the objective, excluding negative feelings, and focusing on rational thoughts. Behaviors stemming from this set of governing variables are thought to be that of control and defense, which limit effectiveness .... Model II has governing variables that are based on valid information, free and informed choice, and internal commitment. Behaviors growing from this set of governing variables are thought to be that of inclusiveness, a sharing of information, and increased participation, which enhances effectiveness. (Karadimos, 2006, p.6)

According to Reason, the use of participatory action research is appropriate with groups that are disenfranchised; the use of co-operative inquiry is appropriate with groups who are already empowered and motivated toward change, and the use of action inquiry is appropriate for individuals seeking to cultivate group participatory inquiry (Reason, 2000). Each of these approaches might apply to different phases of KMb implementation depending on the research being implemented, the characteristics and culture of stakeholders, and the events supporting implementation.

To appreciate is to value. To inquire is the act of exploration and discovery and asking questions.

2.6.2 Appreciative Inquiry
To appreciate is to value, to recognize the best in people and the things around us, while to inquire is the act of exploration and discovery and asking questions. Appreciative

55

inquiry (AI), then, is an approach that discovers and promotes the best in people and those things around us. Hammond describes appreciative inquiry as a way of thinking, seeing and acting to bring about purposeful change (Hammond, 1996).

This approach to discovery was first named in 1990 by Dr. David Cooperrider and his colleagues who were studying at the Weatherhead Graduate School of Management at Case Western Reserve University. In its original form, Cooperrider considered it a mode of action research which embraced the uniqueness of the appreciative mode. Traditional organizational interventions identify problems and hunt for solutions; the appreciative inquiry approach locates and tries to understand that which is working, learning from it and amplifying it, serving as a complement to other interventions, or, perhaps, offering a *way* other interventions can be approached. It is based on the simple premise that organizations (teams, communities, countries) grow in the direction of what they are repeatedly asked questions about and therefore focus their attention on (Srivastva & Cooperrider, 1990).

The four principles Cooperrider & Srivastva lay down for appreciative inquiry are that action research should begin with appreciation, should be applicable, should be provocative, and should be collaborative (Srivastva & Cooperrider, 1990). The principles of AI can be translated into assumptions, the rules that a group follows when making decisions about behavior or performance (Argyris, 1993). These principles are similar to Senge's mental model (Senge, 1990). Hammond translates the principles of AI into the following assumptions:

The past is history, the future is mystery, and the moment is now.

1. In every society, organization or group, something works.
2. What we focus on becomes our reality.
3. Reality is created in the moment and there are multiple realities.
4. The act of asking questions of an organization or group influences the group in some way.
5. People have more confidence and comfort to journey to the future (the unknown) when they carry forward parts of the past (the known).
6. If we carry parts of the past forward, they should be what is best about the past.
7. It is important to value differences.
8. The language we use creates our reality. (Hammond & Hall, 1996, pp.2-3)

The appreciative inquiry approach has been successfully used in community development. As the focus in organizations and communities moves back to people and the knowledge they create, share and use, the empowering aspects of the appreciative inquiry approach can build self-confidence in—and receptivity to—new ideas and accelerate behavioral change.

2.6.3 Community Service-Learning

Community service-learning, rapidly becoming recognized as an integral aspect of education, links established learning objectives with genuine community needs. This approach involves university-level students in voluntary community-based service experiences that are jointly defined, developed, implemented and coordinated by the community and university. In this setting, students earn credits for experiential and collaborative learning while providing service to the community.

Community service-learning provides the opportunity for mutually beneficial interdependent partnering, what Abravanel refers to as equal partnering with a vested interest (Abravanel, 2003). In addition to concrete experiences, students also engage in reflective observation using introspection and dialogue, offering the opportunity to explore how others experience similar events through abstract conceptualization. Students are then in a position to test and modify new concepts and theories (Kolb, 1984). Community service-learning is learning in action, supporting development of lifelong social and professional skills while increasing understanding of various issues such as diversity, ethics and social responsibility. It also builds appreciation and respect for others (Astin & Sax, 1998; Eyler, et al., 1997; Potthoff, et al., 2000). Simultaneously, community service-learning encourages application of research beyond academic circles by drawing on the knowledge and experience of university faculty and staff (Driscoll, et al., 1996). Community stakeholders also contribute knowledge and experience to facilitate student and researcher learning while pursuing their own concerns (Gray, et al., 1998).

Where applicable, community service-learning is both consistent with and highly supportive of knowledge mobilization. The process goes beyond the push and pull illustrated in Figure 3 to the instantiation of collaborative entanglement: *the need drives the research, the research drives the work, the work drives the learning, and the learning improves the needs and helps identify related needs, contributing to future research.*

2.6.4 Social Marketing

Social marketing utilizes commercial marketing concepts and tools to support programs specifically designed to *influence behavior* to improve the well-being and health of individuals and society. Social marketing is customer-driven, seeking to increase the acceptability of an idea, cause or practice in a specific community based on identified needs of that community. Combining business and social objectives, ideas and attitudes are marketed in order to bring about social change. For example, the objective may be to produce understanding (such as the health issues related to smoking); to bring about a one-time action (free chest X-rays); to bring about a behavior change (wearing seat belts); or to change a basic belief (the movement from a control-oriented bureaucracy to a collaborative work environment). Whether local or global, the focus is on learning what people want and need, and proactively responding to those wants and needs in terms of "selling" ideas, attitudes and behavior change.

At some level every person engages in social marketing every day of their lives.

In the early 1970's Kotler and Zaltman forwarded that the same ideas used to sell products could be used to sell ideas, attitudes and behaviors. Kotler and Andreasen see social marketing as differing from traditional marketing only with respect to objectives (Andreasen, 1995). For example, following a normal marketing approach, the social change objective would first be defined; then the attitudes, beliefs, values and behavior of the targeted audience analyzed. This would be followed by development of a marketing plan, either building a marketing group or hiring a marketing organization to do so, and, once the plan is underway, continuously evaluating, adjusting and readjusting the program to ensure effectiveness.

In a sense, all marketing is the marketing of ideas, and everyone is involved. But social marketing is specifically under-girded by the intent to move toward the greater good, certainly an intent often shared by researchers in the social sciences and humanities.

REFLECTIVE QUESTIONS CHAPTER 2

> What categories of knowledge do you use in your daily work environment? At home? When engaging in various community activities?

> What categories of knowledge might research knowledge fall into? How might combining a category of research knowledge with an understanding of the level of knowledge needed by community members to implement drive your knowledge mobilization process?

> Can you recall an issue, problem or opportunity that emerged where a better understanding of the context of the issue, problem or opportunity might have made a difference in your decisions and actions?

> Have you ever had a really good idea that was impossible to link back to anything you could consciously remember? How can this happen?

> Considering the seven categories of knowledge, the eight aspects of context and the subject matter related to complexity it is a wonder that any knowledge can be shared, as it often is. How might this happen? What factors help to facilitate the sharing of knowledge?

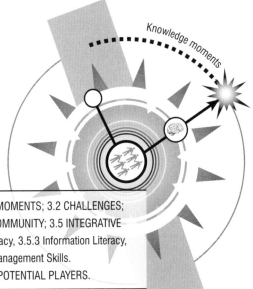
Knowledge moments

CHAPTER 3

THE KMb PROGRAM AND PROCESS

THIS SECTION INCLUDES: 3.0 INTRODUCTION; 3.1 KNOWLEDGE MOMENTS; 3.2 CHALLENGES; 3.3 THE PLAYERS AND THEIR ROLES; 3.4 CHARACTERISTICS OF THE COMMUNITY; 3.5 INTEGRATIVE COMPETENCIES, 3.5.1 Knowledge Mobilization Literacy, 3.5.2 Media Literacy, 3.5.3 Information Literacy, 3.5.4 Research Literacy, 3.5.5 Systems and Complexity Thinking, 3.5.6 Management Skills.
FIGURE: 3-1 THE EIGHT STEPS OF THE GENERIC KMb PROCESS; 3-2 POTENTIAL PLAYERS.

3.0 INTRODUCTION

As introduced in chapter 1, KMb processes combine research and education with praxis through the collaboration of multiple stakeholders having a common goal. Praxis benefits from scientific evidence, and scientific evidence benefits from real world application and feedback. While KMb may be a specific process applied in a given situation, a knowledge mobilization program would consist of a number of specific processes, each designed to create value by moving knowledge from a source of expertise to a local situation. A program would also include the structure of resources, relationships, communication patterns and knowledge systems in support of and across the KMb processes with the goal of ensuring efficiency, coherence and efficacy of the processes to optimize the community's benefit. Thus, where knowledge mobilization creates value, a knowledge mobilization program creates the capacity for a community to simultaneously implement multiple KMb processes. The reason there may be a need for multiple KMb processes is that each specific situation for creating value may require different approaches for effective knowledge mobilization. For example, a community might need a KMb process to maximize new medical responsiveness techniques while simultaneously minimizing drug abuse through education approaches. However, each of these processes will likely contain elements of the generic process shown in Figure 3-1 below.

A KMb program consists of a number of specific KMb processes, each designed to create value by moving knowledge from a source to a situation.

The eight steps in the generic model (Figure 3-1) start with a situation that has been matched to research findings. From that starting point, these steps are:

1. Situation (problem, issue, opportunity) identified.
2. Information gathered about/from the situation and its context.
3. Understanding generated from the information, experience and other multiple related sources.
4. Theoretical knowledge considered in the context of the situation.
5. Pragmatic knowledge from practical experience, similar situations, and systems understanding of the target community integrated with (1) through (4) above.

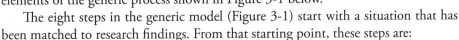

A GENERIC KMb PROCESS

59

6. Action or a set of actions taken.
7. New situation emerges from these actions.
8. Feedback provides the opportunity to assess the effectiveness of actions toward achieving the desired goal, and the opportunity to change or supplement those actions as needed. (See the discussion on project management in chapter 6.)

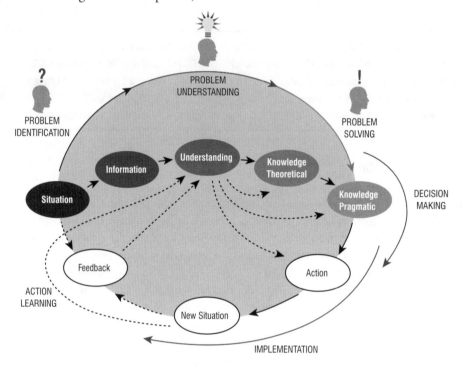

FIGURE 3-1: The eight steps of the generic KMb process.

As shown in the figure, these eight steps move through the focus areas of problem identification to problem understanding to problem solving to decision-making, implementation and action learning. While this model has been couched in terms of an identified "problem", this process would also apply to an identified opportunity. Throughout this process research findings are being explored in the context of the situation, other theoretical knowledge and the pragmatic knowledge of community stakeholders.

The generic process model can be used to address an identified problem or an identified opportunity.

Note that knowledge mobilization as a process goes beyond the omni-directional model of knowledge dissemination by embedding knowledge use and knowledge creation simultaneously within the core of knowledge beneficiaries, moving decision-making to the point of action within the community. The generic KMb process consists of many activities, with each activity serving a distinct purpose, yet with each reinforcing the other, i.e., each activity is connected to and supports other activities. Through the process of sharing and discovery these activities contribute to execution and feedback. Chapter 4 provides a discussion of potential KMb activities.

Since KMb is a process, it can be designed and implemented. However, it is also a process that is driven by three significant—and not simple—factors: people, knowledge, and action. (Recall the earlier discussion of Figure 2-1.) The purpose of the KMb process is to take specific knowledge and apply it locally where it creates value for the local constituents that fulfills a need and improves their welfare. While this purpose appears clear and straight forward, its implementation may be complex and challenging.

While the knowledge mobilization process itself is not emergent, the outcome of the process is often an emergent result as seen by community improvement in behavior and resolution of needs. The efficiency and efficacy of a knowledge mobilization process may also be emergent phenomena dependent upon the nature of the situation and the competency and commitment of everyone involved. These measures of process quality emerge through the multiple interactions of all parties. The quality of these parameters depends upon the energy, dedication, collaboration and coherence of effort of all major stakeholders that play a role in the KMb process.

> *While the knowledge mobilization process itself is not emergent, the outcome of the process is often an emergent result.*

For example, to fulfill a certain community need may require building relationships and connections between university experts in a given domain, knowledgeable practitioners or change agents who understand the community, and local community leaders who can energize and motivate community citizens toward applying knowledge to fulfill community needs. As a second example, a KMb program might require connecting an expert business strategist with a corporation's board of directors and senior managers to develop a strategy for entering new markets in support of community economic development. In this process, the knowledge of the expert strategist would be integrated with the experience and knowledge of the board of directors and senior managers, which then would be transformed into specific plans and actions for creating value. While these two examples may look similar at the highest level, their implementation is very different. Further, as with all human endeavors, the nature, backgrounds and perspectives of the individuals involved will significantly influence the way the process is set up and implemented.

As with all human endeavors, the nature, backgrounds and perspectives of the people involved will influence KMb success.

Because of their generality, overarching knowledge mobilization programs can be applied at the organizational, local or community scale, or perhaps even at the national or international level. The potential contribution that a knowledge mobilization program makes can be enormous. If a community, city, corporation or government can develop the capacity to generate, share, leverage and apply focused knowledge to solve problems and eliminate inequities and weaknesses in its operation, everyone benefits. In essence (reversing the KMb approach that focuses on implementing new research findings and using the same generic process model in Figure 3-1), the purpose could be to identify an area of need, locate the sources of knowledge available and applicable to this need, and connect the two. This, of course, is a gross over-simplification. First, the deep knowledge needed may not have been developed or available. If it is available (and here we address the challenges of KMb), *it may be broad and theoretical rather than pragmatic*, and it may not be understandable by those who need to apply it. Second, there is the problem of convincing those who *can* apply the knowledge that they *should* apply it and, if they do apply it, how to measure the outcome to identify success and build expertise. Third, once the knowledge mobilization process has proven successful, how can it be replicated and applied in other situations or in other communities? Each of these areas, and more, need to be addressed carefully and thoroughly during the development of a knowledge mobilization program.

As a broad-stroke overview, strategic areas in any KMb program would include:

STRATEGIC AREAS IN A KMb PROGRAM

- Designing, developing and executing specific activities needed among stakeholders (see chapter 4).
- Determining how to build knowledge mobilization capacity at all levels (community, organizational, individual) by engaging stakeholders in activities that enhance their knowledge, skills and resources
- Building the capacity of researchers, students, practitioners and community members to build social capital as well as to value, interpret, and use community-based research results.
- Facilitate the flow of information, understanding, purpose and application from its source to the point of value creation (and back).
- Evaluating specific KMb activities to determine how effective they are at moving knowledge into active service within a specific context (see chapter 7).

Areas of critical focus for the knowledge mobilization team include affecting policy-making and public opinion. In the formation of public policy, the role of universities can range from being a social critic to enriching policy development. Policy can embed change into the infrastructure. Policy-making informed by research findings helps ensure long-term gain or sustainability. Even when it appears that the larger community has embraced change, if the community infrastructure does not support that change, there is the potential for behaviors to slip back into old patterns when energy is no longer focused on the area of change. This means that to sustain change in individuals within a community the infrastructure of the community must support that change.

Every action taken in the KMb process will likely affect both public opinion and public welfare, creating both dangers and opportunities for achieving a desired outcome.

3.1 KNOWLEDGE MOMENTS

As the new millennium moves forward, there has been a focus on the transformation of regions and cities into knowledge societies (Carrillo, 2006). For example, among the cities that have made considerable progress toward becoming knowledge cities are Barcelona, Singapore, Munich, Dublin, Boston, Stockholm, and Montreal. Ron Dvir (with the Futures Center in Tel-Aviv, Israel) describes the knowledge city as a collage of human knowledge moments, connecting the daily experiences of citizens as they create, nourish, share and transform knowledge for their individual and collective purposes (Dvir, 2006). These moments happen as individuals move through their lives, occurring at the intersection of people, places, processes and purpose. Since a city or community—whether a place or a group of linked individuals—is *co-evolving*, the quantity of these planned and spontaneous exchanges increases the potential for quality and impact, and thus sustainability. Applying this thinking to implementation of research findings, how might we increase the quantity of knowledge moments for a stakeholder community?

> *Knowledge moments happen as individuals move through their lives, occurring at the intersection of people, places, processes and purpose.*

Since knowledge is defined as the capacity to take effective action, knowledge moments refer to exchanges that provide the potential for, or lead to, effective action. The behavior of a community is enhanced by the result of the interaction of all decisions made and actions taken based on the knowledge moments of every individual in the community. Similar to the butterfly concept in chaos theory, there is the potential for success or failure based on knowledge moments which cannot be specifically identified or tied directly to that success or failure!

This new frame of reference lays the groundwork for understanding knowledge mobilization. One objective of KMb becomes the *nurturing and facilitating of knowledge moments* related to the implementation of research findings. The KMb activities model introduced in chapter 4 suggests ways to create places and spaces for researchers, practitioners and the extended stakeholder community to facilitate knowledge moments that help stakeholders learn and create shared understanding. Creating resonances among and between KMb process stakeholders greatly increases the probability of knowledge moments. When people and their shared ideas resonate, knowledge and understanding flows and grows.

A primary objective of KMb is to nurture and facilitate knowledge moments.

3.2 CHALLENGES

Movement from the deep knowledge of basic research and theory to the arena of daily actions where value is created is the ultimate goal of all knowledge mobilization efforts. For convenience, we have identified five groups of individuals involved in this process as it applies to local communities: researchers, practitioners, community leaders, peripheral stakeholders and members of the community. Researchers are primarily interested in theory and understanding relationships and conceptual issues (and seeing how their theories work); practitioners are in a unique position to observe, understand, and work with organizations and/or community members as change agents; community leaders are concerned community members working for the welfare of the community; peripheral stakeholders are groups with related interests; and members of the community are at the point of action. The groups needed to make the KMb process work usually have very different backgrounds, languages, thinking patterns, goals and mental models. Not only is communication a challenge, but the movement from knowledge to action may be equally challenging. Similarly, moving knowledge from potential to actual effective action is an equally significant challenge. Not only are there translations blocks between theoretical and pragmatic knowledge, but there may also be blocks between pragmatic knowledge

The key to personal change:
AWARENESS
UNDERSTANDING
BELIEVING
FEELING GOOD
OWNERSHIP
EMPOWERMENT

and the process of applying it. For example, before a community member may be willing to take action suggested by the researcher or practitioner, a number of specific activities must occur. First, the community member must be made *aware* of the linkage or possible application of research findings to a specific issue. Once aware, the individual must *understand* the actions driven by the research and the expected results. Then, they must *believe* that the action is real and will work as assumed. Given these three achievements, the individual must then *feel good* about taking the action. These feelings are what make the action important to the individual and worthy of their efforts. Unfortunately, even this is often not enough. Individuals must then feel *ownership* of the action (personal responsibility to act) and feel they are *empowered* to take action. Feeling empowered means they believe they have the right and freedom to take the action (self efficacy). While these elements are not necessarily sequential, together they represent a significant force for energizing action. The challenges presented by these six elements—awareness, understanding, believing, feeling good, ownership and empowerment—make it clear just how difficult it may be to mobilize knowledge such that individuals take action and change their perspective and behavior. On the other hand when necessary they can occur nearly simultaneously. For example, if you are walking past a swimming pool where a small child falls into the water and no one else is around, you would almost instantly experience all of these elements and jump in to save the child.

Another challenge facing knowledge mobilization efforts is the learning needed by practitioners and community members (actors). For learning to be successful at the community level, the actors must have a familiarity with the KMb process and be willing—and capable—of *understanding the results from a research perspective* in terms of their short and long-term impact. During this process, the actors can develop a considerable amount of knowledge and understanding relative to their local community behavior and needs. These results can then be fed back to the practitioners and the researchers to aid in improving their professional competencies and in understanding the degree and quality of knowledge mobilization that has occurred.

3.3 THE PLAYERS AND THEIR ROLES

Figure 3-2 provides an overview of the major constituents of the knowledge mobilization process. This model identifies specific stakeholders and shows their broad relationships to each other. Practitioners are situated in the middle of the inner circle between the researchers (on the left) and the target audience or community members at the point of action (on the right). While this model presents these groups as separate, the researcher may also be a practitioner, or a practitioner may also be a community leader or member. As expected, there will be various advocates and policymakers such as local politicians or other governance bodies involved. Policymakers may or may not play a major role in a specific KMb process. The researchers provide the fundamental research that supports community needs and are usually associated with either universities or research institutes.

Much like the general public, the developers referenced in Figure 3-2 are generally peripheral to the KMb process, yet nevertheless quite important. From a broad perspective, developers create the research and the knowledge needed to understand how to approach a resolution of the beneficiary's needs through a specific knowledge mobilization process. While all bubbles shown represent stakeholders to various degrees, the inner circles of researchers, practitioners and the target audience (or community) represent the major participants in the KMb process.

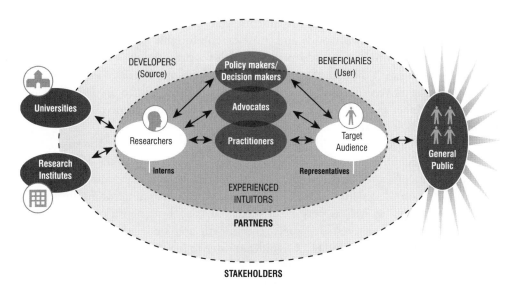

FIGURE 3-2: Potential players.

What are the roles played by these participants? Artificially bounding the KMb process—which is and must be a continuous loop among stakeholders—at the left of the model (Figure 3-2 above) are **researchers** (generally connected with a university, research institute or research-based organization) whose primary role is to research and understand fundamental theories, concepts, relationship and aspects of reality in some specific domain. From a KMb perspective, this fundamental knowledge provides the deep understanding and conceptual grounding for the knowledge mobilization process. At the same time, the output of a knowledge mobilization process is based on feedback to the researcher which either reinforces or modifies previous research findings. This feedback loop is very important for the development of fundamental knowledge as well as validation of the community's actions. It also serves to improve the future capacity of knowledge mobilization programs by providing models for both the broad and iterative application of specific areas of fundamental knowledge. As a specific knowledge mobilization process unfolds, researchers work closely with practitioners and community actors to promote understanding and aid in guiding the approach taken, then learning from stakeholder feedback and working with the KMb team to make changes and take actions driven by those changes. In addition, it is likely that the results from a knowledge mobilization process will yield ideas for further research, potentially outlining community research needs and identifying

RESEARCHERS

The KMb process is a closed loop process which leverages both researcher's expertise and community practices and insights.

65

new collaboration opportunities for researchers and universities.

PRACTITIONERS

The role of **practitioners** in the knowledge mobilization process is a challenging and rewarding one. For those entangled in the KMb process, scholar practitioners is an apt description of this role. Practitioners must be capable of understanding the researcher's knowledge and transforming that knowledge into a language that is understandable to community actors. Since to do this the practitioner must understand the culture and language of the local community, the practitioner's role stands midway between the research theorist and the community actors. In a sense practitioners bridge two worlds and must be comfortable conversing and sharing ideas in both. Simultaneously, a primary role of a practitioner is that of a change agent working with the community to provide insights, advice, direction and energy to create the movement toward action at the community level. To do this effectively, the practitioner must be capable of working with community members as both a respected colleague and an adviser.

Practitioners bridge two worlds and must be comfortable conversing and sharing ideas in both.

The practitioner is also in a position to closely observe the overall results of the knowledge mobilization effort and hence to participate heavily in the assessment of the outcome. As a major player, the practitioner receives and integrates information and builds knowledge from all participating individuals including community actors and researchers, as well as peripheral stakeholders such as politicians, committee leaders and other interested people. The growth and understanding that occurs during the KMb process can be of significant value to practitioners who are initiating other KMb processes and interested in improving community capacity for KMb programs. In addition, as the change agent to the community, the practitioner can learn much about the community and how it can mobilize talent, experience and energy to change behavior and create value that meets its needs.

A joint role of practitioners and researchers is to monitor the systemic effects of the knowledge mobilization process as it unfolds. This role requires a number of competencies such as social skills to interact effectively with community members, the ability to work with groups and facilitate teams, and some understanding of systems theory and complex systems. Familiarity with specific activities such as action learning, dialogue, appreciative inquiry, etc. would also prove helpful. Integrative competencies that can help accelerate the KMb process are discussed later in this chapter.

COMMUNITY LEADER

The role of the **community leader** may possibly be a dual one, that of a community member taking the action (actor) while simultaneously leading the larger community in taking action to change behavior and create value. The role of community leader can be both challenging and fulfilling. Individuals who embrace this role are typically concerned community members who recognize the value of specific research findings and are willing to offer their time and energy to help improve community welfare. They generally have an awareness of the context of the situation (problem/opportunity), are open to change, accept risk, understand their community and their role, develop direction, believe that the process will work, feel good about the effort, accept ownership, and are always ready for action. In other words, they imbue all the qualities of change from within while exerting effort to facilitate change in the community. Note that this follows the pattern of change introduced earlier in this chapter. While knowledgeable people can take active roles in guiding and implementing community action, it requires a significant commitment to work with others in the community to get them to understand and participate in a knowledge mobilization process. Thus, community leaders must be leaders by example as well as by position/status in the community, not only willing to learn and change their own behavior, but also to work with others to try various approaches. As KMb is implemented, community leaders would be constantly monitoring progress and learning from feedback while keeping other members of the community involved and active.

Community leaders must be leaders by example as well as by position and status in the community.

Community leaders represent key decision-makers at the level of implementation, and as such they will be heavily involved in committee meetings and discussions that deal with concerns, fears and anxieties related to proposed actions. These stakeholder leaders are in the best position to understand, assess and learn from community actions as implementation proceeds. In implementing the process, as Lee and Garvin contend, effective knowledge exchange depends on multi-directional, participatory communication among stakeholders (Lee and Garvin, 2003). Community leaders represent the core energizing group within the community and will be a major contributor to the success of the process. Upon them will most likely fall the long-term responsibility of ensuring that the community continues its progress toward self-improvement and growth.

A fourth group could be called **peripheral stakeholders**, although this could be somewhat misleading because they may often play a signfiicant role in determining the success of a KMb effort. These stakeholders would include senior political leaders in the community, educators, businessmen and clergy. All of these people have a stake in the welfare of the community, and can provide considerable assistance and support to a knowledge mobilization effort if they choose to do so. It makes sense that this group be identified and brought into the KMb effort as soon as practical. If they can be sold on the value of the effort, they will play an extremely important role in the activities and in the start-up of other knowledge mobilization efforts in response to other community needs. (See the discussion on social marketing in chapter 2.) If the community is large, this group could be instrumental in building a KMb program that would enable their community to create, share, and apply knowledge to meet their needs. Such an internal capacity provides a major force in rebuilding or growing a community.

PERIPHERAL STAKEHOLDERS

A fifth group of stakeholders is made up of the **members of the community** who are simultaneously the contributors to and recipients of the outcome of the process. This group includes community institutions such as churches, businesses, educational systems, etc., as well as social groups such as families, individuals or children. For KMb processes designed to improve community welfare or to satisfy some specific need within a community, this fifth group of stakeholders represents the individuals that stand to benefit the most from the effort and at the same time have much to contribute to its success. Their actions and the resulting changes in behaviors, attitudes or feelings with respect to a particular issue within the community

COMMUNITY MEMBERS

are critical to solving community problems. When these stakeholders are willing to listen, learn and adapt as they interact with practitioners and community leaders in the KMb effort much can be accomplished. Simultaneously, these individuals are uniquely situated to inform and challenge proposed solutions to ensure that the research being applied and the approach taken to apply it are realistic, appropriate and sensitive to the needs and aspirations of the community.

Those individuals within the community who are most interested in the changes, and who are most knowledgeable concerning related issues, will take on the greatest responsibility and provide the energy, spirit and direction necessary to move the community towards successful implementation. In other words, these individuals—once committed—become the diffused leaders and change agents essential for project success. Since significant change comes from the inside, individual members of the community must decide that change is necessary, worthwhile and achievable. Early implementers in a community are able to share stories, ideas, beliefs and hopes that can lead to acceptance by the larger community of the *need for and possibility of* change. Engaged community members can also provide a source of continuous, realistic, and useful feedback to practitioners, researchers and other stakeholders. This feedback, a natural part of action research, can significantly improve future applications of research findings. Still another role played by this group is to create and support new ideas within the community that will aid in solving the issues at hand and help ensure the sustainability of the gains made through the KMb process.

Once committed, community members become the diffused leaders and change agents that are the cornerstones of the KMb process.

In describing the above five groups in the knowledge mobilization process, it is not implied that each group has its own set of responsibilities independent of the others. As is the case in all complex organization systems, there are many interrelated players. For example, in dealing with overcoming local barriers to change, both practitioners and community leaders will actively engage with researchers in recognizing, identifying and interpreting the latest research results. While researchers undoubtedly play a major role, practitioners provide the community perspective and efficacy of the research relative to community needs. Similarly, whereas the quality of the research would need to be judged by the researcher, the applicability of it to a specific community would be better determined by a team composed of the researcher, the practitioner and community leaders. In assessing the outcome of a specific process, all of these individuals may be involved to varying degrees. (See chapter 7 on assessing outcomes and impacts.)

Each member of the KMb process will have a different approach to the integration of the various knowledges that will arise and have to be understood and acted upon.

Geographical dispersion may cause difficulty in linking partners separated by distance. This could be due to the rural nature of the geographic location, the traffic jams in cities or the physical separation between researcher, practitioner and community members. This issue may be mitigated by travel and use of virtual technologies such as video conferencing and e-mails, although rural areas may have limited cell telephone coverage or high-speed Internet. However, face-to-face meetings, conferences and dialogue will significantly aid in achieving success.

Whatever the venue, the importance of sharing understanding, trust and a truly collaborative approach to working together cannot be overstressed. These form the foundation upon which community actions become successful and long-lasting.

Each member of the knowledge mobilization process will have a different approach to the integration of the various knowledges that will arise and have to be understood and acted upon. (See the knowledge taxonomy in chapter 2.) The researcher, the practitioner, the community member, and the policy-maker will likely all come from different worlds, with different languages, perceptions, ways of thinking and expectations, and *focusing on different types of knowledge*. Yet these groups must somehow collaborate effectively for the good of the community. The common bond and interdependency arises from the objective of the process; to improve the welfare of a specific community. This shared vision and clear understanding of the KMb process, coupled with the learning that naturally arises as the process unfolds, will go far in overcoming the differences among these constituent groups and, of course, expert facilitation and a well-designed project start-up workshop will help.

Another issue may arise from the external responsibilities and pressures on any of the groups discussed above. For example, researchers often have teaching responsibilities and other demands that may minimize their availability. Policy-makers are always balancing the needs and demands of one set of constituents with another. Practitioners may be unable to devote sufficient time to the project or the project may not have sufficient funds available to provide adequate employment. Community members frequently have family and other commitments that must be balanced with their desire to implement the KMb process. Because of these various constraints, prior to beginning a knowledge mobilization process the resources, priorities, needs and importance of the project must be well accepted and understood. (See the discussion on project management in chapter 6.)

3.4 CHARACTERISTICS OF THE COMMUNITY

What would it take to build a knowledge mobilization program focused on community welfare? What has not been addressed so far are the characteristics of the community necessary to support a knowledge mobilization program; that is, to support the capacity to build, maintain and implement knowledge mobilization processes directed toward identified community needs. From a top-level perspective, a community must recognize the benefit of such a program, understand how it works, and be willing to expend the energy and cost of implementation. However, recognition follows cognition, i.e., without an understanding of the negative aspects of the need and the positive aspects of the implementation of the proposed solution it would be difficult to recognize value in a KMb process.

Recognition follows cognition. A need must be recognized before a solution can be accepted and implemented.

The community—as a community—must possess a certain level of willingness, trust and desire for improvement. It should also recognize and respect the importance and power of learning, information and knowledge. This recognition itself may require a KMb effort. As with learning, knowledge mobilization is somewhat of a self-fulfilling prophecy. The initial success of a KMb process is critical to pave the way for community learning and openness to further KMb processes.

69

The following factors play a significant role in determining knowledge mobilization process success. Although wide-ranging, these diverse factors are notable for emphasizing flexibility, collaboration and long-term planning horizons.

- User friendly actionable format
- Commitment and enthusiasm of stakeholders
- Adequate resources
- acilitative strategies
- Attention, time and energy
- Fit between research knowledge and stakeholder needs
- Enabled discussion of findings
- Active collaboration among stakeholders
- Continuing dialogue
- Joint insights
- Choosing a range of activities
- Outreach focused beyond traditional academic circles or community stakeholders
- Experiential approach to implementation
- Willingness to try new things in new settings, open to listening and learning
- An action orientation throughout the process
- Unique opportunity to discover and personalize the sharing of research
- Professionals operating as boundary spanners
- Appreciative inquiry approach
- Action learning

Chapter 4 discusses KMb activities more fully. Appreciative inquiry and action learning are discussed in chapter 2.

3.5 INTEGRATIVE COMPETENCIES

Integrative competencies are knowledge and skill sets that provide connective tissue, creating the capacity, abilities and behaviors that support and enhance other competencies. For example, knowledge management could be considered an integrative competency since it is used to support the creation, sharing, leveraging and application of knowledge in the functional area of interest or practice. Integrative competencies are process accelerators that have a multiplier effect through their capacity to enrich an individual's cognitive abilities while enabling connections to and integration of other competencies, leading to improved understanding, performance, and decisions. In the KMb process they can be used to develop active citizens and stakeholders rather than passive consumers. For example, some of those listed below include skills, capacities and literacies that allow technology to contribute to rather than restrain or restrict individual growth and development.

Integrative competencies create the capacity, abilities and behaviors that support and enhance other competencies.

3.5.1 Knowledge Mobilization Literacy

Knowledge Mobilization Literacy is a new competency arising from the need to develop team member competence in overseeing, integrating and building effective KMb processes. Competencies needed would include meta-knowledge and knowledge management; systems and complexity thinking; facilitation and collaboration skills; and expertise in action research, action learning, appreciative inquiry, social research, learning theory, human and organizational development, critical thinking, dialogue, and creative thinking.

3.5.2 Media Literacy

Media has expanded beyond radio, television, motion pictures and recordings to have a ubiquitous presence. Where there is a proliferation of media and digital technologies into every aspect of social life, the boundaries are blurring between entertainment, business and education. This convergence of life styles and information saturation simultaneously offers the opportunity for embracing new way of learning and the potential for a new digital divide in terms of access to and understanding of new information and communications technologies (ICTs). Thus, as knowledge mobilization embraces new media solutions, media literacy becomes necessary to effectively integrate the activities of the KMb process with the surrounding media presence.

Where there is proliferation of media and digital technologies into every aspect of social life, the boundaries are blurring between environment, business and education.

Media literacy is focused on developing an informed and critical understanding of the nature of mass media, and the techniques and impact of techniques used by the media (Duncan, et al., 2000). The specific focus of media literacy is on how the media contributes to meaning and the construction or perception of reality through hands-on and experiential approaches to learning. A media workshop might also build an understanding of the power of the visual image through hands-on exploration of computer animation and video production techniques. In the first *Media Literacy Resource Guide* published by the Canadian Ontario Ministry of Education, teachers and students were invited to view "media" as texts to be decoded and deconstructed, while encouraged to ask questions about ownership, ideology, bias and representation of social interests, all contributing to critical thinking (Ontario Ministry of Education, 1986). In the KMb process this competency includes the capacity to use the media to improve the process as well as possibly shielding the process from an aggressive media presence, depending on specific circumstances.

3.5.3 Information Literacy

Information literacy is a set of skills that enables individuals to recognize when additional information is and is not needed, and how to locate, evaluate, integrate, use and effectively communicate information. These skills are critical in dealing with the daily barrage of information, whether in community life or in a KMb process, and in using the broad array of available tools to search, organize, and analyze results, and communicate and integrate them for decision-making. Information literacy includes learning how to use the Internet, selecting resources, searching resources, evaluating information, using information, and information ethics. Using the Internet would include understanding common terms and exploring the different types of search tools available and methods for surfing and searching. Selecting resources ties specific types of searching to a search for specific information, including use of the deep web. Searching resources is a strategy for understanding and planning a search approach within documents. Evaluating information can be difficult in an open system where anyone can put anything up on the Internet, and information may or may not be accurate or up to date. Critical thinking is one approach to discerning the value of information resources.

Since information literacy is critical to stakeholders' use of web resources, an information literacy toolkit or virtual course for users may need to be available or perhaps downloadable at the point of interface to web resources. Finally, the Internet has introduced new ethical problems in the areas of intellectual property rights, privacy of information, copyright, plagiarism, filtering, or restricting access to Internet content, and the privacy of users. Information literacy also includes skills in virtual communication.

Information literacy is a critical skill for anyone to achieve in the 21st century.

3.5.4 Research Literacy

Research literacy is a basic requirement for a KMb group because of the continual learning processes that occur during KMb implementation. For example, a virtual course or learning session or event focused on the research process—and how it could impact communities—would be useful in orienting potential community members toward a knowledge mobilization effort. Research literacy would also be instrumental in helping decision-makers and non-academic stakeholders understand research processes and the meaning of research findings, improving communications, facilitating shared understanding and gaining larger participation in—and support of—the KMb process.

Topics in research literacy might include writing grant proposals, introduction to community-based research, research designs, research ethics, and participatory approaches to program assessment. In addition, a case study discussion concerning a previously successful KMb process could be highly informative to non-research oriented individuals. Such a case study could address not only successes and lessons learned but also potential problems and core issues such as multi-university collaboration and commercialization of research results.

3.5.5 Systems and Complexity Thinking

An understanding of systems and complexity thinking provides individuals with a high-level perspective of the KMb process and its potential entanglement (intended and potential unintended effects) within the community. A system is a group of elements or objects, the relationships among them and their attributes, with some defined boundary providing the ability to distinguish whether an element is inside or outside the system. Conceptually, complexity is the condition of a system or situation that is integrated with some degree of order but has too many elements and relationships to understand in simple analytic or logical ways (Bennet & Bennet, 2004).

All organizations or groups of people will naturally operate as complex adaptive systems. To understand their nature, their characteristics and how they react to external changes, an understanding of the language and basics of complexity theory is needed. Since any research that involves people touches both systems and complexity, this becomes an integrative competency for the implementers of research. For example, systems and complexity thinking can support leader and stakeholder understanding of the interconnectedness of a wide array of activities underway, the difficulty of tracking cause and effect relationships, the power of emergence, and potential paths for facilitating and nurturing change.

Knowledge has the ability to mobilize people by creating an atmosphere of collaboration, producing a common vision, and leveraging shared understanding.

3.5.6 Management Skills

A myriad of management skills come into play during the KMb process, ranging from strategic planning and event planning to program administration and project management to conflict resolution and financial management. There is a discussion of project management in chapter 6. As in all programs and projects dealing with multiple stakeholder groups, the quality and level of management and leadership skills engaged may well determine the success of the KMb program.

REFLECTIVE QUESTIONS CHAPTER 3

> Think about a problem that you have recently solved. Are the steps taken to resolve this problem similar to the eight steps of the generic KMb process model?

> Reflect on times during the last few weeks that might be defined as knowledge moments. Have there been any times when you purposefully avoided a knowledge moment? Why?

> Do you identify more with the role of researcher, practitioner, community leader, peripheral stakeholder or community member? In a recent community event, what role did you play?

> How might learning more about one integrative competency introduced in this chapter assist you in your work? In your personal life?

> If you were facilitating a dialogue between a research psychologist, a high school principal and the town mayor on a local problem with teenager DWI (drinking while intoxicated), what knowledge sharing issues would you expect and how would you deal with them?

CHAPTER 4

THE KMb ACTIVITIES MODEL

THIS SECTION INCLUDES: 4.0 INTRODUCTION; 4.1 POINT ACTIONS AS TOOLS; 4.1.1 Events, 4.1.2 Event Intermediation, 4.1.3 The KMb Center, 4.1.4 Published Products; 4.2 META-TOOLS, 4.2.1 Translation, 4.2.2 Consulting Services, 4.2.3 Media Productions, 4.3 Sustainability Tools, 4.3.1 The Living Network, 4.3.2 Living Repositories, 4.3.3 The Living Document, 4.3.4 Media and Web Communications; 4.4 MEMES.
FIGURE: 4-1 KNOWLEDGE MOBILIZATION PROGRAM ACTIVITY.

4.0 INTRODUCTION

The activities that support knowledge mobilization roughly fall into three categories: events occurring at a specific point in time (point events); meta-tools; and sustainability. (See Figure 4-1, Knowledge mobilization program activity.) Point events are product-based and are situation dependent and context sensitive. Research, products and decisions would be considered point events since they occur at a point of time within an identified framework. Examples would be research findings, reports and studies, fact sheets, policy and direction, and books and articles. Events might also include knowledge fairs, town halls, symposia, and conferences. The value of point events is generally understood by those who have engaged in knowledge transfer.

Knowledge mobilization meta-tools reflect set design philosophy, a robust capability in that they can be used in different situations and contexts. Different tools can be used individually or in varying combinations to achieve the desired results. This "set design" approach was introduced in the automobile industry in the 1980's by requiring subsystem contractors to design their subsystems with significant flexibility to adjust their parameters. For example, a manufacturer might make tradeoffs within certain bounds such as designing an item so that it could be used within flexile parameters such as smaller but heavier, or with less power but greater volume. Eventually set design led to open systems design. The concept as used here represents a process in which KMb tools are designed with the flexibility to respond to a number of different situations as they unfold.

> *Knowledge mobilization meta-tools reflect set design philosophy, a robust capability that can be used in different situations and contexts.*

Meta-tools are process accelerators that are repeatable, scalable and robust. Examples would be best practices and best practice patterning (observing the patterns emerging from multiple applications of a best practice in different situations or different best practices in the same situation), andragogy/pedagogy and curriculum for classes or a model for the transfer of research language. Integrative competencies could also be considered meta-tools. Continuing rewards programs and the Knowledge Impact in Society (KIS) program run by The Social Sciences and

Humanities Research Council of Canada (SSHRC) are meta-tools, and any process coming out of a SSHRC-funded program that is repeatable and available for reuse could also be considered a meta-tool. In general, meta-tools are designed for multiuse and multidimensionality, to be used in different ways in different situations.

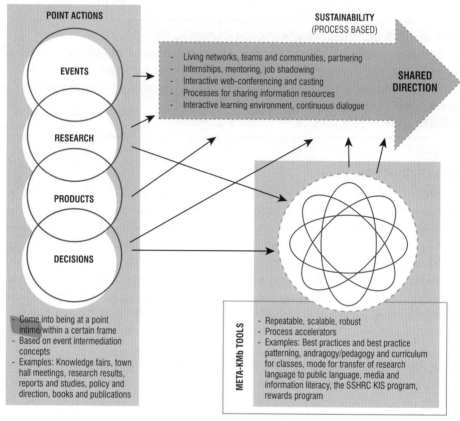

In a KMb process point events provide the venue for knowledge moments, meta-tools serve as process accelerators, and sustainability tools support the continuous flow of knowledge among stakeholders.

FIGURE 4-1: Knowledge mobilization program activity.

Sustainability of knowledge mobilization is based on developing a living network focused on connectivity and open resources, information flows, and the sharing of understanding through trusted relationships. Technology-based examples would be interactive learning environments and interactive web-conferencing and casting. Teams, communities, internships, mentoring, job shadowing, and processes for the continuous sharing of information resources might also be considered sustainability processes.

It is always appropriate to note that any model is an artificial construct, yet models provide a vehicle for focusing on, understanding and sharing concepts. Considerable overlaps in the KMb activities model will occur. For example, while development of a technology system might be considered a point event, the use of that system would be considered either a meta-tool (for example, a process for extracting research summaries) or a sustainability factor (an on-going community of practice support system). Likewise, point events develop resources for sustainability systems, and meta-tools may be technology-enabled for wide dissemination, ease of use, and continuous availability (becoming sustainability tools). Another example would be a KMb Advisory Board. While the Board is a sustainability factor, its meetings could be considered point events. What is important is to ensure that the value of all three activity areas is understood and engaged as appropriate to a specific KMb process.

The following three sections will begin to address the wide range of possibilities in each of the three areas of point events, meta-tools and sustainability. Appendices A, B, C, D, and E support this discussion.

What is important is to ensure that the value of all three activity areas is understood and engaged as appropriate to a specific KMb process.

4.1 POINT ACTIONS AS TOOLS

Point actions provide the venue for knowledge moments, creating a place and space where knowledge can grow. Since knowledge and change come from within the individual or community, not from outside, passive exposure to new ideas is not enough. Interaction among diverse stakeholder viewpoints and active engagement with research questions and research findings through reflection, debate and applying the ideas to day-to-day issues provide fuel for learning and change.

Each stakeholder brings unique experiences and an extensive set of skills, resources and strengths to the KMb process. Whether stakeholders are academics, service providers, policy makers, family members, or other community citizens, they can enhance their knowledge, understanding and awareness through the sharing of knowledge and passions. When stakeholders are engaged in an event, they have the opportunity to *listen to each other*—a diversity of mental models and thoughts in action—and thus they can better understand the range of views on pertinent issues. The key word in the previous sentence alludes to *engagement*, not a passive hearing, but an active talking and listening, moving toward further interaction and potential intermediation as shared understanding emerges.

Since knowledge and change come from within the individual or community, passive exposure to new ideas is not enough.

Implementation of research findings brings with it the responsibility to connect with—and take advantage of—all identifiable sources of energy around the area of research and the stakeholder segment potentially affected by research results. For example, this knowledge might help policy-makers, associations, and community advocates to connect a group of stakeholders with associated groups of stakeholders in other geographical locations to facilitate educational encounters and collective understanding.

In the beginning of relationship building, workshops built around key concepts of KMb (such as action research, participative inquiry, action learning, social marketing, appreciative inquiry, and so forth) as they apply to the specific project of commitment, can be used to build a common understanding of the theory and intent behind actions. In addition, all stakeholders can apply this knowledge from their unique frame of reference to support successful implementation. For example, social marketing techniques can be used in the day-to-day work of advocates and practitioners.

In the KMb Activity Model, Point Actions are presented under the categories of: Events, Event Intermediation, The KMb Center, Consultation Services and Published Products. In addition, there are four representative tools discussed in Appendix A that cross the space of these areas. These are dialogue, rewards programs, storytelling and models. Appendix A (and the other appendices) are intended as idea generators. For example, it may be appropriate for researchers and practitioners to participate in a trade show (that has some connective thread to the research being applied) that offers the potential to reach the target audience.

4.1.1 Events

Events are considered face-to-face activities that provide some level of stakeholder interaction. Events, happenings, or occurrences are designed to be of significance or noteworthy, facilitating the generation of multiple sensory responses which have a greater likelihood of connecting to long-term memory, thus achieving greater impact. This means planning for and nurturing knowledge moments and other memorable moments (stories, announcements, awards, demonstrations, humor, etc.).

Singapore engages the full scope of the human senses in its National Day celebration!

Every year Singapore holds a national parade onto the anniversary of its freedom. While this event is a celebration of independence, it is also used as a means to inculcate Singapore's shared values: Nation before community and society above self; family as the basic unit of society; community support and respect for the individual; consensus, not conflict; and racial and religious harmony. These values are not just said, but shown and felt during the event. For example, in the 2007 national parade called "PosibiCity" (where 27,000 citizens received free tickets for the actual event, and another 54,000 received free tickets to attend the full-event practice sessions), each visitor was provided a colored knapsack filled with food, drinks, coupons, hats, lights, flags, mini-fans, games, and more. Presenting a dynamic defense display, there were large contingents from the Army, Navy, Air Force, Police Force, and Civil Defence Force, including commandos freefalling from 6000 feet on the floating marina stage, F-16s executing afterburner flyovers and bomb bursts, Naval divers jumping off helicopters into the bay, CH-47D Chinook helicopters staging fly-bys, and AH64 Apache helicopters executing maneuvers, and boats and rescue squads. The event offered new music by Singapore artists (played on the radio and television throughout the week), three hours of dancing and marching and fireworks, with hundreds of cheerleaders (National Bay Ambassadors) spread throughout the audience leading interactive cheers and waves, accenting the Singapore event of the year. There was an orchestra of 240 musicians (combined from five separate Singapore music groups); dozens of world-renown, Singapore-based performers; 600 students from primary schools; 600 students from secondary schools, 1600 performers from the Singapore SOKA Association (500 of whom were senior citizens); 400 convent students; and 460 performers from the People's Association. All this was concluded by massive fireworks displays and dancing fountains and moving light visuals created against rising mist. As a Singaporean who had participated in the National Day parade a few years previously said, "We may complain about this and that all through the year, but on National Day we're proud to be Singaporeans." This is clearly a memorable event for both those participating and those in the stands.

WHERE events are held can add value. Events may have a greater impact if locations are in relationship with the research focus or the stakeholder community. For example, the recreation room in an elder care center might be an appropriate setting for a roundtable meeting about the effects of abuse on the elderly. Similarly, a local church or school might serve as the site of a town hall involving stakeholders who live in low-income neighborhoods; or a museum may serve as the backdrop for cultural research.

Where events are held can send a powerful message.

Appendix A offers a wide selection of potential knowledge mobilization events. However, once a specific event is identified as part of the KMb event set, the focus is on HOW the event is designed, HOW it is executed, and HOW the energy generated during the event can continue adding value long after the event is over. Design of an event becomes part of the change strategy, actively engaging multiple stakeholders in the planning process, a process from which some level of ownership emerges and the journey toward shared understanding has begun.

An event does not need to be a one-time affair. Not only can it be part of a larger event set, it is also extended by providing resources and energy through print products, web-based products, meta-tools, or, in the larger scope of social marketing, tools to influence. Sessions are recorded, information aggregated and made available on websites, interviews and speeches are videotaped, or perhaps the event itself is video-streamed to allow real-time, interactive participation to a wide audience, with an asynchronous version stored for future reference. For example, when the U.S. Department of the Navy (DON) held town halls for knowledge fairs, there were three or four camera crews capturing senior leaders talking about their organization's successes in knowledge management. These crews also interviewed project groups. Later, a CD was created that included these videos and sent to DON facilities around the world to expand the level of shared understanding generated from the event.

Events can keep on going through continued networking, reusing resources, and capturing feedback for improvement.

Events also offer the opportunity for data collection and feedback to evaluate and assess progress toward a stated goal. Feedback can be solicited from participants verbally (informally) or in writing (formally). For example, you might ask participants to fill out a brief survey asking whether the event was relevant, useful, energizing, and empowering; what additional information is needed on the topic and how stakeholders can work closer together; and what feelings and insights they might share on the implementation of research findings. The survey itself could be constructed with input from both researchers and practitioners. Results could then be made widely available through a website, and—in a continuous process of improvement— what is learned from one event can be used to improve the next, or expanded over to other delivery and support media. Responses to survey results would also be solicited from stakeholders and placed on the web site. Similarly, any changes or actions taken because of this data collection could be placed on the web site and connected to the original and supplemented survey results.

Events and activities are designed to specifically address the type of outreach and engagement needed to communicate research and research implementation issues. While the listing in Appendix A presents some available options, this is not an exclusive set, but is intended to offer ideas that have worked or have the potential to work in relation to knowledge mobilization of research in the social sciences and humanities.

4.1.2 Event Intermediation

Event intermediation is the use of a planned, collaborative event to move from intention to reality. An intermediary connects knowledge seekers with knowledge sources by relating, researching, validating, reshaping, and transferring information. Planned and supported through communities, event intermediation is a tool for facilitating the horizontal and vertical sharing of knowledge at a point in time as part of a larger change journey. Historically, humans work and strive to create change with only slightly visible results, then some event occurs which connects all this prior activity, the understanding of change pushes everyone to a new strata of recognition, and the entire plain of behavior shifts upward to a new starting point. A good analogy would be the growth of bamboo. For the first four years the young bamboo plant is watered with relatively little visible evidence of growth. But during this time, out of sight, the roots are spreading, interconnecting and becoming strong. Then, during the fifth year, the bamboo plant streaks upward some 20 or more feet.

Historically, humans strive to create change with only slightly visible results, then some event occurs to shift the entire plane of behaviour upward to a new starting point.

Using an appreciative inquiry model, sources are identified where desired actions are successfully occurring, and these are highlighted, shared and rewarded at this event. Although each of these sources may bring to the event only a piece of the process needed to accomplish a desired end state, collectively they provide the evidence that what is being attempted *can* be done, and act as indicators of *how* to accomplish it. This is similar to the amplification and sense and respond approaches in complexity theory. (See the discussion of complexity in chapter 2.)

A larger event approach such as a town hall or a knowledge fair provides the venue for event intermediation. An event of this nature requires wide participation of stakeholders as both presenters and participants, and coordinated, high-level planning for what must be thought of as self-organized local events. For example, in a knowledge fair this might take the form of booths where dozens of stakeholders plan and share their stories. Simultaneously, there might be more formal presentations balanced against demonstrations on the hour. In a town hall format, this might mean simultaneous events such as an expert panel with an audience and live video-feed, a telethon, and a question and answer session being web-cast, with participants moving from one form of media to the next. Other formats might be stand-downs or road shows. Stand-down is a term used in military organizations to refer to a period of time where everyone in the organization "stands-down" from their day-to-day job/requirements to focus on a significant need. For example, during acquisition reform when knowledge needed to be mobilized regarding simplified acquisition procedures, the entire acquisition force of the U.S. Department of Defense spent one day learning and inculcating new procedures, using printed and virtual materials prepared for this event. Regardless of the event(s) used in the KMb process, the aim is to engage a

Event intermediation is the use of a planned and collaborative event to move from intention to reality.

wide array of stakeholders, create conversations, provide take-home resources, and bring all participants to an awareness of and connection with other participants, and a new understanding of the current state of thinking and activity underway, and doing all this in a memorable and influential manner.

As with other events, this might be followed by development of a toolkit which would include video interviews capturing the words of experts and high-level policy-makers; presentations, stories and video clips representing each booth with points of contact; the latest research findings; dialogues from a panel discussion; resource documents; pictures of groups of people; award honorees with descriptions of their work and activity; etc.

4.1.3 The KMb Center

The KMb Center, which could also be considered a sustainability center, is a work place for accomplishing program objectives and developing and assessing new project concepts. It would be a place (or space) for stakeholders to visit, and would include a resource library providing information, knowledge, lessons learned, and state-of-the-art ideas and practices. Most of all, it is a place where stories and anecdotes abound, a place that connects ideas to ideas, people to ideas, and people to people, and a gathering place for stakeholders with common interests and a seed bed for creating knowledge moments.

The KMb Center serves as a work, collaboration and resource center.

A KMb Center might also involve creating a centrally-located community or local university office to coordinate among stakeholders. This office could serve as an interface for groups and organizations to identify and engage with researchers and research in specific areas. This center of excellence concept may also be developed virtually, although that would entail having people and expertise readily available for one-on-one interactions.

4.1.4 Published Products

The listing of published products in Appendix B does not preclude virtual availability, nor should it. Today many scholarly journals are available virtually, and often more virtual subscriptions are sold than print subscriptions. Another notable trend is joint reuse rights of journal articles, i.e., for many publications authors can now re-use their own work where it makes sense. These two trends in journal publication permit wider dissemination of research than in the past.

In like manner, most of the printed materials of today are originally produced on user-friendly software, and thus are easily available for virtual dissemination. While the products in Appendix B are considered print products, they usually are—and should be—made available virtually as long as there is no infringement of copyright. Another approach might be to supply a printed report accompanied with a resource CD that includes an extensive array of data analyses, commentaries, research summaries, and video presentations (which are also downloadable from the website). In all cases, the approach is "both/and", not "either/or".

As with events, published products are designed to take into account the targeted audience of the products. For example, in a research project involved with the elderly, it may be necessary to publish large-print products or develop audio delivery systems to aid accessibility. Or, in an emigrant neighborhood flyers may need to be voiced and published in several languages, and the Internet website equipped with translation capabilities. At many levels, continuously ask: Is this material accessible to the target audience? And further, why would they want to access it?

At many levels continuously ask: Is this material accessible to the target audience? Why would they want to access it?

4.2 META-TOOLS

In this context, meta-tools are fundamental things or processes used to carry out KMb. Generic meta-tools include tools specifically for implementation of KMb. While KMb is the subject matter of various forms of symposia and training, etc., those tools are listed where appropriate in appendix A as events. Generic meta-tools might include academic research papers, environmental scans, a knowledge mobilization handbook, needs assessment study, synthesis, or template. They might also include specific approaches to exploring and getting started such as an experimental project, incubator, matchmaking processes, or a pilot.

Translation, consulting services, and media productions are discussed briefly below. Meta-tools described in Appendix C are organized in the areas of generic, exploring and getting started, developing reference materials, consulting approaches and media productions.

4.2.1 Translation

While research has historically been disseminated through scholarly academic journals, this venue does not serve the non-academic and non-specialist audiences who are the decision-makers for policies, programs and practices that could benefit from that academic research. A challenge for decision-makers is to find appropriate factual information when they need it in a format they can work with to inform actions (Pawson, et al., 2005). Concurrently, the long-term potential of knowledge transformation offered by research findings depends on the capacity of community members to thoroughly understand and participate in the application of research findings.

The responsibility for translation and dissemination of research findings falls primarily on the researcher, the creator or developer of knowledge

Since decision-makers, community members and other stakeholders cannot ask for what they do not know about, the responsibility for translation and dissemination of research findings falls primarily on the researcher, the creator or developer of knowledge. Further, translation and dissemination in terms of knowledge mobilization infer the sharing of understanding and the ability to apply that understanding, bringing the researcher into a partnership with policy-makers and practitioners and the larger community of stakeholders to facilitate implementation of research findings. While this is asking a lot of scholars, the value of KMb to the usefulness of the research itself as well as the application of research findings must be fully recognized by researchers, otherwise KMb may be relegated to a bin called "just another term or condition in the research grant."

The term knowledge translation was popularized by the Canadian Institutes of Health Research (CIHR) to describe the utilization of pure and applied research.

Knowledge translation is interpreted as a complex set of interactions between producers of research and the "translation" of research findings into plain language (CIHR, 2006). "Plain language" (lay language) is used to describe text that is simply written excluding functional and specialty language. Since the translating must be performed by individuals knowledgeable in the functional and specialty language, this is a "push" effort. For example, while plain language research reports for a community would be prepared using a lexicon that high-school students could understand, plain language fact sheets for primary-age children would use a lexicon accessible to the target audience using colorful pictures and symbols to punctuate major themes. Yet the translator may only have a superficial familiarity with the language and imagery of children, necessitating a partnering approach to translation. Similarly, value can be added when translating for a community where the use of cultural language innuendos play a significant role in the understanding of translated words.

Ho described four factors that influence knowledge translation: the role of language in sharing knowledge, effective inter-group communication, accessibility of knowledge, and learning and development in technology-enabled knowledge transfer (Ho, et al., 2003). Davis, who believes that knowledge translation can bridge the gap between what is known and what is practiced, describes five factors that contribute to the success of knowledge translation in effecting change: (1) taking place where practice occurs and acknowledging the social and environmental influences; (2) directing attention to relevant stakeholders; (3) reflecting the interests of relevant stakeholders in a holistic approach; (4) extending practice-based learning and supporting it with evidence-based research findings; and (5) working across disciplines (Davis, et al., 2002).

There are a number of models for knowledge translation and transfer that can add tremendous value to the KMb process.

There have been a number of frameworks forwarded for the transfer of knowledge. One approach is organized in terms of asking five questions: What should be transferred? To whom should it be transferred? By whom should it be transferred? How should it be transferred? And, with what effect (instrumental, conceptual or symbolic) should it be transferred? (Lavis, et al., 2003) In this application, instruction would infer a process or event that would help make knowledge mobilization happen; conceptual would infer the transfer of ideas related to research findings that lay groundwork for knowledge mobilization; and symbolic would infer the bringing together of stakeholders to represent a significant juncture, perhaps the beginning of the KMb process. These effects are not exclusive of each other.

Another approach to translation first identifies the audience the research is trying to influence, then explores their perspective, receptivity to change, capacity to retain knowledge, and learning systems (Ho, et al., 2003). A third approach takes into account the context of the intended user group, the issue, the research itself, and the researcher-user relationship along with dissemination strategies (Jacobsen, et al., 2003).

In bilingual communities, there is the additional requirement to translate plain-language materials into multiple everyday languages. For example, many Canadian provinces have a mixture of French and English literacy. In a virtual environment, this might be accomplished by a multilingual interface and translating key content components. Since many French or English words are not translatable or may have several different representations in an aboriginal native dialect, if there is an aboriginal presence translation might require further steps; for example, specific sounds or expressions or symbols that convey intent. Therefore, a web-based meta-tool might be developed in a specified area of research that could visually, or in story form told by an animated archetypal storyteller, represent the functional concepts that need to be conveyed.

Linking that which is not understood with that which is known can be a challenging problem.

Linking that which is not understood with that which is known can be a challenging problem. Research on individuals who have developed expert knowledge has confirmed that often experts may not know what they know (Ross, 2006). This occurs because much of our knowledge is saved in long-term memory as patterns stored in the unconscious brain instead of detailed explanations of how or why we know. This presents a challenge when research experts, for example, need to communicate aspects of their knowledge to policy-makers, laymen or community members. Formal instruction, facilitated group discussion, dialogue, graphics, stories and anecdotes are all potential ways of communicating insights, "aha" experiences, and intuitive understanding. Presenting information in different formats, using metaphors, analogies, examples, and Socratic questioning can all help translate one person's deep knowledge into a form recognizable and useable by someone else.

Interpretative materials (providing background and context such as historical relevance, economic significance, or future potential to areas of focus) may also be considered aids to translation since they may change the frame of reference from which a user views other material. For example, since there is a significant amount of background material contained in literature reviews key points of these reviews would be rewritten to: (1) exclude any terminology beyond standard research terms; (2) eliminate or rewrite any terminology functionally-specific to the research; and (3) translate language into that understandable by a high-school level.

Interpretative material in support of knowledge mobilization may be information prepared for dissemination and use by community members that supports the relevance and importance of research implementation. For example, there may be historical information that would demonstrate the significance of a specific research effort, or a story that conveys meaning, or a series of quotes from respected and trusted sources, or a study regarding the economic influence of similar research implementation in another community. Following a similar pattern to the discussion of context in chapter 2, the availability of interpretative materials provides expanded opportunities to develop shared understanding across the stakeholder community. The research synthesis process is itself a form of translating research findings into a shorter, more easily consumed form while sustaining core meaning. The difference between translation and synthesis is that thoughts, not language, are the focus of the synthesis. A synthesis would include specific research knowledge pulled from a specific area or concerning a specific issue.

There is a delicate balance between mass dissemination and targeting messages for stakeholders.

There is a delicate balance between mass dissemination and targeting messages for stakeholders. The development of new knowledge is only part of the solution to decision-making. As is becoming clear, new knowledge must be communicated in ways that people can understand and use it.

4.2.2 Consulting Services

One approach to connecting researchers and community stakeholders is to offer consulting services. For example, this could involve university-sponsored faculty members participating in a community planning process, program development, or crisis management. Clearly researchers should be readily available for consultation to research implementers. Conversely, community members may serve as consultants to researchers, a benefit from reciprocal relationships. Several specific consultation approaches are included in Appendix C.

4.2.3 Media Productions

In large or special stakeholder communities, there may be a strong need for producing acceptable and alternative presentations of the audio/visual content of television or movie programming. Tremendous in-roads have been made in improving accessibility for users who are deaf or blind, hard of hearing or with weak vision; for example, closed captioned video (also called video information or described video), or the translation of emotive indicators into animated captions.

Media tools offer the opportunity to not only provide reusable products in support of research findings and implementation, but to bring stakeholders into planning, development and distribution of the media. Feedback from the community can also be embedded during the final editing process. Outside of the content, two underlying themes are universal design and accessible media. See Appendix C for a brief listing of some forms of media production that could be used in KMb.

Two underlying themes for media productions are universal design and accessible media.

4.3 SUSTAINABILITY TOOLS

Sustainability tools provide a central point for collecting and distributing information that supports the activities and processes necessary for implementation of research findings. For example, sustainability is supported by the development of information technology-driven tools that enable information and knowledge sharing among stakeholders. These tools can contribute to the development of trust and respect among stakeholders by supporting the creation or expansion of communities of interest, learning and practice. KMb can be a significant contributing element toward sustainable high performance, especially if it is first built on sustainable relationships.

Electronic venues can be loosely categorized in terms of intranet, extranet, Internet and contact databases. The Internet (also generally called world wide web) is a decentralized set of networks and gateways that crisscross around the world using the same group of protocols (where open information resources and community support programs would reside, and project deliverables diffused as knowledge and training). The intranet is an internal network sharing information management system that acts as a small, contained Internet (where sensitive discussion forums and list servers might reside). While an intranet may be connected to the Internet, it is usually embedded behind a firewall, with controlled stakeholder access. The extranet is generally an extension of a group's intranet, using the public telephone system to expand access to a larger group of stakeholders (where an information clearinghouse might reside). While an open systems approach to knowledge sharing (Internet) may serve as the baseline for providing information to stakeholders, there may also be a need to contain sensitive findings and exchanges within a bounded location or framework, in which case an intranet or extranet may be required. Wherever possible, an open, sharing approach offers the best opportunity for building community. Contact databases such as those offered by iPod use have rapidly gained market share in the attention economy of younger adults. For example, Pod-casts may offer value in rural areas that have a high-speed Internet deficit.

Internet resources are available when they are needed, can be accessed from any Internet computer, and, with a well-thought-out portal, can be made easily available for stakeholders. Information can be both structured and unstructured, and customized to the individual's needs. Communities and online collaboration for research or the research implementation can be included. Open standards allow the combining of systems to meet special needs and wants, and functionality can be built in to allow users to add content. Information can be self-organized, self-archiving, and summaries and newsletters self-generated. In a geographically dispersed and time-limited stakeholder population, there is increasing confidence in Internet sources. For example, in a multi-lingual world, continued momentum is accomplished by a multilingual interface and translating key content components. Strategically mobilized networks can locally, nationally and internationally examine important themes.

Open standards allow the combining of systems to meet special needs and wants.

A technology-based sustainability strategy provides unlimited access to information and knowledge (people) and can overcome barriers of distance and time. By hosting both synchronous and asynchronous approaches, web-based information systems meet the continuous need for stakeholder communication and integration. In this usage, synchronous means fixed, or predictive, such that there is a specific timing to an event. Asynchronous means that the timing is arbitrary, such that a stakeholder could log into an event or exchange at their convenience.

Clumping is organizing data and information driven by the decisions that need to be made using that data and information.

Sustainability issues go beyond hosting and design regarding a web site. Questions to ask include: How will it be interactive? What other resources can we link to? Who will update the information resources hosted on this site? How will it be kept current? Who will have access to it? How will access be made known? How will its value be assessed and continuously improved?

From a user's viewpoint, it is important that the web site have all the necessary information needed to make good decisions. This is a different approach to organizing information. Historically information is clustered, bringing together those things that are similar or related. This way of organizing is *driven by the content* of the data and information. Clumping is organizing data and information *driven by the decisions that need to be made* using that data and information. Considering data and information from this frame of reference changes the way we organize and connect content. It means including or linking to secondary data and information needed by individuals using the primary information for decision-making. This approach requires a change in behavior since the provider of information now takes responsibility for connecting users to additional information that may be required. Thus the provider needs to know something about the situation and the nature and context of decisions that will be made based on system content.

This section does not intend to cover the available approaches and technologies that are emerging in a connected world. The intent is to provide ideas from which to springboard. Ultimately, all of the areas touched in Appendix D deal with connectivity, relationships, information and knowledge around research, research implementation, and the people who touch these. The areas addressed below are: The Living Network, Living Repositories, Media and Web Communications and Virtual Communities. Sustainability tools that are featured in the appendix are cybercartography and best practices/lessons learned.

No tool will be effective unless it is accessible and accessed. Active involvement and ongoing training of users is critical for aggregated data and information to be valued and used. Therefore, outreach work is necessary to ensure that stakeholders become aware of the existence of these resources, and know how to access them. Further, with the recognition of value added, there will be an ever-growing community of seekers, users, and contributors. To ensure continued ease of use, an on-line survey could ask visitors to provide their feelings about the site, the information presented, and its ease of use. Feedback offers the opportunity to continuously improve and refine knowledge mobilization strategies.

4.3.1 The Living Network

The living network brings knowledge sources and knowledge users together in an information exchange that can grow to a collaborative dialogue in virtual spaces for the exchange of ideas and experiences among researchers and stakeholders. By living is meant an iterative and interactive communication and resource network composed of changing content, people and processes but with a focused purpose and scope. A living network can change size, form and means of communication. It would be flexible and adaptable to the changing needs of its members and its environment, and often rather informal based on interests, trust and cooperation. Thus, it will live or die depending on the allegiance of its members, and may even go to sleep for awhile and yet still be available when someone seeks help. Its purpose is to provide efficient and effective knowledge, ideas, opinions and suggestions from trusted colleagues to any of its members.

A living network is an iterative and interactive communication and resource network composed of changing content, people and processes but with a focused purpose and scope.

Designed with open and dynamic systems, both definitive and ever-evolving, and user driven, the living network is composed of systems, connections and links, meta-systems and information repositories that can literally span the world in terms of geographic location and research subjects and approaches. Networks themselves provide the linking function, a means of accessing contact information and short updates on activities. Since the collection and dissemination of information and the creation, sharing and application of knowledge are quite different things, the living network supports interfaces and interactions among members, providing the platform for on-going communities of interest, learning and practice. Question and answer opportunities offer virtual access to personalized resources. Following the Wikipedia model, community members can add their own information in individualized subject modules, or comment on the views and perspectives of others.

To support both browsing and systematic research, the living network is embedded with discovery tools far beyond simple search capabilities and keywords. Tools and widgets such as modeling, data analysis and idea and web mapping support the overlaying of information in new ways. Visualization and representation techniques provide multiple points of view to look at the same phenomena. Contributors and users collaboratively develop organizational schema, and catalogue and review resources.

4.3.2 Living Repositories

The repository is the collection and connection of databases filled with high quality information, research findings, and a myriad of related resources. *What information* is included, how *context* of that information is ensured, and *what is connected* and *how it is connected* become critical issues. While people-to-information connections play an important role in sustainability, documents within repositories are also connected to people, whether it be the individual who wrote them, the individual who championed the ideas written about, the individuals who are implementing these ideas, or an intermediary who can answer questions. Links to these individuals are embedded throughout the living repository.

In a living repository, what information is included, how context of that information is ensured, and what is connected and how it is connected become critical issues.

Repositories need not be static. Diverse search approaches and reference materials hyperlinked to resource materials provide ease of access. Video and audio materials may be embedded or linked. In short, there is the ability to access, integrate, visualize and analyze vast amounts of data and information. Interfaces may be personalized for specific stakeholder groups or specific individuals, automated notification of new content can be programmed on a topic-by-topic basis to specific individuals (via e-mail or cell phone instant text messaging, etc.), and e-bulletins and e-newsletters can be automatically generated and disseminated that summarize new content.

Finally, repositories are *not archives*. They evolve. They need to be updated and rotated, with documents added and removed as needed, becoming an integrated pool of knowledge from a variety of relevant *disciplines* and relevant *people*. Appendix D includes some forms KMb repositories may take. Again, this list is not exclusive, rather a scattering of approaches provided to communicate the spirit of the KMb approach.

4.3.3 The Living Document

Any document must be trustworthy, and convey a sense of legitimacy. That means providing context, identifying the qualifications of the source, and ensuring accuracy and currency of the information. Questions to ask include: Is it clearly written? Is it accessible, easily understood? Can it be put into action? Is additional material or training required to use this material? It is relevant to the issues? What else might be needed?

Other requirements for sustainable materials are that they be user-friendly with feedback mechanisms in place; and, where appropriate, interactive. As part of a living repository, a living document cannot be static. It is flexible and adaptable, providing for the efficient inclusion of and connection to additional expertise. As new information is learned or discovered, additional links are added. As information changes, a rewrite may be necessary (again and again). The living document evolves; and is visibly related to people, so that frames of reference can be assessed and questions vetted.

Since a living document must be flexible and adaptable, and a document can't do that by itself, that means people must make it that way!

4.3.4 Media And Web Communications

While a few generations ago media meant books, newspapers, and magazines (in print format)—and then expanded to include radio, television, motion pictures, and recordings—today media is generally considered to include materials used "in the entry or storage of data in a computer, or in the recording of results from a computer." (Illingworth & Daintith, 2001, p. 128) These are generically described as output media, input media and storage media, although this distinction may overlap. For example, CDs and DVDs could serve all three functions.

This category includes all of the forms of media specifically delivered via the computer. It is expected that products published in print and products from events would also be made available as appropriate via the Internet. For example, bulletins, fact sheets, and reports might become e-bulletins (that could be used to disseminate breaking news), e-fact sheets (that could be available on-line to download and distribute) and e-reports (that could be available as a resource when questions arise). Therefore, while the tools described in chapters 4 and 5 may be delivered in some format via the web, they are not repeated here.

New information systems and "knowledge systems" (those that focus on facilitating the creation of knowledge in users) are emerging every day, presenting new capabilities and offering new ways to work. Yet the concepts of living networks, repositories and documents can serve as stretch goals for imaginative and creative designers, administrators and users. For example, since the human mind is associative (versus the sequential and parallel processing of most computers), how might a system be used to make materials more accessible to stakeholders? The idea is to *keep asking questions* and drawing on the rich intellectual capital of the larger stakeholder group to help facilitate community improvement.

The concepts of living networks, repositories and documents can serve as stretch goals for imaginative and creative designers, administrators and users.

4.4 MEMES

A meme is an idea, behavior, pattern, or piece of information that is passed on, again and again, through the process of imitation such that it takes on a life of its own (Blackmore, 1999). The role that memes play in learning comes from their capability to remain in the memory because of their sound and meaning. Memes become stronger (more memorable) when they are delivered in connection with an emotional event that engages the listener's/participant's feelings.

Another role memes play is to act as replicators of information (that may become knowledge) as they spread throughout groups of individuals. Of course, learning only occurs if their meaning and relevance is understood by individuals within the group. This means that for memes to spread they need to relate to the culture, attitudes, expectations and interests of the group. Learning can be greatly enhanced by the effective choice and use of memes throughout the communication process. People using similar memes, together with common syntax and semantics, can understand each other much more effectively and rapidly, thereby more easily creating social networks which facilitate the transmission of information and the creation of knowledge.

Since memes take on a life of their own, memes can be powerful aids to facilitate change.

Memes can be powerful aids to facilitate change. For example, a meme employed during the 1990's in the U.S. Department of the Navy acquisition system was "Change Thru Ex-Change." The government needed to rapidly facilitate the sharing of ideas during reform of their acquisition system processes. "Change Thru Ex-Change" involved an initial process of collecting best practices and then creating a manual with cross-search mechanisms. This also included implementing a highly-visible program that rewarded the best and the innovative aimed at improving the system, and a culminating event for presentation of those ideas. Since the date this event was scheduled coincided with St. Patrick's Day, the opening and closing precessions were led by a bagpiper. In addition, several entertainers were hired to create humor and music themes that engaged the theme of "Change Thru Ex-Change," and short messages from senior leaders showed their commitment to this project. Attendees (representing every acquisition office) were all provided "dance cards" that were signed by other attendees when they had conversations during regular free-flow periods throughout the day. These cards also had a place to jot down any learning or new ideas that emerged from the exchange.

The event was highly successful. This event wound up being "the gift that kept on giving" (another meme?) Several months later this "Change Thru Ex-Change" process was repeated (with other creative ideas embedded) in other geographically-dispersed parts of the Department with the focus on their own learning needs and new initiatives. The following year there were several more events, quite different at this point, but still focused on "Change Thru Ex-Change." It is clear from this example that memes offer the potential to facilitate the "change thru ex-change" which must occur in a KMb process.

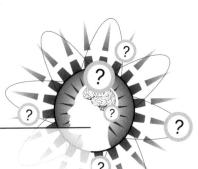

REFLECTIVE QUESTIONS CHAPTER 4

> What are some point actions, meta-tools and sustainability tools that you've participated in or used in your organization or community? What was the result of your participation or use?

> How does event intermediation participate in bringing about change?

> In your day-to-day personal and professional life, what percentage of your time is spent participating in events, what percentage is spent using printed materials, and what percentage is involved in virtual media? How do you think your neighbor would respond to this question? What about your parent, spouse, son or daughter?

> Think of a recent conversation with a colleague where an important message was conveyed. How would you go about conveying this to a high school student? How would you convey this to an elementary school student?

> How might the concepts of a living network, living repository, and living document help you think differently about the way you design and use your personal and professional web pages?

CHAPTER 5

INVOLVING AND EVOLVING LEARNERS

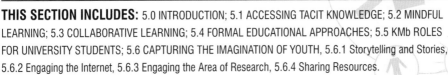

THIS SECTION INCLUDES: 5.0 INTRODUCTION; 5.1 ACCESSING TACIT KNOWLEDGE; 5.2 MINDFUL LEARNING; 5.3 COLLABORATIVE LEARNING; 5.4 FORMAL EDUCATIONAL APPROACHES; 5.5 KMb ROLES FOR UNIVERSITY STUDENTS; 5.6 CAPTURING THE IMAGINATION OF YOUTH, 5.6.1 Storytelling and Stories, 5.6.2 Engaging the Internet, 5.6.3 Engaging the Area of Research, 5.6.4 Sharing Resources. **FIGURE:** 5-1 EXAMPLE OF SOME FORMAL EDUCATIONAL APPROACHES.

5.0 INTRODUCTION

All KMb stakeholders have the dual role of mobilizing knowledge to aid communities and expanding their own knowledge, understanding while appreciating the needs and complexities of their target communities. Thus continuous learning is a very desirable factor in effective KMb implementation.

Learning is the process of acquiring information and creating knowledge so that individuals can change their understanding and behavior to successfully adapt or influence their environment. Thus learning and knowledge are closely related, with learning the process that creates new meaning from experience and new capabilities for action, and knowledge (the capacity for taking effective action) being the result of learning. For purposes of this chapter, a learner is any individual engaged in acquiring information or knowledge related to the area of research, research findings, the implementation of those findings within the stakeholder community and the myriad of disciplines and skills required to successfully administer a process or program.

Learning is the process that creates new meaning from experience and new capabilities for action. Knowledge is the result of learning.

To put learning in perspective, consider several closely related concepts: training, teaching, education, and what might be called acquiring deep knowledge. All of these are forms of learning, each emphasizing a different goal with varying processes used for each. Training deals with developing skills and abilities that do not require abstract concepts or a great deal of experience, and usually has a narrow focus and results that achieve a specific capability. Training would normally emphasize Kaction and Kpraxis (see Figure 2-2). Education is usually thought of as a process of learning about things that provide the learner with a broad, balanced perspective on the world and the ability to understand and deal with many areas of life. It would normally emphasize Klearn and Kstrategic (Figure 2-2). Deep learning refers to the acquisition and understanding of highly abstract and complex concepts, systems and information. It would normally emphasize Kresearch and Kmeta (Figure 2-2). For example, a deep knowledge of calculus would be the ability to solve calculus problems which would include understanding the foundations of the theory, its limitations, and domain of application. Deep knowledge is created by study, reflection, assimilation, practice, problem-solving and "living with the subject." In the KMb process, community leaders or members may possess deep knowledge about the culture of the community created through years of living in the community and interacting, observing and building relationships with its members. It should be noted that considering these three concepts—training, education and deep knowledge—all of them would use all of the seven categories of knowledge at one time or another. A normal distinction in these knowledge categories is pointed out above to give visibility to the challenges of communication and collaboration due to different frames of reference and experiences.

> *Learning underpins the entire KMb process—whether that learning is occurring in researchers, research assistants, students, practitioners, community leaders, policy-makers, or other members of the stakeholder community.*

As introduced in chapter 1, KMb promotes learning and behavioral change through the application of developed knowledge, i.e., research findings. Learning underpins the entire KMb process—whether that learning is occurring in researchers, research assistants, students, practitioners, community leaders, policy-makers, or other members of the stakeholder community. In other words, every participant in the KMb process should be involved in learning, and this learning—primarily social in nature—in turn binds stakeholders together. As Brown and Duguid assert, people are enmeshed in society; that is, language "is a social artifact, and as people learn their way into it, they are simultaneously inserting themselves into a variety of complex, interwoven social systems." (Brown & Duguid, 2000, p. 140) Further,

> *Social learning can occur when individuals with experience and knowledge share their understanding with each other through conversations, storytelling, or dialogue.*

> Looking at learning as a demand-driven, identity forming, social act, it's possible to see how learning binds people together. People with similar practices and similar resources develop similar identities … These practices in common … allow people to form social networks along which knowledge about that practice can both travel rapidly and be assimilated readily. (Brown & Duguid, 2000, pp. 140-141)

This is a description of the desired social system that a KMb process works within to jumpstart change through community learning, reinforced by practitioners, advocates and policy makers. Social learning can occur when individuals with experience and knowledge share their understanding with each other through conversations, storytelling, or dialogue, either formally or casually. The activities of the KMb process support the creation of knowledge moments where "aha's" can erupt and social learning can occur.

Many organizational learning models can be extrapolated across to the KMb process for use with specific community groups focused on implementation of research findings. For example, Crossan, Lane and White (1999), present the four mental model process of intuiting, interpreting, integrating and institutionalizing occurring across individual, group and organizational (community) levels. While these authors describe intuiting as pre-consciously perceived patterns or possibilities in an individual's experience, intuiting could also build upon conversations, observations and study, and connections and relationships (Tomblin, 2007). Interpreting is the process of meaning-making within the particular domain of research; integrating moves community members toward shared understanding resulting in coordinated action; and institutionalizing would describe an end state when the behaviors affected by research findings become embedded in community and community member routines and processes.

The discussions below on accessing tacit knowledge, mindful learning and collaborative learning are provided in light of their contribution to the ongoing KMb process.

5.1 ACCESSING TACIT KNOWLEDGE

Although we have so far been talking about collaboration among individuals and/ or groups, there is another collaboration that is less understood. This is the process of individuals collaborating with themselves. What this means is the conscious mind learning to communicate with, and listen to, the unconscious mind. As individuals observe, experience, study and learn throughout life they generate a large amount of information and knowledge that becomes stored in their unconscious mind. Even though an individual may have difficulty pulling it up when needed, learning how to access the unconscious—and listen to it—can become an extremely valuable learning process. (See the discussion regarding internalized knowledge in chapter 3.)

An individual is able to collaborate with himself when the conscious mind learns to communicate and listen to the unconscious mind.

Knowledge exists in two principal forms (explicit and tacit) and at three levels (the individual, the team (family), and the organization (community)). Regardless of the setting, primary knowledge typically lies within the individual, with secondary knowledge in the major core competencies and the ability of a family (team) or community (organization) to pull people together to implement that core knowledge. All three levels of knowledge become significant when the environment becomes surprise prone and full of uncertainty and complexity. The knowledge at each of these three levels can contribute significantly to overall success by providing a wider capacity for creative thinking, problem solving, decision-making and implementation. While it is explicit knowledge that is normally considered as the primary source of action, there is always a wide and deep basin of tacit knowledge embedded throughout a community that operates quietly to ensure effective day-to-day implementation of KMb. Recognition of the value of this tacit knowledge and the capacity to bring it to the surface and make it explicit is a challenge. This tacit knowledge that the typical individual, family or community does not know it has represents a potential, unused resource awaiting the opportunity to contribute. These same considerations apply to KMb processes, projects and programs.

It has only been in the past few decades that cognitive psychology and neuroscience has begun to seriously explore unconscious mental life with the understanding that conscious experience, thought and action are influenced by concepts, memories and other mental constructs that are inaccessible to conscious awareness and somehow independent of voluntary control (Eich, et al., 2000). At the same time, research in neuroscience is also digging deeper into the understanding of the emotions, working memory and unconscious processing that occur within the human mind, and to some extent throughout the body.

What you know but don't know you know: that's tacit knowledge.

Much knowledge within the individual is invisible, particularly a most valuable knowledge—tacit knowledge. Michael Polanyi, a chemist, was the first to identify and define this type of knowledge. His definition was simple: tacit knowledge is knowledge that cannot be articulated. (Polanyi, 1958) Tacit knowledge will play a significant role in the way KMb team members do their work and communicate with each other. Every individual knows much more than they know they know, and this "hidden knowledge" needs to be surfaced, shared and implemented when appropriate. Because this tacit knowledge is so valuable to project success, learning how to surface, interpret and apply it will greatly enhance the KMb team's performance.

Several factors come into play when considering the challenge of sharing tacit knowledge and making it explicit across a stakeholder group. Clearly one needs a common language, common interests, a common knowledge base and preferably commonality of thinking styles. Context is addressed extensively in chapter 2. A second factor is the degree or level of tacitness of the knowledge itself, which is highly dependent upon the nature of the knowledge as well as its depth and complexity.

According to the description above, it seems clear why sharing tacit knowledge is usually so difficult. If an individual has tacit knowledge but cannot dive down and provide a full linguistic description of its content, then how can a full and open dialogue occur? How can the reasons for or explanation of intuitive decisions be communicated?

Meditation practices, questioning, lucid dreaming, hemispheric synchronization and active reflection can help access tacit knowledge.

Where physical tacit knowledge is concerned (such as riding a bicycle), mimicry is the classic approach that evolution has provided to transfer such abilities, and it seems to work quite well. More recently it has been discovered that there are mirror neurons in the brain which create patterns and associate connections within the mind of an observer; for example, while watching someone perform an act such as a broad jump. If the observer were to perform exactly the same broad jump, these same mirror neurons would be firing within their mind whether they are performing the broad jump or watching themselves on video as they performed the jump. Thus mimicry is a highly successful practice for transferring tacit knowledge of action. Unfortunately, transferring other forms of tacit knowledge such as abstract and cognitive knowledge are not so easy.

The challenge of sharing non-physical tacit knowledge rests with the fact that the knowledge itself exists within the unconscious mind of its owner. In fact, what actually exists in the mind are patterns of neuronal connections and interactions that are subjectively experienced as thought and information. However, when the individual takes action or makes a decision based upon intuition, gut feel, etc. the appropriate part of the unconscious mind moves into action and creates the information which then influences and drives its owners decision, behavior and action. Thus the source of intuition or gut feel, while not usually apparent to the conscious mind of its owner, nevertheless creates the knowledge which drives the thinking and behavior of the individual.

A number of techniques are readily available for those who choose to expand this expertise; for example, meditation practices, questioning, lucid dreaming, hemispherical synchronization (Atwater, 2004), or active reflection with oneself. Meditation practices have the ability to quiet the conscious mind, thus moving into greater access to the unconscious. Another way to access tacit knowledge is to ask yourself a lot of questions related to the task at hand. Even if you don't think you know the answers, reflect carefully on the questions and be patient. Often sleeping on a question can yield an answer the next morning. Lucid dreaming is a particularly powerful way to access tacit knowledge. Tell yourself, as you fall asleep at night, to work on a problem or question. The next morning when you wake up, but before you get up, lie in bed and ask the same question, listening patiently to your own, quiet, passive thoughts. Frequently, but not always, the answer will appear, although it must be written down quickly before it is lost from the conscious mind.

Hemispheric synchronization is when both hemispheres of the brain are in unison, providing the conscious increased access to the subconscious.

Hemispheric synchronization is the use of sound coupled with a binaural beat to bring both hemispheres of the brain into unison (thus the name hemispheric synchronization). Sound and its relationship to humans has been studied by philosophers throughout recorded history; extensive treatments appear in the work of Plato, Kant and Nietzsche. Through the last century scientists have delved into studies focused on acoustics (the science of sound itself), psychoacoustics (the study of how our minds perceive sound) and musical psychoacoustics (the discipline that involves every aspect of musical perception and performance). Simultaneously, neuroscience (the science of the brain) has slowly begun to recognize the capability of internal thoughts and external incoming information (including sound) to affect the physical structure of the brain—its synaptic connection strength, its neuronal connections and the growth of additional neurons (Pinker, 2007).

Binaural beats were identified in 1839 by H. W. Dove, a German experimenter. In the human mind, binaural beats are detected with carrier tones (audio tones of slightly different frequencies, one to each ear) below approximately 1500 Hz (Oster, 1973). The mind perceives the frequency differences of the sound coming into each ear, integrating the two sounds as a fluctuating rhythm. This perceived rhythm originates in the brainstem (Oster, 1973), is neurologically routed to the reticular activating formation (Swann, et al., 1982) and then to the cortex where it can be measured as a frequency-following response (Marsh, Brown & Smith, 1975; Smith et al., 1978; Hink, et al., 1980). This inter-hemispheric communication is the setting for brain-wave coherence which facilitates whole-brain cognition, assuming an elevated status in subjective experience (Ritchey, 2003).

While this sounds complicated (and clearly it is), what can occur during hemispheric synchronization is a physiologically reduced state of arousal *while maintaining conscious awareness* (Mavromatis, 1991; Atwater, 2004; Fischer, 1971; West, 1980; Delmonte, 1984; Goleman, 1988; Jevning, Wallace & Beidenbach, 1992), providing a doorway into the subconscious. It is difficult to imagine the amount of learning and insights that might reside therein and the expanded mental capabilities such access could provide, much less the depth and breadth of experience and emotion that has been hidden there, making such access a mixed blessing.

Another approach would be to use thought reflection, introspection, and

97

dialogue to pull out the key patterns and factors that supports the tacit knowledge as they would apply to a specific situation or problem. Through this process as it may be possible to surface and hence be able to understand and built upon the specific elements, factors, and patterns that the unconscious mind has used in making its recommendation conscious.

Von Krogh suggests that the best way to share tacit knowledge is through what is called micro communities of knowledge. These are small teams of five to seven members who are socialized through team projects and come to understand each other through a common language and purpose. This approach will facilitate the transfer or sharing of meaning and understanding provided the participants are able to verbalize their tacit knowledge (Von Krogh, et al., 2000). Such communication can never be perfect because tacit knowledge comes with emotions, memories and perhaps deeper meanings that may not be known to its owner, and may be truly unaccessible. What can happen is that the listener may receive sufficient information to re-create a significant part of their knowledge within their own cognitive capabilities. When this happens, the listener's perceptions, understanding, and meaning may be close enough for the effective re-creation of the speaker's tacit knowledge. This result—a learning process—is highly contingent upon the listener being receptive to the information and finding the results compatible with their own knowledge, beliefs and assumptions. If this does not occur, the listener may reject what is heard, misinterpret what was said, or experience a "disorienting experience" that leads them to question their own beliefs and assumptions through critical analysis. Clearly, the best transfer will occur if there is a compatible and reinforcing dialogue between the listener and the owner of tacit knowledge.

Re-creation of a speaker's knowledge is highly contingent upon the listener's own knowledge, beliefs and assumptions.

As a final point, what you think and talk about and act on drives your perceptions of the things around you *within your threshold*, a functioning space within which knowledge and events make sense (A Bennet, 2006). At any given moment in time, each individual, team, organization, community or country functions from a very definable band or region of thinking, talking and acting. If a proposed new idea (or strategy or initiative) is outside that functioning space—beyond that individual's comprehension space which reaches out slightly beyond that individual's functioning space—it is not understood and has no perceived value. Conversely, a new idea (or strategy or initiative) may be so far within an individual's functioning space that it is dismissed as unimportant or obvious. An individual's level of knowledge and the frame of reference from which that knowledge is driven define this space. As tacit knowledge is made explicit the individual's functioning space widens and available knowledge and internal complexity rises, providing that individual with more options to implement the KMb process.

5.2 MINDFUL LEARNING

Mindful learning is based on an understanding of context and the recognition of the ever-changing nature of information and knowledge. This approach, also called conditional learning, surfaces the myths or mindset of individuals, similar to the concept of mental models (Senge, 1990). As Langer explains,

Wherever learning takes place—in school, on the job in the home—these myths are also at work and the opportunity for mindful learning is present. Whether the learning is practical or theoretical, personal or interpersonal; whether it involves abstract concepts, such as physics, or concrete skills, such as how to play a sport, the way the information is learned will determine how, why, and when it is used. (Langer, 1997, p. 3)

The mindful person stays open to new ideas; looks for similarities, differences, and patterns; seeks to understand the context of what is learned; and looks at what is learned from different perspectives. Discernment and discretion are individual capabilities that describe an individual's ability to identify and choose what is of value and the equally difficult ability to toss aside that which is not of value. With the exponential rise of available information in an increasingly connected world comes the need to hone these skills. A clear understanding of the purposes of the KMb process and the *intent behind those purposes* will help stakeholders discern what information is of value to the process and what information can be considered noise, and of no consequence to the community. Noise is defined as data or information that while appearing relevant is in fact misleading, distracting and potentially harmful; for example, information relative to a previous experience that is used to justify non-support of a current effort which upon closer observation is found to be unrelated to the proposed effort, is noise that can distract or derail a proposed project. This "noise" might be recognized by the words "we've done this before and it didn't work" conveyed by a community member. In this example, a mindful learner would also recognize that perception is almost as important to KMb effectiveness as reality and must therefore be managed as part of the KMb process.

> What you think and talk about and act on drives your perceptions of the things around you within your threshold, a functioning space within which knowledge and events make sense.

With the realization that what is memorized today may not make sense tomorrow, the mindful learner looks for patterns that communicate deeper value for the future. This recognition leads to questioning the "illusion of right answers" (Langer, 1997, p. 117) and recognition of the need for continuous learning as KMb implementers search for the "best" answers in terms of time and place, then move forward to quickly discover the next "best" answer for a new time and place.

With the realization that what is memorized today may not make sense tomorrow, the mindful learner looks for patterns that communicate deeper value for the future.

5.3 COLLABORATIVE LEARNING

Collaborative learning—or learning through collaboration—is one of the most effective ways to create a learning environment as well as facilitate a shared understanding throughout an organization or community. Considering collaboration as the interdependent cooperation and working together of individuals to achieve some joint effort or activity, it is easy to envision the power of such interactions in sharing, generating and leveraging knowledge. Collaborative learning not only generates both individual and group knowledge, it also pulls a group together socially and emotionally, which in turn reinforces the effectiveness of communication in the generation and application of new ideas. Where collaboration exists across social

Collaborative learning serves to broaden perspectives through a higher appreciation and respect: each for the other, their knowledge and their values.

groups—for example between researchers, practitioners and community members— collaborative learning will serve to broaden all perspectives through a higher appreciation and respect each for the other, their knowledge and their values.

When stakeholders of all ages at all levels of education engage in the collaborative setting of community, their learning is facilitated through the day-to-day actions and successes of a knowledge mobilization project. What the researchers and practitioners of KMb are learning is *how to look through the community lens* in order to fully engage and excite the community. With this new understanding of community problems, situations and perspectives, researchers and practitioners can communicate far more effectively, thereby adjusting underlying theory or the implementation approach. This action oriented learning, occurring continuously as the KMb process unfolds, allows adjustments throughout the process that can keep it on track and result in maximum benefit to the stakeholder community.

Although most educational systems emphasize teaching, *most adults much prefer learning.* The difference is significant. Teaching can be considered the presentation and transmission of information to others with the intent of improving their understanding or knowledge of a certain topic. Learning, on the other hand, is the internal creation of knowledge by an individual. Using Malcolm Knowles theory of adult learning, i.e. andragogy, as a reference, adults are: (a) motivated to learn by internal factors rather than external ones, (b) use their past experiences as a resource for learning, and (c) are primarily self-directed human beings who desire to control their own learning (Merriam & Cafferella, 1999). This provides a backdrop for recognizing and harnessing the power of collaborative learning in the KMb process.

5.4 FORMAL EDUCATIONAL APPROACHES

Before the advent of the Internet and virtual learning, students desiring to learn could go to a place of learning (the university or an extended campus), a place of learning could come to them (community workshops or those held at the place of business) or both the learner and the teacher could meet in a third venue (conferences, etc.). Figure 5-1 expands these three approaches in terms of the relationships among the university, the practitioner and the community itself (of which the researcher may or may not be a part). The "practitioner on campus" approach moves the practitioner into the university setting, directly involving the practitioner with research efforts underway (similar to a visiting scholar arrangement). The practitioner would audit courses, and have full access to university student facilities, including library resources. The "practitioner residence program" would be a residential program more formally connected to academic credit. An inverted approach to the residence fellowship would be to move the researcher or assistant researcher into the practitioner organization, what might be called a practitioner fellowship program. This would be similar to serving an internship, except participants would be researchers and professionals with a high level of education and experience.

The term "field school" in Figure 5-1 is used to denote a formal setting for collaborative learning among researchers, practitioners, interns, community leaders and other members of the stakeholder community. While this formal setting does not need to be geographically located within the target community, grounding the field school in the community setting can potentially provide higher significance and impact. According to Gray and Egbert, this approach promotes retention of material and a feeling of ownership and builds relationships while providing applied or practical experience (Gray & Egbert, 1993).

The "field school" of knowledge mobilization encourages not only the transmission of information among relevant parties but also respects the need for individual empowerment, ownership of learning, a shared recognition of the common goals of the project and acceptance of personal responsibility for actions. It is these latter factors that stimulate an individual's desire to learn, and willingness to listen and engage in a dialogue of mutual exploration and enlightenment. The Tourism Research Innovation Project led by Malaspina University-College presented in chapter 8 is an example of how this might be accomplished in the KMb process.

The KMb "field school" respects the need for individual empowerment, ownership of learning, and acceptance of personal responsibility for actions.

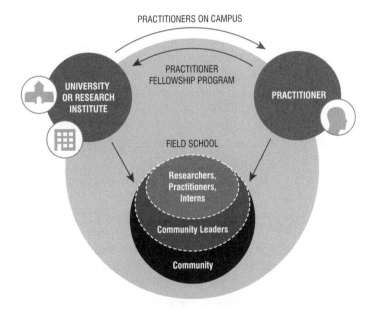

FIGURE 5-1: Example of some formal educational approaches.

With the advent of the Internet, education venues have expanded into virtual environments. Along with this expansion, the ideas of "schedule" and "place" are fading in favor of self-selection, connection and direction. In other words, because of advancement in technological support, it would be possible to simultaneously implement a KMb project around the world. Given what is being implemented resonates with a virtual implementation approach, advantages include the ease of both synchronous and asynchronous communication and the range and reach. However, disadvantages arise from lack of face-to-face communication; for example, the development of trust, understanding and collaboration are much more challenging in a virtual community. This is particularly apparent if multi-cultures and multi-languages are involved.

5.5 KMb ROLES FOR UNIVERSITY STUDENTS

Formal students can play important roles in the KMb process. As the role of the university shifts from locality to ubiquitous, from an ordered structure for dissemination to nurturing self-learning environments, connecting students to community service can facilitate discovery, create excitement, and build commitment to high professional standards (Nikolova Eddins & Williams, 1997). In the community setting, students can hone knowledge mobilization skills while interacting with researchers, practitioners, community leaders, and the larger stakeholder community. The KMb process can expose them to real-time relationship building among partners and stakeholders as well as consensus building and collaborative decision-making. They can participate in translating research findings, supporting volunteer functions, building case studies and leading community workshops.

The KMb process can expose students to real-time relationship building among partners and stakeholders as well as consensus building and collaborative decision-making.

Some student activities directly associated with degree fulfillment may involve volunteer work; others (such as summer jobs or graduate internships) may offer salaries at an established university student rate. Students and the community can both benefit from service-learning approaches (discussed in chapter 2). In addition to improving academic performance in general, the benefits to students from participating in service-learning projects would include skill development in the areas of communication, leadership, problem analysis, critical thinking, citizenship and personal development (Eyler & Giles, 1999). Regardless of reimbursement possibilities, student participation in KMb projects can provide holistic learning experiences, a wide array of learning opportunities, and/or relevant career experience in a specific area of study. They could also spend time working in partnering organizations.

Students can support—or serve in—many of the roles on the KMb project team described in chapter 6. For example, with some level of mentoring a student could serve as an activity coordinator or part of the assessment team. Depending on their education and skill set, they could support web-based information systems, architecting the organization of information, developing user interfaces, creating web maintenance tools, managing the web-site and actively leading discussion forums and blogs. They could present at events and draft and edit papers and reports. Through developing bibliographies and literature reviews they would scan the breadth of the subject matter while learning what databases are available and how to navigate them. Preparing lay summaries and synthesizing research materials develop library research skills. Assisting with surveys provides experience with quantitative and qualitative data analysis.

Participating in planning, developing and executing workshops builds project management, social networking and organizational skills, and hands-on knowledge of how to structure a successful program. By listening to presentations and interactions while taking notes at events, then compiling and synthesizing those notes, students have cross-sensory involvement with diverse frames of reference. Through the gathering of questions from community stakeholders and the seeking for answers from researchers, practitioners and community leaders, students begin to understand the difficulties in translation of research findings to end users. The list of hands-on activities and involvement potentially available to students is endless, and many of the tasks could be tailored to the level of a specific student's readiness. Emersion in these varied activities accelerates learning and lays the groundwork for critical thinking, further honed by involvement in the assessment process.

While all of the activities called out in the above paragraphs can contribute to the successful implementation of KMb, the execution of program activities by high school or college students might contribute significantly in those areas where the domain of application includes communities experiencing high school or young adult level needs. In other words, there may well be a role for high school and college students in a KMb process that requires interactions with community high school students or young adults. All students involved in the KMb process should be used to their full capacity and perhaps a little more—moving beyond support tasks to leading roles when it makes sense—so that they may fully contribute to and learn from the KMb process.

Students involved in the KMb process should be used to their fullest capacity, and perhaps a little bit more ...

Since public opinion and public policy are critical aspects in support of long-term sustainability, students may also have the opportunity to build an understanding of and actively engage in changing the community infrastructure. Policies are considered principles or procedures that guide individuals in their day-to-day decision-making and actions. As guidelines for decision-making, behaviors, and interactions, policies can have a large impact on the learning effectiveness of a community. Student participation with policy-makers could range from working with and supporting those policy-makers to building a public discourse on the value of research findings; for example, students might be involved in discussing the implications of specific research with industry and government actors and representatives, particularly when it involves community members similar in age or background.

Special activities and learning opportunities related directly to the area of research may emerge for students. For example, to implement research findings related to museums as learning platforms might require special training in building learning exhibits. In like manner, research findings centered on the use of communication technologies with pre-school children might offer the opportunity for learning how to design, produce, act in, and distribute video programming. Other special knowledge needs could include understanding choices of media for the representation of specific information to specific target groups, developing a sensitivity to universal design theory and how it impacts people with disabilities, or techniques for conserving historical and archaeological materials.

> *Student emersion in the varied KMb activities accelerates learning and lays the groundwork for critical thinking.*

The journaling process can be a precursor to sense making and learning.

As part of their involvement with the KMb process, students can be tasked to keep a reflection journal which not only tracks learning but could later be used to prepare a scholarly paper. While capturing pertinent details of their work, journaling provides a reflection process, helping students relate the new to what is known through making comparisons, interpreting and expressing opinions and judgments side-by-side with events. The journaling process can also be a precursor to sense making and learning.

Throughout the KMb process, researchers, practitioners and community leaders would develop coaching and mentoring relationships with students, ensuring that they are on track and processing and integrating what they are learning. Over the course of a project, a network of research mentorships is built up, simultaneously increasing student skill sets while building project capacity. In addition, development of a student network for students involved in KMb, with regular participation required of the student, will help share and support what is being experienced and learned. Once a student's skills are observed as both efficient and effective, the student becomes the teacher as knowledge is mobilized throughout the student network as well as the stakeholder community.

Bringing students from multi-disciplines onto the implementation team can add value to the KMb process. Student team members are in the unique position of viewing the implementation of research findings from the outside in—making observations from a significantly different viewpoint than researchers and practitioners. In addition, when student team members are not continually focused on a specific task, but generally helping across the board and throughout the KMb process, they have a wide exposure to the activities and interactions underway. Given the opportunity (facilitated through scheduled interviews with researchers and community partners), student team members can help identify, observe, annotate and integrate KMb best practices with a fresh perspective. This can prove quite valuable to seasoned teams.

In the KMb process there is an ever expanding role for the university in the day-to-day lives of students of all ages and with varied experiences and educational levels. KMb moves the nurturing of learning fully into the community: For the community, of the community, by the community. Further, the KMb process does not need to be limited to implementation of research findings. It offers an approach to moving critical areas of learning resident in the university setting into the larger community, where stakeholders can benefit both themselves and others.

The university is, of course, a community within itself. As such, it may well apply and value knowledge mobilization as a process of knowledge creation via multi-disciplined assimilation and integration. This parallels Wilson's use of William Whewell's concept of conciliation "... literally a' jumping together of knowledge by the linking of facts and fact-based theory across disciplines to create a common ground work of explanation." (Wilson, 1998, p. 8) While the KMb objective may be to mobilize specific theoretical research knowledge to create practical results from empirical research, just the reverse can occur, i.e., *mobilizing empirical results to create new theoretical understandings.* As an example, consider the application of recent findings in neuroscience to the upgrading of extant adult learning theories.

While the KMb objective may be to mobilize specific theoretical research knowledge to create practical results from empirical research, just the reverse can also occur.

This discussion leads to an interesting question: Does knowledge mobilization scale? For instance, would a knowledge mobilization process apply to a community of universities, or perhaps a community of communities? A community of communities would be a tiered, hierarchical approach to large-scale interaction, learning and contribution. Hierarchies can serve as learning platforms (A. Bennet, 2006). Not to be confused with a bureaucracy, a hierarchy is "an order of some complexity, in which the elements are distributed along the gradient of importance." (Kuntz, 1968, p. 162) Two points are pertinent to this discussion: (1) there is a central theme and dominant center point to a system with levels of hierarchy; and (2) the function of any one part can only be understood in its relation to the whole, that is, to the parts above and below it. In the example of a community of communities, this would infer that each sub-community was focusing on an aspect of the research findings and implementation approach which, in turn, would only make sense when combined with the other aspects developing in other communities. The community of communities would be the focal point for bringing together and considering these aspects from a larger systems perspective

Although the answer to the question posed in the previous paragraph would appear to be yes, it would be necessary to develop a knowledge mobilization strategy and implementation process within the specific context of a multi-community system and apply the KMb process accordingly. (See chapter 9.)

5.6 CAPTURING THE IMAGINATION OF YOUTH
Students ranging from preschool through high school may also be stakeholders in the KMb process and the implementation of research findings. While many of the events and publications listed in Appendices A and B offer approaches for engaging youth, when they are stakeholders the further question must be asked and explored: How can projects be designed, implemented and sustained to optimize learning for youth?

As generation after generation moves forward, most adults would agree that children today are different (Kehoe & Fisher, 2002; Lerner, 2004). Depending on whom you ask, this might mean that they are children of the media or children of the moment, more focused on celebrities than historic figures (DeGaetano, 2004) or unconcerned with the future. In the first case, this means that using media and connections with famous people offer the potential for gaining children's attention; for example, developing leadership models based on carefully-selected celebrities.

Depending on whom you ask, children of today are either children of the media or of the moment.

As discussed in chapter 4, experiences that engage multiple senses with incoming patterns have the greatest opportunity of engaging internal patterns of historical significance. Recursive interactions between external patterns and internal patterns of historical significance creates recognition, sense-making, meaning, and ultimately knowledge (Bennet & Bennet, 2006). For example, through media, artwork and dance, movement and emotion can be linked with specific areas of research. Further, written texts could be enhanced with images and sound.

Engaging and ensuring continuing support for students in a target group could include creating a structure for parental involvement and community member mentoring. Inner-city schools could set up teacher interactions with students outside the classroom to demonstrate what is being communicated in the classroom. Community partners could support special community learning days accented by movies, games and prizes in a downtown mall, all related to the specific area of research.

Further, the best learning often occurs in a low-stress, small-group environment that is positively reinforcing, with some enthusiasm and humor (Rose & Nicholl, 1997). An example would be bringing disparate groups together during school break in a joyful setting to exchange ideas.

5.6.1 Storytelling And Stories

Good metaphors, analogies, stories and storytelling can be used to connect places and events to learning patterns, providing tools to help understand an issue or problem (Bennet & Bennet, 2004). In addition to offering the potential to entertain, stories and storytelling can be used to share knowledge and teach behavior and morals. A story is an account or recital of an event or series of events which may or may not be fictional. Storytelling is "an oral art form that provides a means of preserving and transmitting ideas, images, motives, and emotions that are universal." (Cassady, 1990, p. 5). In a storytelling setting, the ideas, images, motives and emotions that are being transmitted cannot be separated from the storyteller, the one who is transmitting. Nor can they be separated from the one listening to the story, the one interpreting and responding to the story.

Knowledge is made up of experiences and stories, with our knowledge of the world more or less equivalent to our experiences (Schank, 1990). In other words and as forwarded throughout this book, new experiences are understood in terms of those experiences already in memory so that new ideas are dependent on old ideas. Context helps relate incoming information to those experiences already in memory, and *stories can provide that context*. A story could be equated to mental software; it can be run again (and again) at a future point when new input comes in from a specific situation. As Simmons explains, "Once installed, a good story replays itself and continues to process new experience through a filter, channeling future experiences toward the perceptions and choices you desire." (Simmons, 2001, p. 42) So a good story transmits images that listeners make their own, continually adapting and changing these images to make sense out of new inputs.

Context helps relate incoming information to those experiences already in memory, and stories can provide that context.

Stories can be designed to help translate and build awareness and understanding of key concepts in the KMb process. They can be specifically developed to reflect the breadth and depth appropriate to the age and experience of the target audience and their ability to understand the concepts being addressed. One approach would be to create these stories collaboratively, hold storytelling sessions for children, train-the-storyteller sessions for adult community volunteers, and then developing a set of children's books around these stories to facilitate continued use.

Alternately, children and youth could be engaged in *discovering and telling their own stories*. As appropriate, these might be verbal or written; one-on-one, small group, or submitted for publication. Or, children could picture themselves in future stories about their lives and careers. An example of this is the Pow-Wow, an exchange of knowledge through story and music named after the Native American gathering involving dance, music and socializing. Children's literature could also be used to engage focused discussion on specific values and issues related to research findings, and youth might participate in story and poetry readings.

5.6.2 Engaging The Internet

As children are increasingly engaged by and interacting with computers, the challenge becomes that of embracing this medium as a learning tool, interjecting creative and interest-building approaches to everyday computer usage. The point to be made here is that media—in particular the media that have moved into everyday usage in children's lives—must be part of the KMb change strategy when children and youth are involved.

For example, a web site might be customizable, with spaces and places for discussions, and games and interactive role-playing related to the content area of KMb implementation. A short set of questions could move participating youth through a series of learning pages designed to intersect with their areas of interest. The interactive, partner-based virtual games could be on-going, with "wins" counted in terms of change and gain, not destruction or loss, an important psychological difference of which the full consequences are not yet understood and recognized by game designers and the general public. Discovery tools would support specific needs as determined by research findings. All these approaches, of course, would be accompanied by visuals and music and opportunities to literally make the screen "dance" with figures and patterns that help make sense out of research results.

Media must be part of the KMb change strategy when children and youth are involved.

> *New experiences are understood in terms of those experiences already in memory so that new ideas are dependent on old ideas.*

Whether the focus is on adults or children, the level of media literacy significantly contributes to the effective use of media. Media literacy was introduced in chapter 3 as an integrative competency, a skill set that has broad application to most KMb processes. A media divide (a digital divide in terms of media and Internet access and the skill sets for their effective and efficient use) is still prevalent in "affluent and poor communities, cities, regions and nations. It impedes progress toward an equitable, educated information society." (Berry, 2000, pp. 9-10) For example, access to Internet service is unevenly distributed. Making research findings available by creating a website does not mean the target audience will be able to access those findings. The audience would be, in effect, structurally "deaf" to what is being said if they don't have access to the Internet or the skill set to use it when it is available.

The second, and in some ways much larger, issue is the capacity to understand and use what is found; hence the importance of interpretation, translation and shared learning in any KMb activity. (See the discussion on translation in chapter 4.) The technical "fix" of using the Internet just isn't enough. The media divide, coupled with the opportunity for misuse of the media by children and youth, makes youth media literacy a primary concern (and opportunity) for engaged community leaders such as those participating in KMb implementation projects. With the use of media to implement research findings comes the responsibility to provide constructive guidance and contextual knowledge along with critical tools for accessing, navigating and using media.

As demonstrated throughout this text, the subject area of research cannot be separated from the KMb process.

5.6.3 Engaging The Area Of Research

As demonstrated throughout this text, the subject area of research findings cannot be separated from the KMb process or project. For example, a meaningful site for conveying tribal values and cultural history might be an archeological dig or a museum with the appropriate format through storytelling. The process of an event then reinforces the content that is being conveyed, providing the opportunity for participants to *experience learning*. Another example conveying the value of hands-on (constructivist-based) science teaching would be engaging youths in two-hour, night-time, ears-on "listening" sessions at facilities like the U.S. National Radio Astronomy Observatory (NRAO) located in West Virginia, which supports youth programs of this nature.

These approaches are consistent with the concept of KMb implementation or any other change effort. When the process of implementation (or change) emulates the change that is being promoted, then demonstrated learning is experienced beyond that which is being taught. This approach melds *that which is being taught with what is already understood and what is being experienced and felt*. Accelerated learning, an approach designed to take advantage of the whole brain's capability to learn (Gardner, 1993), can then be facilitated by practicing—and reflecting on—what has been learned.

5.6.4 Sharing Resources

As iterated throughout this book, KMb does not focus only on the transfer and application of research findings, but also on the *building of shared understanding* across the target community. Shared understanding can be facilitated through an individual's *personal* story. (See the discussion above on stories and storytelling.)

> Fully engaging students of all ages throughout the KMb process is consistent with the holistic approach needed to effect lasting change.

For example, youth could develop papers describing what they were learning and how this learning is affecting their behaviors, sharing these papers with youth at other schools, community centers, etc., during a jointly-sponsored event. Conversely, teachers and other individuals in guidance roles could begin to share their own learning, teaching strategies and tools across school and organization boundaries to bring the larger community into the change process, and facilitate expansion of local successes through reuse and adaptation of materials and approaches. For example, curricula used in a KMb project might be downloadable to multiple schools.

> The more partnering relationships across the community, the more opportunity for seeing the world from different frames of reference.

The more partnering relationships that can be developed and supported across the community in support of community youth, the more opportunity there is for seeing the world from different frames of reference and understanding the viewpoints and stories that underpin them. For example, inner-city young people whose families may be consumed in the every-day struggle for survival may not have the energy—nor ability—to focus on future health difficulties from substance abuse since they cannot see beyond current circumstances. Simultaneously, the more consistency across partnering relationships and support systems, the greater the opportunity to serve these children. Research indicates that the greater the integration of multiple support systems in the lives of youths, the greater their resiliency (Flach, 1988; Richardson, 2002).

Fully engaging students of all ages throughout the KMb process is consistent with the holistic approach needed to effect lasting change. By engaging is meant directing worthwhile and challenging work that contributes both to the KMb process and to personal growth and learning. Students should be encouraged to learn not only KMb processes but also the competencies of teamwork, dialogue, empathy, assessment, etc. Indeed, empathy moves beyond shared understanding and context to a willingness to imagine yourself in the place of another. As a result of the insights gained from such an empathetic effort, adjust actions and choices to improve the efficacy of the KMb process and the benefits of shared learning.

REFLECTIVE QUESTIONS CHAPTER 5

> What is the best way you personally learn?

> Which is more important in learning, questions or answers? Why?

> As the practitioner and change agent in a knowledge mobilization project, how might you surface the tacit knowledge of community leaders to help in local economic development?

> As a team leader, what actions might you take to enhance the learning capacity of your team?

> Putting yourself in the shoes of a colleague, think about their frames of reference and how they see the world. How does it feel? What are the insights to be gained from this point of view?

CHAPTER 6

EXECUTION IN THE ACTION SPACE

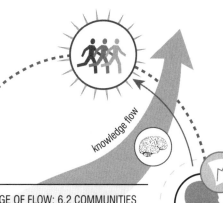

THIS SECTION INCLUDES: 6.0 INTRODUCTION; 6.1 THE CHALLENGE OF FLOW; 6.2 COMMUNITIES AND THE COMMUNITY, 6.2.1 Community of Interest, 6.2.2 Community of Learning, 6.2.3 Community of Practice, 6.2.4 Community of Research; 6.3 A NOMINAL STRUCTURE FOR GOVERNANCE, 6.3.1 The Project Team; 6.3.2 The Steering Committee, 6.3.3 The Advisory Board, 6.3.4 The Assessment Team, 6.3.5 Content Communities of Learning and Practice, 6.3.6 The Larger Knowledge Network; 6.4 MOVING FROM KNOWLEDGE BROKER TO CHANGE AGENT; 6.5 THE KMb PROJECT/PROGRAM LIFE CYCLE, 6.5.1 Initiation and Planning, 6.5.2 Start-Up, 6.5.3 Expansion and Growth, 6.5.4 Sustainability, 6.5.5 Close-Out.

FIGURES: 6-1 KMb PROCESS AND KNOWLEDGE FLOWS; 6-2 NOMINAL GOVERNANCE STRUCTURE FOR A LARGE-SCALE KMb APPROACH.

6.0 INTRODUCTION

Execution of a project is one of the most challenging responsibilities of project personnel. A Booze Allen and Hamilton survey of 3800 senior executives asked them to prioritize their most significant challenges. The number one item of most concern was execution, that is, the ability to implement and take action upon some strategy or direction. While often ignored, execution frequently plays the dominant role in determining success or mediocrity of a project's results (Kleiner, 2005).

Rosbeth Moss Kanter says that "Execution means having the mental and organizational flexibility to put new business models into practice, even if they counter what you're currently doing." (Kanter, 2005, p. 39) Bossidy and Charan proposed that to understand execution one has to keep three key points in mind: (1) execution is a discipline and a major part of strategy, (2) execution is a major job of the leader, and (3) execution must be a core element in an organization's or team's culture (Bossidy & Charan, 2002). Applying these three points to a KMb process, execution must be considered throughout all phases and areas of the process. While research knowledge and pragmatic know-how may be the foundation of a successful knowledge mobilization effort, without effective and timely execution throughout all aspects of the project as it unfolds, the likelihood of success remains questionable. Execution plays a critical role in translating research into layman's language that is accessible to the practitioner and community members. It also influences community member willingness and capability to understand and communicate the need for change and take clear and appropriate action to model that change.

Knowledge may tell you what to do and where to go, but execution is what gets you there!!

To appreciate the challenges of effective execution, consider Bossidy and Charan's statement, "Conceiving a grand idea or broad picture is usually intuitive. Shaping the broad picture into a set of executable actions is analytical, and it's a huge intellectual, emotional, and creative challenge." (Bossidy & Charan, 2002, p. 32) While the foundation of knowledge mobilization lies in the transformation of knowledge into action that creates value, the source and outcome of that transformation is found in the execution capability of everyone involved in the project.

After the seven essential behaviours for execution comes the framework for cultural change.

If execution is that important to success, what can a project leader and KMb team partners do? Bossidy and Charan suggest three building blocks of execution. The first block is composed of seven essential behaviors: (1) know your people and your business; (2) insist on realism; (3) set clear goals and priorities; (4) follow-through; (5) reward the doers; (6) expand people's capabilities; and (7) know yourself (Bossidy & Charan, 2002).

For building block two, they propose creating a framework for cultural change. This would carry over directly to the community in implementing the KMb process, and highlights the importance of the stakeholder community being action-oriented with strong follow-through. An action-oriented culture is an empowered culture within which community members have the capability and motivation to act on their own to meet local needs while at the same time being supported by practitioners and key decision-makers throughout their community. Frequent and effective communication plays a strong role in execution efficacy. To execute well one must clearly understand the desired results. Community leaders must also understand how to achieve those results and the impact of those results on others in their community.

> *While the foundation of KMb lies in the transformation of knowledge into action that creates value, the source and outcome of that transformation is found in the execution capability of everyone involved in the project.*

The third building block is the job of the leader to delegate—ensuring the right people in the right place (Bossidy & Charan, 2002). Although the project leader may not have control over community membership and involvement, the third building block emphasizes the importance of identifying the best people possible, and working with them in support of the program's success.

6.1 THE CHALLENGE OF FLOW

Observing the KMb process from a bird's eye view (Figure 6-1), we can identify three major forces for success, with each of the these forces representing individuals and the knowledge they possess. Recognizing that in reality there is no beginning and no end, we begin our discussion with the researchers who have deep knowledge of the research findings and are usually found in universities or research institutions. The second significant force in the KMb process is the practitioner who typically has strong knowledge of change management and how to get things done. The third major force is those individuals throughout the community at the point of action where local actions are taken to change behavior and create opportunities. Community leaders possess experiential knowledge and a strong understanding of their local culture, its beliefs and values. In summary, there are three major forces (researchers, practitioners and community members), all with their own backgrounds, experiences, belief sets and unique knowledges created through years of study and experience.

Recall that the objective of the KMb process is to take the deep knowledge developed from research and transform it into pragmatic knowledge implemented by community members to create value, although (as noted in Chapter 5) it is also possible to mobilize experiential knowledge to create new theoretical understandings. Referencing Figure 6-1 below, the three outer ovals represent the three primary forces involved in the KMb process (researcher, practitioner and community member).

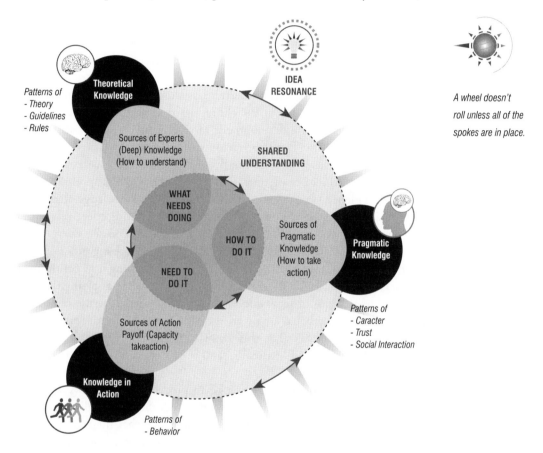

FIGURE 6-1: KMb process and knowledge flows.

The other three ovals represent their corresponding knowledge brought to the KMb process. The traditional flow of the process is from the researcher to the practitioner to the community member. This flow of knowledge is from the theory of the researcher to the pragmatic knowledge of the practitioner to knowledge-in-action of the community member. While this flow is essential to KMb, so, too, is the simultaneous flow of knowledge from community member to practitioner to researcher as well as direct flows among researchers and community members where it makes sense. The challenge is to facilitate: (1) this flow of knowledge, (2) the transformation of knowledge from theory to action and back, and (3) the interactions necessary among the three groups to nurture that flow.

The energy output of the three groups (or roles) moves beyond the generation and movement of knowledge to the management and implementation of the KMb process. These individuals must not only work closely together from the project perspective of accomplishing results, but they must also, in that process, communicate with and understand each other's knowledge base and their frame of reference (or mental model). This is no small task. Each individual with their own history and experience possesses some level of knowledge in their area of expertise and in related areas of interest and passion. They may also hold this knowledge within a framework of perception and sense-making that often extensively differs from other KMb stakeholders. For convenience it is assumed that each of these three groups possess deep knowledge in their area of expertise.

As introduced earlier, recent research has shown that experts become experts by effortful study that results in the chunking of ideas and concepts and creating understanding through the development of significant patterns useful for solving problems and anticipating future behavior within their area of interest (Ross, 2006). For example, researchers focus primarily on a mental theory, basic concepts and guidelines, laws, principles of operation and frameworks grounded in empirical testing and evidence. Practitioners would have deep knowledge that consists of patterns relating to knowing how to take action or to working effectively with people based on study, experience and intuition. They would also possess a large number of patterns related to influencing, communicating, and energizing others. In a change agent role, they would have learned many patterns describing how communities and individuals change and would have significant experience in applying those patterns to real-world situations. This would enable them to recognize the best approaches needed to change the behavior of an individual or the culture of a community or an organization. Recall that this knowledge may be very different from that of the researcher interested in theories and broad concepts. (See the discussion of knowledge in chapter 2.)

The third set of individuals in the KMb process is community leaders. While these leaders may or may not be formally educated, they will undoubtedly have had considerable experience within their community such that their knowledge will be primarily experiential, real and close to their day-to-day actions of life. They will understand their culture, their friends and their beliefs and hopes. While they may or may not be experts in any given area, they will have ideas and opinions that can significantly influence the outcome of the KMb process. For the knowledge mobilization process to be highly successful, researchers, practitioners and community leaders must be able to communicate effectively and to work together as a team. For this to happen there must exist a positive chemistry among them, or a resonance that encourages and reinforces their capacity to relate to, learn from, and trust each other. Since they have unique backgrounds, this *resonance* will come from a strong belief in the value of the project, a personal willingness to learn and grow, and a feeling of respect and trust among them. Although these can be nurtured by the participants, these latter feelings will most often come through interactions with each other as the KMb process evolves.

For researchers, practitioners and community leaders to function as a team, there must be a resonance that encourages and reinforces their capacity to relate to, learn from, and trust each other.

6.2 COMMUNITIES AND THE COMMUNITY

Communities of learning, interest, practice and research are designed to communicate and create shared understanding across interdisciplinary academic and practitioner areas and inter-functional community areas of stakeholders. They are vehicles for facilitating the flow of information (and knowledge) across stakeholder groups.

Although communities have always formed a social basis for learning and knowledge exchange, more recent forms of virtual communities are Communities of Interest (CoIs), communities of learning (CoLs), communities of practice (CoPs), and communities of research (CoRs). While these communities are supported in terms of the information technology infrastructure of the knowledge network, the trails of thought are very much a product of self organization. As Etienne Wenger states, "… you cannot force a plant to grow by pulling its leaves … what you can do is create the infrastructure in which it can prosper." (Wenger, 1998) Critical factors for community success would include respect, trust, open communications and personal passion. It is also beneficial to have a *sense of urgency* surrounding the areas of focus. Involvement of key thought leaders in these key areas serves to elevate the exchange of ideas and increase the flow of new ideas, and thereby enhance the learning that occurs.

While technology enables the exchange of information—and can seed the creation of knowledge through context, learning programs, and interactive systems—it is the relationships among the people who create and use information that actually mobilizes knowledge. As in face-to-face relationships, trust and respect make information and shared experiences more meaningful and useful (Landry, et al., 2001).

Because of their unique focus on knowledge, learning and research, communities can cross cultural, racial, geographical and gender issues, linking and learning from communities and society at large. The social capital promoted through community interaction can be a major resource for KMb and support development of the larger communities in which participants work.

Knowledge cuts across cultural, racial, geographical and gender issues.

6.2.1 Community Of Interest

A CoI is focused on a specific domain of knowledge and made up of individuals who have an *interest* in that knowledge domain. A CoI is defined by knowledge, not task, has an evolving agenda driven by members of the community, and is managed by making connections and building relationships. The focus is on value added, mutual exchange and continuous learning. Since participants will usually have differing levels of interest, this is a more loosely connected community, not developing the close relationships found in communities of learning and practice.

6.2.2 Community Of Learning

While CoLs may be domain related, they are *part of a learning process*, often moving from domain to domain, or perhaps focusing on the process of research itself. CoLs promote shared learning and shared "knowing" through the cooperative construction of knowledge (Tinto, 1998). They are particularly effective for fueling innovation in areas that cross domains where understanding can be very difficult to convey. Tinto forwards that CoL's amplify the voices of their members. When members of a CoL find themselves for the first time in an e-learning setting that requires their active involvement, "they discover a 'voice' that they may not have previously recognized or had not been recognized by others." (Tinto, 1998, p. 172) A CoL can help individual participants increase their benefit from participating in the KMb process through expanding learning opportunities. Ideally, the results of these exchanges would be kept in files or summary reports for broader distribution.

6.2.3 Community Of Practice

Similar to a community of interest, a CoP is focused on a specific domain of knowledge, but it is comprised of people who actually work (practice) in that domain. A CoP is also defined by knowledge within some domain (not by task), has an evolving agenda driven by members of the community, and is managed by making connections and building relationships (Wenger, 1998). While the focus is on value added, mutual exchange and continuous learning, CoPs are more likely to brainstorm and seek solutions to specific issues and problems forwarded by community members than communities of interest. Thus, participation in and reliance on CoPs increases over time. Allee states that as people move beyond routine processes into more complex challenges they increasingly rely on their CoPs as a primary knowledge resource (Allee, 2000). This powerful form of community can prove a continuing source of ideas and energy for long-term KMb implementation.

6.2.4 Community Of Research

Made up of researchers (from academia and private and public sector research institutions) and others *interested in research*, a community of research may be focused on a specific area or a number of related areas. This is similar to the community of practice, with the "practice" being the practice of research in a specific domain. However, it is *not* limited to university and institute researchers, but engages all those who have a passion for and understanding of the research process supporting the KMb project.

Governance should be distributed, flexible, collaborative and cohesive, and designed to guide and support (not control) the KMb process.

6.3 A NOMINAL STRUCTURE FOR GOVERNANCE

In this section an overview of how a large-scale KMb project might be governed is provided in order to highlight possibilities and identify governance aspects that could be easily overlooked. Although each aspect of governance is treated separately, e.g., project team, steering committee, etc., it is understood that several of these functions will often be done by a single group, or several jobs by the same individual.

The knowledge mobilization governance structure must reflect the intent of the process, i.e. implementation of research findings to fulfill a community need. This requires a balance of academics, practitioners, community representatives and any other key decision-makers from the larger stakeholder population. In addition, governance may include policy-makers, advocates and independent consultant experts to provide the diversity and scope of expertise needed, ensuring that the perspectives and voices of stakeholders are heard and that these perspectives feed into the underlying structure, goals and priorities of the implementation program.

In keeping with complexity theory, *the governance structure would be decentralized* to support skilled collaborators and partners taking the lead in their geographical locations or specialized areas of expertise. While providing a solid foundation of support, it would also encourage and nurture self-organization within the community setting to ensure ownership and sustainability of implementation efforts. The characteristics of decentralization and self-organization do not preclude a supportive structure; rather, they are more about *how* implementation proceeds (process and empowerment) than what needs to be done.

Figure 6-2 demonstrates a nominal governance structure for a large-scale KMb project. Since KMb cannot be separated from the knowledge that is to be mobilized (research findings), the structure supports the continued interaction among researchers and practitioners and other stakeholders throughout the process of implementation, with a continuous process of assessment and change supporting those interactions. *This discussion is more about roles than positions, and a different combination of roles may be required for different projects.* Conversely, some of these roles may be double-hatted within the university, research institute, not-for-profit or practitioner organization, or other partner structures.

> *The knowledge mobilization governance structure must reflect the intent of the process.*

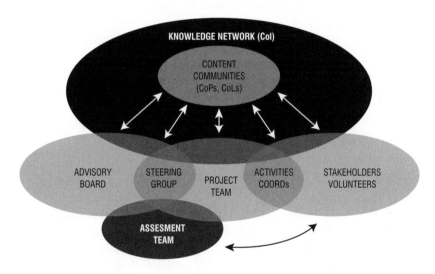

FIGURE 6-2: Nominal governance structure for a large-scale KMb approach.

The terms used for this nominal KMb structure are descriptive, not prescriptive. For example, the steering group could also be considered the executive committee or the executive management team and might serve the function of a senior management committee. Similarly, the project director (who leads the project team and is a member of the steering group) might be called the program or project manager. The activity coordinators (who are both stakeholder volunteers and part of the project team) might be thought of as KMb coordinators. The advisory board could be called an advisory group or council. Content communities (communities of practice and learning) might be thought of as research committees supported by cross-stakeholder communities and interconnected throughout the knowledge network.

All team, board, group, and community members and volunteers have the responsibility for actively engaging in knowledge mobilization and ensuring a shared understanding throughout the larger stakeholder community. A dynamic balance is necessary between the process and implementation of the process. While the overall process must be guided to ensure progress and consistency of direction, local implementation of the process should be performed by individuals empowered with the competency, freedom and authority to adapt to local issues, opportunities and needs.

To understand the functions of the bodies shown in Figure 6-2, and some of the roles played, the following nominal descriptions are provided below in this order: the project team (the project leader, the project coordinator, activity coordinators), the steering committee, the advisory board, the assessment team, content communities, the knowledge network, advocates, policy-makers, opinion leaders, and champions. In addition to these groups/roles, working groups and research committees comprised of appropriate partners and stakeholders may be organized for the length of need. While such a need may be forwarded by any group across the KMb structure, working groups and research committees would be tasked through the project leader and supported by the project team.

Note that the sphere of roles covered in this chapter is maximized to encourage detailed thought on the potential types of roles needed in a specific KMb process or program. While all should be considered, it will most likely not be possible to include all stakeholders on the KMb team. However, by extension they may be included in focus groups, surveys, and other KMb activities.

All team, board, group and community members, and volunteers, have the responsibility for ensuring a shared understanding throughout the larger stakeholder community.

6.3.1 The Project Team

The project team includes representatives of major stakeholder groups with their inherent expertise and knowledge. The intent is to ensure incorporation of academic, practitioner and community perspectives with active partners in the KMb project represented. This group makes the key implementation decisions, both developing and supporting operational design and ensuring goals are achieved. This core project team requires a high level of commitment, expertise in KMb, and the ability to provide hands-on assistance as needed. For a significant project, the team will have to spend time learning how to work together, sharing values and developing a clear consensus on the purpose, vision and implementation strategy for the project. This is a good starting strategy for any group effort.

The core project team requires a high level of commitment, and the ability to provide hands-on assistance as needed.

The team might include an advocate who has in-roads to policy-makers and decision-makers; a functional expert who manages virtual support systems; a researcher who has continuous liaison with academia partners and content communities; and a practitioner who has continuous liaison with community leaders and content communities. The researcher and practitioner would work with the project leader to ensure the availability of the best resources to stakeholders. This team might be assisted by a writer/editor/communications person (paid or volunteer, reporting to the project coordinator) and several interns, as needed, drawn from university resources as well as the larger stakeholder community. Interns could assist the writer/editor/communications person in translation of materials, and provide KMb support functions for events, publications, development of sustainability tools, assessing, etc. (See the discussion on students in chapter 5.) As needed or appropriate, additional members of the project team might include a representative from a committed policy-maker, an advocate, or a key community decision-maker. A member of the project team might also serve on the assessment team. In other words, obtaining a balance of skills and experience must be considered while simultaneously engaging stakeholder representatives. Typical skills sought include:

- Management skills such as motivation, planning and resource allocation;
- Technical skills such as IT platform development, research translation or interpretive design;
- Administrative skill such as payroll, record management and routine correspondence;
- Interpersonal, social networking, and conflict resolution skills;
- Problem solving skills;
- Knowledge of the organization(s)/stakeholders; and
- Experience with similar projects.

TEAM MEMBER SKILLS

Integrative competencies should also be considered and training/learning workshops scheduled when gaps exist. (See the discussion on integrative competencies in chapter 3.)

Project leaders build process cohesion and flexibility through collaboration, not control.

6.3.1.1 The Project Leader

Project Leader is a full-time job. This individual, drawn from academic or practitioner partners, has the responsibility for overall implementation of the project and for developing partnering relationships, exploring avenues of additional funding support, and overseeing the allocation and approval of expenditures. This individual relies on the functional expertise of the project team, engaging in dialogue and providing a sounding board as needed, and interceding when significant issues arise. Serving as a member of the steering committee, the project leader stays in open, continuous dialogue

Collaborative leaders represent a mobilizing force within any organization.

with steering committee members, partners, policy-makers, and key decision-makers. Leading a KMb project requires a flexible and collaborative leadership approach.

Collaborative leaders represent a mobilizing force within any organization. By working at multiple levels and networking they can build organizational cohesion and local flexibility, nurturing subordinates rather than "controlling" them. They can be characterized by the kinds of actions they take (Bennet & Bennet, 2004). For example, collaborative leaders:

- Insist that everyone always be treated with respect, fairness, and equality.
- Maintain strong moral and ethical values and apply them to all areas of their working life.
- Treat people as individuals and professionals, giving them the benefit of the doubt until proven otherwise.
- Inspire others through positive thinking with an optimistic but not naïve outlook, pursuing appreciative inquiry.
- Ask how and why things happen, and how and why an action is taken.
- Use networks to align the team, leverage knowledge, and support all team members.
- Focus on quality, effectiveness, and team health.
- Lead by example and collaboration, not by ego.
- Build other leaders, and leaders who can build other leaders.
- Facilitate loyalty, respect, competence, synergy, and learning among team members.
- Do not pretend to know when they don't.
- When confronted with very complex issues, admit they don't know and suggest that "If we work together we can figure this out."
- Always share context with team members.
- Leverage knowledge wherever possible.

The project leader would be experienced in leading teams, and in facilitating team creativity, problem solving, decision-making and implementation. In addition, the team would have a written charter that addresses the authority, resources, responsibility, purpose, project and desired outcome. The charter should be signed by all team members, funding sources, and other senior individuals who have a stake in the project's success. See Katzenbach and Smith (1993) and Bennet (1996) for further information on team creation, facilitating, leadership and operation.

All teams should have written and signed charters to ensure clarity of task and support from sponsors.

6.3.1.2 The Project Coordinator

Project coordinator can be a full-time job or part-time job, depending on the size of the project, and is either a practitioner partner or an opinion-leader in the stakeholder community. This individual leads the activity coordinators, supports the steering committee as needed, and acts as the administrative support coordinator for the project team. Working closely with the project manager and utilizing input from the advisory board and steering committee, this individual develops models and plans for KMb outreach and engagement. The project coordinator also oversees development and maintenance of a project records system documenting decisions, activities and feedback. In short, this individual is an integrator with the primary function of ensuring connection of people and activities across the project team and among the project team and other implementation groups. This individual also serves as a liaison with other stakeholder groups as needed.

6.3.1.3 Activity Coordinators

Led by the project coordinator, activity coordinators are volunteers drawn from the stakeholder community. According to their individual knowledge, commitment, and passion, they co-lead and design and coordinate events, publications, and develop and ensure the upkeep of sustainability tools. These individuals engage in quality control for the translation of research findings and in the usability of virtual tools, as well as participating in focus groups to help understand stakeholder needs. This group is not static, with stakeholders moving in and out of the group driven by self-selection, skill sets, and community needs.

6.3.2 The Steering Commitee

The steering committee may include the project leader, the project coordinator, a rotating member of the advisory board, a rotating member from the stakeholder community, and one other (if the project leader is an academic, this is a practitioner; if the project leader is a practitioner, this is an academic). The steering committee operates as a team, self-organizing and rotating leadership depending on the issues at hand and member expertise and experience. This committee makes policy decisions; provides operational guidance; reviews goals, guidelines and assessments including an annual program review; oversees any personnel or financial issues deemed appropriate by the project team; and considers any implementation issues that may arise. While staying in touch with the project office virtually, the steering committee would meet face-to-face quarterly (or as often as needed) to monitor the progress of the project. They also have formal and informal interaction with members of the advisory board and academic and professional partners. The project leader reports to the steering committee for advice and support.

The steering committee operates as a team, self-organizing and rotating leadership depending on the issues at hand and member expertise and experience.

6.3.3 The Advisory Board

The advisory board is comprised of key stakeholders with direct and indirect expertise in the areas of focus. They represent the political, academic, professional and community sectors. They are the arms-length advisors to the steering group, project team and assessment team, and to members of the larger knowledge network and content communities as appropriate. One or two members (rotating and self-selected) serve on the steering group.

Advisory board members are charged with ensuring that community capacity building is fostered, and that the project is consistent with and supportive of the long-term interests of the community. They meet quarterly to look at patterns across content areas, discuss policy changes and potential stakeholder shifts (culture, behavior, etc.), review funding and progress, and provide input, feedback and advice to the steering group and project team on specific activities. Between meetings they are kept apprised by periodic interaction with the project leader and through membership on content communities, the assessment team and the steering group. Available as information sources, members also participate in events and publications according to their ability and availability. Their primary focus is to support the project team through their experience, professional knowledge and relationship networking.

Advisory board members are charged with ensuring that the project is consistent with and supportive of the long-term interests of the community.

121

6.3.4 The Assesment Team

The assessment team may be made up of a member of the steering committee, a member of the project team, an intern from the project team, and stakeholder volunteers. While this may be a self-selected and rotating membership, it is involved in continuous assessment, with at least one active member from academia, one practitioner, one individual who represents the larger stakeholder community, and most desirable, one experienced individual who has no other relationship (formal or otherwise) with any of the KMb stakeholders.

Project assessment must be for guidance and progress monitoring, not fault finding.

The assessment team will work with the project team to develop and apply assessment tools. The process of assessment is continuous as data is collected from virtual support systems, events, publications, and various other feedback mechanisms. Special assessment events are undertaken as needed and in concert with the project office, with periodic reports and recommendations made to the steering committee. Assessment data and findings of the assessment team are available to all steering committee and project team members, and passed on to the advisory board and larger stakeholder community as appropriate. It is very important to recognize that the purpose of assessment is to *guide the project and identify changes and adjustment needed to maintain progress toward the end objectives.* Assessment must not be used (or interpreted as) a vehicle for fault finding, excuse generation or manipulating the process. (See chapter 7.) While all participants in the larger stakeholder community may be involved in change, the project team has responsibility for having the right information, making decisions based on input, and ensuring implementation of changes in response to incoming assessment material. (An extensive treatment of the assessment process is in chapter 7.)

> The purpose of assessment is to guide the project and identify changes needed to maintain progress toward the end objective.

6.3.5 Content Communities Of Learning And Practice

As communities of learning and practice, content communities (supported and nurtured by the project team) are focused on the specific knowledge areas involved in the KMb process, project or program. While academic partners may choose to champion these communities in order to ensure representation of different perspectives these content communities are comprised of committed academics, practitioners and other self-selected stakeholders. *They have a collective responsibility for providing intellectual leadership and identifying gaps in content areas.* Focused on knowledge and shared understanding, they look for connections and patterns across content, review user feedback in context areas, engage in continuous dialogue, and help translate their learning into a practical and accessible format for the larger stakeholder community.

While on-going connectivity and interaction is primarily virtual—and members of the content communities serve as contributors to, and auditors of, virtual network content in their areas of focus—they also actively participate in KMb activities and publications.

6.3.6 The Larger Knowledge Network

The knowledge network is the larger community of interest, and is more about relationships and adding potential value than sustained interaction. Since participation is open to all stakeholders and interested parties, members may or may not have relationships and connections with members of the content communities or any of the implementing groups. Participation is self-selected drawn by interest, passion, and advocacy, or maybe in response to questions solicited by a content community, the project team, or another member of the stakeholder community. The knowledge network would include universities and research institutes who have related research underway. It could also include local, provincial and national partners doing related work; for example, practitioners in other geographical locations who have a vested interest in successful implementation of research findings.

Participation in the larger knowledge network is self-selected drawn by interest, passion and advocacy.

The knowledge network would also connect to other related networks and communities of interest, supporting greater access to on-going research in related areas. While supported by the project office in terms of offering connectivity and virtual resources, forums and blogs, the knowledge network is also supported by its participants such that advocates, opinion leaders and champions emerge from this group.

As part of the knowledge network, virtual teams and other stakeholder communities of practice, learning and research are connected and supported. They are also major content contributors.

6.4 MOVING FROM KNOWLEDGE BROKER TO CHANGE AGENT

With the rise of knowledge management in the early 1990's came a focus on the need for knowledge intermediaries to (1) capture and codify tacit knowledge for re-use; (2) search, retrieve and disseminate explicit knowledge; and (3) connect knowledge seekers and users to sources of tacit and explicit knowledge (Horvath, et al., 2000). When implementing research findings, practitioners and community leaders act as knowledge brokers, both connecting and translating knowledge to the end users, i.e., the target audience.

> *The unique relationships between practitioners and the people they work with provide a foundation for trust and respect that supports the flow of knowledge and the seeding of new ideas.*

The unique relationships and networks developed over time between practitioners and the people they work with, and between community leaders and the larger community, provides a foundation for trust and respect that supports the flow of knowledge and the seeding of new ideas. This trust is a valuable, almost sacred, capital. De Furia (1997) proposed five behaviors that help build trust: sharing relevant information, reducing controls, allowing for mutual influence, clarifying mutual expectations, and meeting expectations. Further, he noted that the consequences of violated trust, because they carry far into the future, are often greater than the value of the potential desired outcome (De Furia, 1997). What this means is that small successes in implementation of research findings can lead to larger successes, but without trust one failure in a closely-linked community makes future successes much more difficult.

Grounded through research, insights and anecdotes, the knowledge broker role becomes that of a change agent. Addressing multifaceted issues in a complex environment (the community, target audience) while also dealing with complex systems (people) requires a multifaceted change strategy. Paraphrasing Ashby's (1964) law of requisite variety, there must be more variety in the change strategy than in the system you are trying to change. This means a KMb strategy would engage a variety of relationship networks such as advisory boards, community and advocacy groups, communities of interest and practice, and local businesses and other institutions. It also means that the KMb process is likely to include multiple events and publications, meta tools, the strategic use of media, and education and community service incentives. *It is through the interaction of all of these relationships and activities and the sharing of understanding that desired change emerges.* As discussed in chapter 2, emergence is a unique and wide-spread property of a complex system that results from the interactions and relationships among people and between people and their environment (Bennet & Bennet, 2004).

Emergence is a property of complex systems resulting from the untraceable causal connections within the system.

To head the community (target audience) in the desired direction requires a *connectedness of choices*. This means that decisions made by people, while different, are clearly based not only on a clear direction for the future, but on an understanding of both why that direction is desirable, *the role* that an individual decision plays with respect to immediate objectives, and *how well* the decision supports the shared vision. What this means is that the decisions made by people as part of their KMb process implementation are based on an understanding of the actions necessary to achieve a desirable goal or objective. The theoretical force behind this connectedness of choices is a common set of beliefs, values and purpose nurtured through knowledge and sharing across trusted networks.

6.5 THE KMB PROJECT/PROGRAM LIFE CYCLE

The composition of the project team will usually change as the project passes through its life cycle. While the description of the life cycle can vary based on the type of project, all projects pass through several distinct stages. One way of describing these stages is to think about them in terms of: initiation and planning, start-up, growth and expansion, sustainability, and close-out. While we take a pragmatic look at each of these stages below, in real life their boundaries are not necessarily clear; for example, planning, although critical during initiation and start-up, extends throughout the life cycle of the project.

6.5.1 Initiations And Planning

It is at the initiation of the project when organizations begin their planning effort. The rationale for undertaking a particular project can come from many sources: an action item flowing from the university's strategic planning; a new discovery from research; a decision by community partners; a new community need; or a new opportunity such as a new funding resource.

For some KMb projects, an initial feasibility review might be completed. If the outcome is negative, the project is shelved before detailed planning is undertaken. Organizations might decide at this stage not to pursue the project or to continue a low level of research of studies. Reasons for this could include:

- The project is not consistent with the organization's strategic focus.
- Resource limitations (time, people, funds) which would make successful completion of the project unlikely.
- There are many other potential projects which are more important to the organization/community than the project being considered.
- The project is not economically feasible.
- More data or information is needed to make a sound decision.

There are many elements to planning a project; for example, defining scope, developing schedule, budgeting, manpower, risk planning, etc. A written plan is developed which outlines the various stages and activities of the project. Planners usually start with a vision of the desired project outcomes and determine, at a high level, the characteristics and major elements of the project required to achieve these outcomes. Major elements are divided and broken down into smaller pieces which lend themselves to scheduling and costing (also known as decomposition). This plan identifies all the things that must be accomplished during the life of the project. There are a variety of software programs available to assist in the development of program plans.

6.5.2 Start-Up

In the context of the life cycle process, start-up of the project usually means the beginning of execution or implementation of the project plan. If the planning has been thorough, then start-up is focused on identifying participants, building relationships across stakeholders, and setting project and KMb activities in motion. Project activities at start-up include allocating resources, contract administration, distributing information, and communicating the project plan to stakeholders and the project team, which must be managed, motivated, informed, encouraged, empowered and supported.

6.5.3 Expansion And Growth

While managing is necessary from the beginning to the end of the project, the expansion and growth phase of the project establishes the processes and approaches needed to sustain the project. Managing involves measuring performance to identify variances between planned and actual results, taking appropriate corrective action when required, and controlling changes to the project or its end product. There are several steps which must be taken to ensure project expectations are being fulfilled. These usually involve selecting appropriate objectives, setting targets which challenge and create pressure for high performance, development milestones and selecting appropriate measures.

6.5.3.1 Selecting appropriate objectives.

The project requirements must be made explicit for all personnel involved in the project to understand. Project objectives are often defined in terms of being SMART: **S**pecific, **M**easurable, **A**ttainable, **R**ealistic (and Relevant) and **T**ime based. While this approach works well for complicated systems such as engineers would design and build, parts of SMART may have to be dropped or modified in a KMb project where the desired outcome is an emergent phenomenon of the complex system (community).

6.5.3.2 Setting targets which challenge and create pressure for high performance.

In any case, these targets are sometimes referred to as "stretch" goals or targets. They are challenging but not so challenging that they are viewed as non achievable.

6.5.3.3 Developing milestones.

These are usually significant events in the project such as completion of deliverables or significant phases of the project. These milestones can be used to evaluate performance by comparing planned results at a point in time to actual results. Deviation should be checked throughout the life of the project. There is little point of being informed of a major cost overrun at the end of the project, or of ignoring a counter intuitive result that creates unintended and harmful consequences to the project outcome.

By the sustainability phase the KMb team understands expectations and is a cohesive connected body, empowered and making decisions at the points of action.

6.5.3.4 Selecting appropriate measures.

While there is a need to measure expenses, schedule, scope, and quality, there are also subjective measures for things like your organization's relationship with other project partners, HR relations, community buy-in, etc. Any measure is appropriate if it helps ensure the project is on track with its strategic intent. The measuring or assessing process and potential measures are discussed in detail in chapter 7.

6.5.4 Sustainability

All the steps taken to ensure project expectations are being fulfilled during the growth and expansion phase are in place during the sustainability phase. At this point the KMb team understands expectations and is a cohesive connected body, empowered and making decisions at the points of action. As detailed earlier, the primary job of the project leader is to monitor and assess project progress, and provide resources and guidance to the team. Information on progress must be evaluated, comprehended and acted upon. Variations must be investigated, and adjustments made where necessary, while keeping the entire KMb project team informed. Typical adjustments include: hiring additional staff to reduce a time overrun or stopping project overtime to reduce costs. If actual performance is radically different than planned performance, the project may require implementation of a contingency plan.

While an in-depth treatment of project management actions is beyond the scope of this text, included here (with prejudice) is a quick synopsis of management actions underway during the sustainability phase:

- Check the progress of activities against the plan and make adjustments where necessary, ensuring that all stakeholders are informed of any changes and, where possible, included in the decision-making process.
- Review performance regularly and at the pre-planned review points, and confirm the validity and relevance of the remainder of the plan.
- Adjust the plan if necessary in light of performance, changing circumstances, and new information, but remaining on track and within the original terms of reference.
- Use transparent, pre-agreed assessment measures when judging performance.
- Identify, agree and delegate new actions as appropriate.
- Inform team members and those in authority about developments, clearly, concisely and in writing.
- Plan and execute team review meetings.
- Stick to established monitoring systems.
- Probe the apparent situations to get at the real facts and figures.
- Analyze causes and learn from mistakes.
- Identify reliable advisors and experts on the team and use them.
- Keep talking to people, and make time *available to all*.
- Share everything possible with all team members.

6.5.5 Close-Out

Closing out the project is often overlooked and if not done, many loose ends will be left hanging. Close-out can involve things such as settling contracts and outstanding billing issues, having a final meeting of the project team to review the overall effort, filing away project records, saying good-bye to everyone, submitting a final project report, etc. In general, there are four important elements in the closeout stage:

6.5.5.1 Performance Assessment

Understanding and describing how well the project performed in terms of its deliverables, schedule and budget, and most importantly, the end result in the community.

6.5.5.2 Documentation

The collection and storage of project records for use in future KMb process and other KMb project teams.

6.5.5.3 Lessons Learned

Determining what can be learned from the effort. Team members should identify their successes, mistakes, unjustified assumptions, and things that could have been done better.

6.5.5.4 Celebration

Thanking all of those who helped with the project and formally recognizing the impact of the project in the community. The celebration will help team members make the "work-life transition" from this project to their new roles.

The lessons learned from the KMb project are particularly important. At the end of the project a review of the entire effort is held with all stakeholders in attendance (sometimes called a post-mortem meeting). The assessment should examine what happened and why, what went well and what did not, etc. Failures and mistakes are reflected on positively, objectively, and without allocating personal blame. Successes are gratefully and realistically discussed. Finally, a review report is prepared which includes systems-level observations and recommendations on follow-up issues and priorities.

REFLECTIVE QUESTIONS CHAPTER 6

> How might communities of practice, interest or learning improve decision-making in your organization? In your community?

> As a project leader, what leadership characteristics would you use to inspire your team and to ensure maximum cooperation from the community and the advisory board?

> As a project leader implementing a KMb process, it is imperative that you get, and give, timely and accurate feedback from project activities. How would you go about doing this in a manner that creates a learning atmosphere and a focus on excellence?

> What contributions can community stakeholders make to a knowledge mobilization process that would accelerate research implementation?

> You've just been selected as the project leader for a knowledge mobilization project in a small, remotely-situated community of 3,000 people who are struggling to provide medical assistance for their elderly population. Funding for a KMb project has been approved, and you are familiar with the university that has the relevant research. Make reasonable assumptions about the situation and develop your management structure for KMb implementation considering and selecting from the proposed elements in this chapter and any others required. Develop brief explanations of your decisions. Working with this project team, do you feel empowered to succeed?

CHAPTER 7

OUTCOMES AND IMPACTS

THIS SECTION INCLUDES: 7.0 INTRODUCTION; 7.1 ASSESSMENT; 7.2 THE ASSESSMENT PROCESS; 7.3 QUALITATIVE AND QUANTITATIVE MEASURES; 7.4 MEASURES OF FEELING; 7.5 BROAD AREAS OF ASSESSMENT MEASURES, 7.5.1 Outcome and Impact Measures, 7.5.2 Input Measures, 7.5.3 Output Measures, 7.5.4 Process Measures, 7.,5.5 Technology Systems Measures, 7.5.6 Sustainability Measures; 7.6 ADDITIONAL APPROACHES TO ASSESSMENT.
FIGURES: 7-1 REPRESENTATIVE QUESTIONS IN THE ASSESSMENT PROCESS; 7-2 BROAD AREAS OF ASSESSMENT MEASURES.

7.0 INTRODUCTION

The terms outcomes and impacts are often used interchangeably. However, there is the subtle difference that an outcome can stand alone while an impact is on something. Ultimately, the outcome of any research implementation in the social sciences and humanities is going to be the impact on humans and the social change brought about by that impact. This means that impact represents the difference between the key social characteristics at the beginning of KMb project and those same characteristics at the end of the project.

While some impacts can be directly attributed to identifiable changes, many are indirect, and therefore it may be difficult to identify specific causal relationships between actions and impacts (see the discussion on complex systems in chapter 2). However, everything is as it should be, i.e., the current state is a result of multiple and competing factors and forces and the interactions among them. Consistent with complexity theory, a small perturbation may result in large-scale change (butterfly effect), or conversely, a large number of events and processes may be needed over time before the system will finally (and quickly) move in the desired direction (the tipping point).

> *The outcome of the implementation of social sciences and humanities research is its impact on people and the social change brought about by that impact.*

Indirect impacts may have to do with the personal development of individuals in the stakeholder group, or the building of relationships across communities. Therefore, focal points for assessment may be individual and collective as well as offering potential evidence of larger cultural and social change. For participating individuals, a significant outcome may be the amount and nature of learning that has occurred, shifts in their frame of reference, and behavior changes, many of which would be reflected in decisions made or actions taken. Another outcome may be a pattern of learning across all participants, resulting in a visible collective behavior change. For example, consider the impact of professional development activities on practice, and how this might have impacted stakeholder groups.

The best approach to developing an assessment plan is collaborative. Partners and representatives of the larger stakeholder community can best express what is important to them, what they perceive as value added. If what they express is not aligned with the intent of research implementation, then pre-work is necessary to build a shared understanding before moving forward. Collaborative assessment planning facilitates the development of shared ownership through a process of reflection, communication and growth.

Collaborative assessment planning facilitates the development of shared ownership through a process of reflection, communication and growth.

The intent of this chapter is not to be all inclusive. There are many excellent studies and texts in both academic and popular literature on assessment. Rather, here is offered a collection of ideas with specific focus on knowledge mobilization in the implementation of social sciences and humanities research findings. Since knowledge mobilization processes are heavily situation-dependent and context sensitive, a continuous process of assessment based on qualitative information regarding the strengths and weaknesses of specific activities associated with the process will provide the opportunity for focusing limited resources in those areas most important to project success.

7.1 ASSESSMENT

Assessment is the process of using measures or indicators to judge progress toward achieving predetermined goals, including efficiency, quality, outcomes and the effectiveness of specific actions and activities in terms of their contribution to the overall objective. In the implementation of social sciences research, assessment measures can also validate (or guide) research findings. Therefore, the design, process, and implementation of assessments may significantly affect the outcome of implementation.

Taking an appreciative inquiry approach, the concept of assessment can be far more effective than the concept of evaluation. Evaluation is a judgment on how well or poorly someone or something is doing. Assessment looks at the current state in a longer journey and asks: is it on track? Similar to a sense and respond strategy used in complex systems, it can be viewed as a testing approach where the system has been perturbed and the response is being studied. If everything is on track, then the implementation process continues forward. If not, then some shift or change occurs to head the system in the desired direction. Although assessment occurs at a point in time, it is a periodic process, a series of points in a longer journey. While evaluation is judgment on a project's status, an assessment can be used to improve or help a project achieve its goals. Assessment can also aid in uncovering factors or actions that may later lead to problems. For example, a project may or may not be on target at a point in time.

Taking an appreciative inquiry approach, assessment can prove far more effective than evaluation.

In a conversation between a senior military officer and a contractor, the officer used the expression "make it so naturally." At first glance it appears ironic to juxtapose the word "make" and "naturally." However, the concept he introduced was one of putting enough of the right pieces in place to nurture learning focused on a specific area that in turn would lead to decisions and action in the desirable direction. This "make it so naturally" approach would then lead to a connectedness of choices (introduced in chapter 6), where different decisions and actions made in different parts of community life would nonetheless support community development in the desired direction. Similarly, the challenge in a KMb project is to create an assessment process that "makes it so naturally."

A connectedness of choices is where different decisions and actions made in different parts of community life move the community in the same direction.

While assessment measures may be thought of in terms of formative and summative (process and outcome), these concepts apply only to the specific project underway, which in a complex setting is only one point of change in a larger journey toward long-term community goals. There may be no ending point to knowledge mobilization. During the start-up phase of implementing research findings, there is considerable effort and activity required as the knowledge mobilization process begins to build awareness. As implementation expands and grows, encompassing larger stakeholder populations, the knowledge that is mobilized may resonate with that population and take on a life of its own. This is much like the idea of a meme introduced in chapter 4, something (an idea, a behavior or a pattern or piece of information) that can be passed on, again and again, through the process of imitation, taking on a life of its own (Blackmore, 1999). Effective implementation of social sciences research often nurtures learning and behavioral change. The meme that has been nurtured passes from individual to individual, community to community, long after the project has formally "ended." If KMb has been successfully implemented, then the process will have propagated to various levels in the community and will continue building upon itself as long as there is the need. In its highest form of success, the process will have influenced people who will influence other people to learn, act and solve problems; this is the secret of sustainability, "making it so naturally."

> *Measure for the future. What gets measured is what gets attention.*

Measure for the future. Since what gets measured is what gets attention, it is important to think forward to the desired end state and identify performance measures that move beyond reflecting specific goals to serving as part of the implementation change strategy. In this discussion, assessment measures are considered standards used to measure success in achieving an identified objective where applicable. They describe the metric that is *expected* to qualitatively or quantitatively, explicitly or implicitly, indicate progress towards achieving the objective.

The secret of sustainability is to "make it so naturally."

While the primary focus of assessment in the implementation of research findings is effectiveness (in terms of input, output, systems and outcomes), assessment measures also address efficiency and sustainability of the implementation process. Effectiveness is doing the right or best *things*; efficiency is doing things the right way by employing the right or best *use* of available resources. Further, community member *self-efficacy* for implementing the KMb process—the belief of having the power and capacity to achieve an objective—is critical for process sustainability, and therefore a candidate for assessment. For example, an efficacy measure might be the ability to attract top researchers as partners, the level of advocacy for this area of research and at what levels (policy-makers, local and international, etc.), or even the number of web sites that link to and from the research site.

The process of collecting information that can be used to assess value is inherent in the participatory action research approach. This information may take a variety of forms; for example, observation, level of participation and anecdotes. Both structured and unstructured feedback from the target audience is a source for continuous assessment. A feedback loop can serve as a source of quality control, and can help build understanding of the value of KMb approaches. Virtual resources such as discussion forums and blogs provide on-going opportunities for assessing stakeholder perceptions.

While a nominal assessment process (complete with broad areas of assessment measures and examples) is presented below, additional approaches are mentioned at the end of the chapter. These additional approaches include: after action reviews, action assessment and learning (AAL), benchmarking, case studies, cost benefit analysis, grounded theory, inquiry groups, inventories, surveys, and social network analysis.

7.2 THE ASSESSMENT PROCESS

The assessment process starts with a series of steps to clearly identify what should and should not be assessed, how to measure it, and how to use the measures. Each step includes a series of questions that help guide the assessment process—defining, choosing and using the best measures for a specific implementation approach. Provided in the following paragraphs are brief descriptions of these steps and the types of questions that might be asked for project assessment at each step. Figure 7-2 provides an overview of these questions. Remember that each KMb project will be unique and measures will need to be tailored to each phase of the project.

7.2.1 Step One

The first step of this process is to identify the KMb project objectives and the target goals along the implementation journey, and have an understanding of how the selected KMb approach will move identified stakeholders toward the objective. Therefore, *the first three questions become*: What is the objective of the project? What are the target goals in the journey toward that objective? What methods and tools will be used to measure the success of these objectives?

7.2.2 Step Two

Ask: Who are the stakeholders? What do they need to know? How will this assessment improve the projects chances of success?

In generic terms, there are the developers of knowledge and the beneficiaries of knowledge, the researchers (in universities, research institutes, etc.) and the target audience (a community, or defined segment of the general public). Practitioners have day-to-day interactions with the target audience in the course of their role as change agents; advocates are opinion leaders and champions; policy-makers are high-level decision-makers, generally inferring political impact. The target audience is called community and the term decision-makers would include those stakeholders who hold positions of authority or leadership in regards to implementation of research findings. (See Figure 3-1 and the related discussion on stakeholder groups in chapter 3.)

7.2.3 Step Three

Ask: What is the framework within which we will measure?

Implementation of social sciences and humanities research findings is built on a framework that emerges out of the content of the research, the nature of the targeted change, the characteristics of the stakeholders, and the commitment and resources of researchers, decision-makers, advocates and practitioners. Making this framework explicit provides a useful setting to convey how actions contribute to overall goals and the ways they produce benefits. These actions and their benefits can then be assessed for timeliness, quality, impact and long-term consequences.

There is no standard framework for assessment. Some examples would include flow, matrix, and causal diagrams. A flow framework traces implementation activities to impacts (with related measures) and is effective for showing how activities lead to benefits. Since a matrix can condense many interdependent factors into a readily understood format, it might be an effective framework for demonstrating choices made during the implementation process. Causal loop diagrams are effective to show cause-and-effect relationships of a complicated system; but would not capture the interactions among elements in a complex situation (DON, 2001). Pert charts and POA&Ms (plan of actions and milestones) are standard ways of displaying, describing and managing projects. Whichever framework is selected, it can help ensure that metrics are aligned to the overall objective and target goals during the journey toward that objective.

There is no standard framework for assessment.

7.2.4 Step Four

Ask: What should be measured? Will assessing these things contribute to desired behaviors and aid project personnel in their decision-making and resource allocation?

Measures are tied to the maturity of implementation, which has a life cycle and progresses through a series of phases as understanding expands and behaviors begin to change. Loosely, these might be thought of in terms of pre-planning (initiation and planning), the start-up phase, implementation (expansion and growth), sustainability and close-out. In the pre-planning phase, researchers, partners and practitioners are developing strategies and anticipating results, perhaps looking at process and risk analyses. In the start-up phase, the goals would be to generate interest and support, so there would be a high value on measures that demonstrate interest such as anecdotes and levels of participation (O'Dell, 2001). During the growth and expansion phase, measures would demonstrate larger stakeholder involvement meeting planned milestones and behavior changes, evidence of success. During the sustainability phase, measures would attempt to convey cultural change and to identify larger and long-term stakeholder benefits. The point is that when the implementation approach is phased, each phase requires a different set of measures, and if a pilot or incubator approach is used, these would need their own special measures. For example, when these approaches are used, the effective transfer of best practices and lessons learned might be assessed through anecdotes and measures of feeling (discussed below).

7.2.5 Step Five

Ask: Who will measure? How should measures be collected and analyzed?

Decision-makers must be actively engaged in the assessment loop.

The important point here is to structure information gathering such that the information can help guide decisions at all levels. This means that decision-makers must be actively engaged in the assessment loop.

Input measures are generally qualitative in terms of accessibility and understanding of research materials and the ability to act on what is accessed and understood. For system measures there are automated data collection systems, such as tools that measure website access, downloads, and visit times. A system performance log can also provide measures. Output and outcome measures may contain a mixture of qualitative and quantitative information, thereby requiring a larger investment in time to collect, analyze and understand. Process measures are continuous and should be addressed during periodic meetings of key personnel.

The process has its own outcome. If it achieves a comfort level with stakeholders in terms of value added, this process could become a self-reinforcing loop. For example, as you start to implement the process you get results. Taking an action research approach, these results are fed back to the researcher and practitioner partners, and this new learning drives new actions that are then made part of the KMb process. As this feedback loop becomes more effective, more learning occurs. The more learning that occurs, the more effective the results, creating a powerful reinforcing feedback loop.

7.2.6 Step Six

Ask: How will we embed assessment feedback into the implementation process?

This is a critical step in the assessment process as well as the KMb process. The complex and dynamic nature of social sciences research implementation and the knowledge mobilization process may make it difficult to pre-plan what measures can best assess the process. Therefore, whatever assessment framework is put in place needs to be flexible and adaptive to what is learned during the implementation process. Good assessments often start with key questions. What has been discovered about stakeholders and stakeholder participation? Are stakeholders using the knowledge that is being mobilized? Are they sharing meaningful experiences and knowledge openly? Are there any anecdotes or stories that show success to guide future actions? These are representative of the questions that need to be asked during the on-going

Good assessments often start with key questions. Even if there are no firm answers, the search for answers provides valuable insights and ideas.

assessment process. As answers emerge, the next step is to ask why, and when an answer comes, ask why again. One valuable contribution of assessment is to help all participants better understand what is really happening as the project evolves. The insights that result can be of enormous benefit to the project and professionally to its constituents. Even if there are no firm answers, the search for answers can provide valuable insights and ideas on how to improve the implementation and assessment process. By collecting and prioritizing these ideas, original plans and assumptions can be challenged and changed as needed, with new assessment measures identified in response to these changes (Porter, et al., 2003).

As answers emerge to the questions asked in the assessment process, the next step is to ask why, and when an answer comes, ask why again.

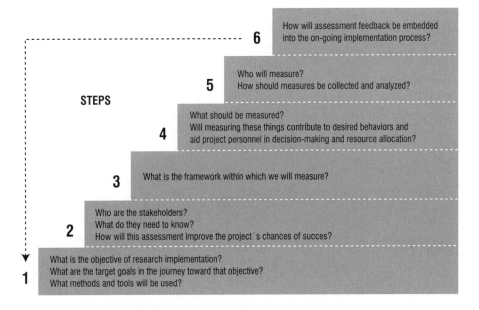

FIGURE 7-1: Representative Questions in the Assessment Process.

7.3 QUALITATIVE AND QUANTITATIVE MEASURES

Assessment approaches usually combine quantitative and qualitative indicators. Quantitative measures are those that use numbers (referred to as hard data) to identify trends or assess changes between specific points (from week to week, etc.). Qualitative measures (soft data) pull from the context of a situation to provide a sense of value or indication of the magnitude of some attribute such as level of morale or resistance to change. These indicators include stories and anecdotes. For example, to measure the value of participation in a community, a story from a community member about how the community provided information critical to solving a dilemma might have a greater impact on stakeholders than the number of people helped.

Qualitative measures are particularly suited to evaluating effectiveness of the implementation of social sciences and humanities research findings. Even when quantitative measures are available and make sense, qualitative measures can add context, meaning and insight.

7.4 MEASURES OF FEELING

The concepts of tangible and intangible benefits are closely related to the concepts behind the use of quantitative and qualitative measures. Since tangible benefits are concrete and easily identified and described, they are relatively easy to measure in quantitative terms. However, while intangible benefits may be felt, they are difficult to describe in quantitative terms. They deal more with feelings, perceptions, beliefs and other qualitative concepts. Here is where qualitative measures come into play; for example, how stakeholders feel about a project underway can be highly significant in the implementation of research findings.

Measures of feeling are a specific form of qualitative measures. They can loosely be divided into two areas. First, they can be the result of the practitioner or a partner scanning and interacting with the stakeholder environment and recording what they personally feel about implementation progress (a form of self-reflection). While all people tend to find what they are looking for, a practitioner or partner who steps back and looks at implementation from a systemic point of view can generally get an intuitive feeling of how things are going. By following up with other stakeholders to get their perspectives on this feeling, some strong insights may emerge.

While all people tend to find what they are looking for, a partner who steps back and looks at implementation from a systemic point of view can generally get an intuitive feeling of how things are going.

Second, these measures can be the result of the practitioner or a partner scanning and interacting with the stakeholder environment and recording how stakeholders feel about implementation progress. In a more formal approach, interviews can serve as a one-on-one vehicle for creating dialogue and allowing stakeholders to share their feelings about the research results and/or implementation of the project. They may use a phenomenological approach or come in the form of stories and anecdotes.

A combination of these approaches would be a 360 degree assessment process where all stakeholders are asked how they feel about aspects of implementation that are outside their areas of focus as well as their own area. A variation of this approach would be the use of learning circles—dynamic knowledge exchanges, both planned and spontaneous—to capture local stakeholder feelings and perceptions.

Community random sampling can provide a larger "feeling" base. While small samples may provide greater benefit from one-on-one interactions (surfacing feelings such as self-efficacy and confidence of stakeholders and/or practitioners and partners), larger samplings can help build an understanding of intent (what knowledge do you feel is the most useful to you and how will it be used?) through surveys and virtual Internet approaches.

Anecdotes can reflect the overall impressions of research implementation, its usefulness and the resulting changes in behaviors of the target audience. A single anecdote can convey an individual feeling. A pattern emerging from a series or group of anecdotes from stakeholders conveys a sampling of feeling. Once a critical number of anecdotes are captured from a community, the value set or rules underlying the behavior of that community may be determined (Snowden, 1999). That critical number would be similar to the concept of a tipping point in complexity theory. Similarly, these anecdotes can be used to measure change when that change is directly related to the value set or rules underlying the behavior of the community, which may be the case in implementation of social science research results.

7.5 BROAD AREAS OF ASSESSMENT MEASURES

While the Internet offers expanded opportunities for collecting assessment measures, there are situations where it is inappropriate. For example, face-to-face interactions would be necessary in rural communities with a lower density of computer access, or when stakeholders are a low-income, migrant population. Conversely, where access to information and computer skill sets are contributors to implementation of research results, these would be encouraged, promoted, taught and supported. However, virtual communication is never the same as face-to-face dialogue.

Taking an appreciative inquiry approach, since what is being measured is indicative of future desired states and every small movement in that direction is of value, assessment measures may be considered measures for success in terms of interim or final outcomes. While it is easy to forget, the major focus of the project is not the implementation of research results but *achieving a specific objective across the stakeholder group by implementing research knowledge that is transformed into actions and new behavior of community citizens.*

Since what is being measured is indicative of future desired states and every small movement in that direction is of value, assessment measures may be considered measures for success.

As shown in Figure 7.2, broad areas of assessment measures discussed below include outcome and impact measures, input measures, output measures, process measures and technology system measures.

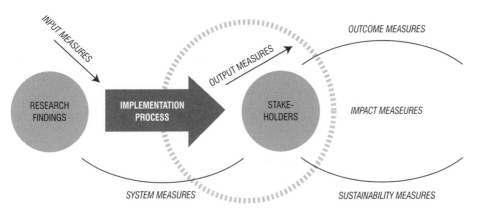

FIGURE 7-2: Broad areas of assessment measures.

7.5.1 Outcome and Impact Measures

Tied directly to the contribution of research findings to targeted stakeholders, outcome measures concern the overall result (value) of the project and measure large-scale characteristics such as the degree of achieving the objectives related to the target community, and the quality and effectiveness of researcher-practitioner-community partnering. An indirect outcome may be the process of learning that has occurred, or even *learning how to learn*. Additionally, the relevance, extent and quality of learning and how that learning is put into action might be of significance. An array of measures may have to be considered since indicators of these desired outcomes may not emerge through a single assessment process.

An indirect outcome may be the process of learning that has occurred, or even learning how to learn.

While the primary outcome is benefit for the community, the total outcome

137

includes the benefit to researchers, practitioners, the community, and other stakeholders (policy-makers, advocates, etc.) and future community members! Each stakeholder would have their own desirable outcome. The researcher would seek feedback on the efficacy of research theories used, potentially using what has been learned from practical application to guide future research. Practitioners would be interested in learning more about the theoretical foundations of their practice as well as evaluating their own effectiveness in terms of application of practice relative to the research area and the community. The practitioner may also learn more about the community in the process of implementation. The community would want improvement in terms of the original identified need, and in the process of this improvement would have acquired good practices and an understanding of why the practices were effective. Policy-makers would have learned a little about the whole program and benefited from their constituents gain. They are also in a position to understand the process and, as appropriate, to initiate policy change, transfer what has been learned to other locations, and potentially support related knowledge programs for their constituents.

OUTCOME AND IMPACT MEASURES

7.5.1.1 Examples of Outcome and Impact Measures

Policy change (scans before and after)
Cultural changes
Related stakeholder innovations
Replication of KMb processes by stakeholders at local levels and nearby communities
Individual and community follow-on activities
Cross-fertilization across knowledge fields
Positive economic impact
Transferable community models
Additional funding through research and local community grants
Ability of key community members to use research knowledge
References to research in new research

7.5.2 Input Measures

Input measures are specific to knowledge mobilization in terms of (1) the ability of researchers and practitioners to convey or translate the intent and capacity of the research to help the stakeholder population, and (2) the ability of the stakeholder community to understand the intent and engage in implementation of the research. Input measures are significant measures during start-up and early growth and expansion, but become less significant as the project moves into the sustainability stage and the language most appropriate for the exchange of information and shared understanding has been developed such that there is a connectedness of choices.

Input measures are significant measures during start-up and early growth and expansion.

7.5.2.1 Examples of Input Measures

Feedback from stakeholder community reflecting ability to understand and apply the research findings

Nature of requests for additional information
Number of requests for translation of research language
Membership of relevant stakeholders in communities and on project teams
Adequacy of resources allocated to the project
Quality of project design, structure and personnel

7.5.3 Output Measures

Output measures are focused on achieving specific goals along the implementation journey. For example, they may deal with the effectiveness of a specific event, or the transfer and/or improvement of a specific lesson learned.

The amount of media coverage about implementation of research findings could serve as a KMb indicator of the broader public interest. Discourse analysis of that coverage could then provide an indicator of value to implementation. As with all measures, the measure itself must be understood within the context in which it occurred and in which it was collected.

Output measures are focused on achieving specific goals along the implementation journey.

7.5.3.1 Examples of Output Measures

Participation in and feedback from events
Changes in discourse
Satisfaction surveys (what works?)
Event evaluations
Co-authoring of publications
Number of requests for information
Sales of publications
Number of activities
Audience reaction testing
Academic peer reviews
Number of creative ideas forwarded
Presentations requested and made to policy-makers
Reflective writings
Improved conceptual and practical tools
Citations in policy documents
Increased stakeholder contributions to publications
Number of collaborative projects across functional areas

7.5.4 Process Measures

On-going records of the process such as meeting minutes and other dialogues in scheduled events, focus groups, e-journals and production blogs (daily, weekly, monthly) can serve as instruments of process assessment. Such records become even more effective in terms of offering wider perspectives with stakeholder contributions. The action research method provides for the study of processes as they unfold. Sources for assessments might include: active reflection, milestone accomplishments, field notes, observations, interviews, questionnaires and surveys, and organizational or community records and documents.

When used, student participation in the KMb process can be specifically addressed. For example, the number of students involved (graduate and undergraduate), number of community placements, or the extent to which the research performed by students is informed by the project.

Process measures are periodic (or continuous as appropriate) over time. For this reason, measures can be compared (over time) to provide an indicator of overall impact. As best practices and lessons learned emerge, the sharing and application of what has been learned becomes a process assessment measure. It must be remembered that best practices are very sensitive to context and cannot easily be transferred to other situations or KMb projects.

7.5.4.1 Examples of Process Measures

Improved KMb among stakeholders
Participation on committees
Collaboration in planning events
Suggestions from stakeholders on topics for events
Requests for additional events
Requests by special interest groups
Degree of interaction during meetings
Advice from stakeholders
Frequency and duration of media exposure
Involvement in communities of learning, practice and interest
Activity in communities of learning, practice and interest
Openness of information and knowledge exchange
Solicited periodic feedback
Panel discussions
Measures of feeling (discussed earlier in this chapter)

7.5.5 Technology System Measures

In this usage, system refers specifically to technology systems supporting knowledge mobilization. System measures deal with the effectiveness and efficiency of the communications structure, monitoring the usefulness and responsiveness of technology support tools. Value added and user satisfaction can be assessed by surveying stakeholder partners on whether the material they need is available, and the extent to which the materials provided support their work (service delivery, program planning, etc.) Some of these measures could be collected via on-line monitoring devices and additional feedback could be solicited. For example, a feedback form built into the website might query stakeholders regarding the usefulness of materials and the ease of use, as well as ask for suggestions for improvement and what additional resources may be needed. Valuing what has been learned through knowledge management, an overarching design measure might be the percentage of materials that include summaries, context, links to related materials, and points of contact for additional information. Think in terms of the living system, the living networks, repositories and documents described in chapter 4.

PROCESS MEASURES

Content analysis of the materials on the website can ensure the site is supporting the goals of research implementation. Comparing patterns of use across materials can provide insights; for example, identifying those areas of greatest need/interest to stakeholders, or identifying those materials quickly scanned but not downloaded (either not of interest or inaccessible). Similarly, content analysis of discussion forums, blogs, etc. will surface patterns that show areas of concern or passion.

7.5.5.1 Examples of Technology System Measures

Website traffic
Number of resources available
Number of resources contributed by stakeholders
Number of downloads of pertinent information
Participation in sponsored virtual dialogue forums
The use of virtual tools
Increased participation in communities
Number of questions forwarded
Number of responses to an Internet survey
Take-up of webcasting
Continuous engagement
Increased access to resources
Increased access to expertise
Amount of interaction in discussion forums
Use of learning systems
Expansion of network
Level of self-organization in the system
Number of interactive links (both ways)
Patterns of use

7.5.6 Sustainability Measures

Loosely related to the sustainability stage of the project life cycle, these assessment measures are used to identify and assess those factors that determine the capacity of the KMb project to maintain the quality of the outcome after the initial objective has been achieved. Although these factors are often unique to the specific project, there are a few generic characteristics that tend to support sustainability. Examples would be: cohesiveness and energy of the community members after achieving the objective; political and media backing and support of the project; downstream funding to support future activities in the project; citizen recognition and involvement in planning future objectives and the adaptability and learning rate of the community as the project achieves the desired outcome.

The cohesiveness and energy displayed by community members after achieving the objective helps support sustainability.

7.6 ADDITIONAL APPROACHES TO ASSESSMENT

As noted earlier, all models are artificial constructs, specifically developed to explore relationships within a structure. They aid in focusing and learning, and serve as vehicles for sharing what is learned. The six-step assessment process presented at the beginning of this chapter represents one way to develop an approach to and measures for assessment. Other approaches that can contribute to the assessment process might include: after action reviews, action assessment and learning (AAL), benchmarking, the use of case studies, a cost benefit analysis, grounded theory, inquiry groups, inventories, surveys, and social network analysis. These are cursorily addressed below.

After action reviews were initiated by the military a number of years ago. The concept is that key questions are answered by engaged stakeholders following every event or situation to assess the context of the event and capture the learning that has occurred. These then serve as real-time on-going assessment vehicles as well as to build understanding in those who participated and those who later read and analyze them.

Action Assessment and Learning (AAL) is an action learning-while-assessing approach that ensures what is planned stays in resonance with emerging community needs. AAL would be based on a series of periodic "reviews" throughout the KMb process. These reviews are similar to the "after action reviews" described above, except they are process-driven rather than action-driven. Both a pre-AAL and post-AAL become part of the process. The pre-AAL brings the KMb team together to focus on the direction ahead, how progress will be assessed, and sharing lessons learned from previous KMb projects or related community projects. After each AAL session the KMb team would continue to learn from actions taken and actions underway to ensure the relevance of continuing and future actions.

The AAL is process-driven rather than action-driven.

While **benchmarking** has historically proven useful where transfer of best practices (APQC, 2000) has been successful, much of the research and humanities has not been previously implemented in a common context. In addition, the social sciences are highly context and situation dependent, making it difficult to locate a community with which to benchmark. However, in the process of implementation, segments of the target audience may show demonstrated results before other segments. While not necessarily providing an easy comparison due to the complexity of communities, here is where benchmarking might provide useful insights and guidelines for actions or questions.

The **case study** is a formal and comprehensive report about a specific individual or group (organization, community, etc.) who has implemented related research findings, or a similar process implementing different findings. It is often used to build an understanding of connections and causes thereby creating patterns that may be applicable to future situations. Since the case study is a detailed description of a project, situation or group, including heavy context, it provides a setting to examine numerous elements within a component of the implementation process. For example, the focus might be on stakeholder awareness, understanding, commitment and actions, or on reactions, learnings, transfer and results (Kirkpatrick's four levels of evaluation). Since case studies are intended as learning vehicles, implementation results may have been successful or failed, or both. A mini-case study is a shorter, less-detailed version that covers primary points but still includes details and context of the group or situation.

Cost benefit analysis can be used to assess the value of the KMb project in terms of its real costs to stakeholders, the qualitative outcome and overall project costs. What were the resources spent and what was the result? One of the costs is time;

another is knowledge created or lost. Part of the outcome is the peripheral benefits. For example, for the researcher and practitioner, that might include what has been learned about the KMb process that might be transferred to future efforts. (See the discussion above under outcome and impact measures.)

The **grounded theory** approach enables theory to emerge from data and information through in-depth interviews with stakeholders (Tesch, 1990). This rigorous qualitative approach seeks to understand stakeholder viewpoints through their own eyes. Analysis would focus on the patterns emerging across stakeholder interviews andwould have the potential to contribute to the development of theory of community practice, leadership and self-efficacy.

Inquiry groups are brought together to investigate or examine some specific issue. These can be held both face-to-face and through interactive technologies (video conference, conference calls, e-discussion groups). They may include the full or partial group of stakeholders with invited outside resources, with a minimum of one representative from each sector (policy, practitioner, consumer and advocate) and other related inquiry groups as required. Inquiry groups provide the opportunity for each stakeholder to share diverse perspectives and build capacity through learning and teaching. Basic inquiry procedures are used, including questioning and cycling between action and reflection.

The **inventory** is a detailed account of items. It may be either a listing of research related to a specific area of focus or a listing and linking of research implementation strategies that are working and those that are not. This latter approach is an assessment tool.

The **survey** process can provide a baseline for community behaviors and attitudes. For example, data taken at start-up and again a year or two into implementation can be used to identify attitudinal changes over time (Robson, 1993). In addition, surveys can take many formats, and questions can be structured, semi-structured or open ended, providing different points of reference for exploring core issues. They can also help identify sustainability factors that are working.

Social network analysis can be used for mapping the relationships among community stakeholders. It is particularly effective in assessing the flow of information through communication and collaboration and can help identify people who are central or peripheral within a stakeholder group, and the extent to which the group is connected or split into subgroups. The process of SNA begins by collecting data through interviews or surveys. Focused on the implementation of research results, the questions asked might be: From whom do you seek information? To whom do you give information? When you need information or advice, is this person accessible to you? When you need information or advice, does this person respond within a sufficient amount of time to help you solve your issue? How frequently have you received information from this person in the past? From the answers to these or similar questions a map is created that connects people who receive information with people who have provided that information. When combined with other sources of information, this approach allows stakeholders to assess their ability to create and share knowledge, and once the current state is recognized, it becomes an enabler for

Social network analysis is particularly effective in assessing the flow of information through communication and collaboration.

143

improving these abilities (Cross & Prusack, 2002; Cross, et al., 2002).

Determining outcomes and impacts and assessing along the way is not a science, but more of an art.

There are several software products available to do SNA mapping. These programs use simple screen-oriented interfaces, allowing the user to drag nodes with the mouse and click to add new modes. Each node is assigned a number of attributes, which are highlighted using colors and shapes. There are also several tools for automatic layout of the network. Once the mapping is complete, analysis of this structure of connections can provide information on relationships among stakeholders that facilitate or impede knowledge sharing or mobilization, offering intervention opportunities.

As can be seen by the wide variety of available assessment approaches and potential measures, determining outcomes and impacts and assessing along the way is not a science but more of an art, a human effort to consciously supplement the work of nature. How can the KMb process be formed and moved, arranged and grouped such that it emerges as a community work of art?

REFLECTIVE QUESTIONS CHAPTER 7

> Thinking about the measurement processes and instruments with which you are familiar, reflect on the role people's feelings may have played in the measures these processes and instruments produced.

> How can you, as a project leader, ensure that the assessment process is implemented in a manner that identifies all issues, mistakes and successes without embarrassing the people making the mistakes and thereby lowering morale and the spirit of the workforce?

> Reflect on the distinctions between outcome measures and impact measures introduced in the first paragraph of this chapter. Recognizing that you would need to qualitatively assess the critical factors in current state and then reassess those same factors at the end of the project, how would you measure the impact of project implementation?

> How might you apply the AAL approach in your every-day work? In community efforts? What benefit would be gained?

> Since social network analysis is based on behaviors as well as knowledge, how would you ensure it was used for assessment and learning rather than punishment?

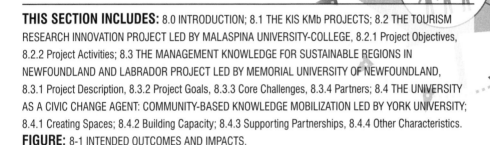

CHAPTER 8

THE KIS OF SSHRC

(A MINI CASE STUDY)

THIS SECTION INCLUDES: 8.0 INTRODUCTION; 8.1 THE KIS KMb PROJECTS; 8.2 THE TOURISM RESEARCH INNOVATION PROJECT LED BY MALASPINA UNIVERSITY-COLLEGE, 8.2.1 Project Objectives, 8.2.2 Project Activities; 8.3 THE MANAGEMENT KNOWLEDGE FOR SUSTAINABLE REGIONS IN NEWFOUNDLAND AND LABRADOR PROJECT LED BY MEMORIAL UNIVERSITY OF NEWFOUNDLAND, 8.3.1 Project Description, 8.3.2 Project Goals, 8.3.3 Core Challenges, 8.3.4 Partners; 8.4 THE UNIVERSITY AS A CIVIC CHANGE AGENT: COMMUNITY-BASED KNOWLEDGE MOBILIZATION LED BY YORK UNIVERSITY; 8.4.1 Creating Spaces; 8.4.2 Building Capacity; 8.4.3 Supporting Partnerships, 8.4.4 Other Characteristics.
FIGURE: 8-1 INTENDED OUTCOMES AND IMPACTS.

8.0 INTRODUCTION

The Social Sciences and Humanities Research Council of Canada (SSHRC) is committed to "a future where humanities and social sciences research provides Canadians with the knowledge and understanding to strengthen our social and intellectual foundations, to build an economy based on principles of fairness and equity for all, and to bring Canadian ideas onto the world stage." By all accounts, SSHRC is not only bringing Canadian ideas onto the world stage, but leading development of a process to close the gap between research and action, what they define as knowledge mobilization, making knowledge readily *accessible*—and thereby *useful* to any number of individuals and groups in society—by developing ways in which groups can work together collaboratively to produce and share and apply knowledge.

Knowledge dissemination of academic research findings to practitioners has historically been fragmented and too disconnected from applied settings to ensure wide distribution about effective programs and to permit replicability (Dufour & Cumberland, 2003). To address this challenge, SSHRC has embarked on an ambitious series of initiatives to transform itself into a knowledge council. For example, in the Fall of 2005 SSHRC sponsored an invitation-only event—a first of its kind—bringing together a diverse group of experts with a wide range of concerns to focus on knowledge mobilization for the Human Sciences. This group included participants from academic research environments, public and private sectors, charitable and community organizations, and the media. Initial challenges identified for mobilizing knowledge across the humanities and social sciences included: (1) How to index and translate the knowledge produced by a variety of disciplines and fields such that it can be accessed by any number of

> *SSHRC is leading development of a process to close the gap between research and action, making knowledge readily accessible—and thereby useful—to any number of individuals and groups in society.*

145

researchers; (2) How to disseminate academic research to the public at large in an easily understandable language; and (3) How to enhance the way in which researchers can access and understand other forms of experience and lay knowledge resident in academic organizations and cultures.

During the course of this three-day event participants explored a myriad of questions from the different viewpoints of the academic, private, aboriginal, volunteer, and policy sectors. What are the most difficult challenges for building and sharing knowledge? How would you characterize and gauge the interest and motivation for engaging in knowledge mobilization? Is there a significant commitment for developing this broader dimension of knowledge mobilization? Who should take the lead in a knowledge mobilization initiative? Do partnerships across sectors make sense? What are your principal knowledge needs, knowledge resources and pathways connecting them? What are the most promising developments and opportunities for knowledge mobilization?

SSHRC's first event on its journey toward becoming a knowledge council surfaced more questions than answers.

The Fall of 2005 also saw SSHRC issuing their 2006-2011 Strategic Plan aimed at continuing the transformation into a value-added knowledge council committed to improving "by several orders of magnitude" the effectiveness of sharing knowledge gained from basic and applied research across families, community groups, policy-makers, legislators, business leaders and the media. The powerful end result is seen as sustainability, wealth creation and a higher quality of life, *"a more connected nation that reaps unprecedented benefits from both the scale of its geography and the rich diversity of its population."*

In the case of SSHRC, words do lead to action. For more than 25 years the Canadian government has funded academic research in the social sciences and humanities. However, SSHRC began to realize that there were significant difficulties in moving this research beyond academia into the wider public domain, and that SSHRC's responsibility as a publicly-funded organization was to ensure the transfer and uptake of research for the benefit of Canadian citizens.

The initial approach was to fund university-based strategic knowledge mobilization initiatives that would benefit both researchers and non-academic stakeholder communities.

As part of this transformation the Knowledge Impact in Society (KIS) Pilot Initiative was also underway. The overarching objective of the pilot was to explore potential methods of support for effective knowledge exchange and mobilization. Specifically, the objectives were (1) develop or expand strategies to systematically move social sciences and humanities knowledge from areas in which a university has recognized research strength into active service beyond academic circles; (2) build or expand relationships and facilitate knowledge exchange between specific non-academic stakeholders and researchers whose expertise is relevant to those stakeholders' interests and concerns; and (3) create or expand opportunities for students in the social sciences and humanities to develop knowledge mobilization skills through hands-on experience.

The initial approach was to fund university-based strategic knowledge mobilization initiatives that would benefit both researchers and non-academic stakeholder communities. In this instance, SSHRC defined knowledge mobilization as *moving knowledge into active service for the broadest possible common good.* The knowledge focus was understood to mean any or all of the following: (1) findings from specific social sciences and humanities research, (2) the accumulated knowledge and experience of social sciences and humanities researchers, and (3) the accumulated knowledge and experience of stakeholders concerned with social, cultural, economic and related issues. In addition to the primary focus of building cross-sector partnering to move research to action, the KIS initiative provided a platform for facilitating two-way communication and understanding (researchers to stakeholders, and stakeholders to researchers) and for expanding opportunities for students to develop knowledge mobilization skills through hands-on experience.

KMb was defined as moving knowledge into active service for the broadest possible common good.

SSHRC received 151 letters of interest for KIS resulting in 86 separate applications representing academic institutions from across Canada and literally hundreds of researchers and stakeholders. Each application described systematic and sustained activities to mobilize accumulated social sciences and humanities expertise for the broader common good. Each proposal was based on the cooperative participation of researchers and non-academic stakeholders, and included letters of institutional and stakeholder support as well as commitments from stakeholder groups of cash and in-kind support.

A significant benefit that Canada has already reaped is the learning and awakening that occurred as the proposal teams prepared their proposals.

SSHRC awarded eleven grants as part of the KIS pilot initiative, each tenable for three years. The evaluation criteria for adjudication were based on (1) the overall quality and coherence of the proposed knowledge mobilization initiative; (2) the nature of and potential for sustained engagement with internal and external stakeholders; (3) the nature and quality of confirmed institutional support of the proposed initiative; and (4) the quality of the plans for assessing the degree of success of the proposed initiative.

A significant benefit that Canada has already achieved from this KMb effort is the learning and awakening that occurred as the proposal teams prepared their proposals, with some of the unfunded initiatives moving forward through other means. Further, as the pilot projects share what they are learning across the university, practitioner and larger stakeholder communities, this seeding could pay off as awareness of KMb, and appreciation for its nature and its potential for helping to resolve social problems as they emerge in the future.

There appear to be two dominant styles of approach to these initiatives: one focused on processes and relationships, and the other focused on development of tools.

8.1 THE KIS KMB PROJECTS

While SSHRC found it difficult to select from the many qualified submissions, awards were made to: University of Alberta, Malaspina University-College, McGill University, Memorial University of Newfoundland, Université de Montréal, Université du Québec à Montréal, Université du Québec à Trois-Rivières, Ryerson University, University of Saskatchewan, University of Victoria, and York University. Each of these universities has pulled together a KMb team that crosses the sphere of stakeholders in each area of focus.

Despite the diversity of fields of inquiry, there appear to be two dominant styles of approach to these initiatives: one is to focus on the development of processes and relationships, and the other is to focus on the development of tools. The process approach is multi-faceted, collaborative, and iterative, and emphasizes personal interaction in various forms to engage in knowledge creation, knowledge sharing, knowledge use, and capacity development. Institutional capacity for externally-focused dissemination of information, combined with the adaptation of research questions and activities in the context of stakeholder needs, drives research uptake and problem resolution. Uptake is enhanced by sustained and multiple forms of interaction among researchers and research users at all stages of knowledge mobilization activities.

This seeding could pay off as awareness of KMb and appreciation for its nature and potential for helping resolve social problems emerges.

A key distinguishing characteristic of this approach is that constructive and mutually beneficial relationships among individuals and among organizations are cornerstones of success. As one successful applicant wrote, "our research partnerships have added to the growing body of evidence [in this field] … and have also demonstrated the considerable benefits of academic-community collaboration in the conduct of such research." The process approach integrates both activities and tools to produce a variety of outputs and outcomes that are best measured in terms of behavioral and cognitive change.

A key distinguishing characteristic of the process approach is that constructive and mutually beneficial relationships among individuals and among organizations are cornerstones of success.

The tools approach is based largely on developing specific responses to narrowly defined needs, often applying an economic model of demand and supply to identify knowledge gaps, i.e., a place where improved KMb could help bring the demand for and supply of research knowledge into closer alignment. Such gap analysis is a potentially very powerful KMb activity. It not only carries the potential of showing clearly where short-term needs lie, e.g., immediate opportunities for the creation of knowledge sharing tools, but it can also point both researchers and research users towards new areas of demand for knowledge, thereby shaping future supplies of knowledge. In this approach, the supply of knowledge would appear to be dominated by academic institutions and individual researchers in their capacities as producers of research; demand originates among stakeholders who are seeking answers to questions and solutions to problems. Less common, but equally important, is a situation in which stakeholders provide knowledge to answer inquiries from academics.

One of the attractions of the tools approach is that the results are more easily quantifiable than those of the process approach since outputs are essentially commodities.

One of the attractions of this approach is that the results are more easily quantifiable than those of the process approach since outputs are essentially commodities, e.g., databases, questionnaires, and assessment frameworks. This approach also has the potential to generate quantifiable outputs more quickly since narrow short-term needs can lead to tightly-focused responses involving greater use of pre-existing information products, e.g., published journal articles.

Interactions among academics, researchers and non-academics also play an important role in the tools approach, but are more bounded in that they are established primarily to initiate a very specific and usually fairly narrow exchange of information. Horizontal interaction among non-academics, i.e., the exchange of information and knowledge among stakeholder groups without mediation by researchers, does not figure prominently in the tools approach, and the output of the interactions between researchers and non-academics is largely pre-determined; for example, creation of a database. Thus, production of a mutually agreed upon commodity is the dominant focus of this approach.

148

These different approaches also produce different interpretations of capacity building among researchers and non-academics, and of the nature and purpose of training that is provided to students. The process approach emphasizes mutual learning arising from interactions among all parties. Through this learning process each group of participants improves both their potential and actual abilities (i.e., capacity) in one or more areas of expertise. From the perspectives of project outcomes and impacts, the emphasis on process and extensive interaction may present some challenges to the eventual and effective uptake and application of the knowledge that is shared when inadequate resources are allocated to problem resolution.

The two approaches produce different interpretations of capacity building among researchers and non-academics, and of the nature and purpose of training that is provided to students..

The tool-based approach, on the other hand, focuses less on skills and capacity development and more on the production of specific knowledge products. By concentrating on knowledge needs identification, or gap analysis, the tools approach assumes capacity at the outset (on the parts of non-academic stakeholders) to understand and articulate their knowledge needs and to engage in meaningful dialogue. This approach further assumes that users of research can express needs in ways to which researchers can meaningfully respond by way of developing appropriate knowledge mobilization tools. Successful application of the resulting knowledge tools may be difficult to achieve depending on the extent to which potential users have the capacity to gain access to and have the skills to use both the knowledge revealed through the identification process and the new knowledge tools.

The KIS KMb projects led by Malaspina University-College, Memorial University of Newfoundland, and York University provided details of their projects to serve as examples for this book. These are presented in detail as 8.2, 8.3 and 8.4 below.

8.2 THE TOURISM RESEARCH INNOVATION PROJECT LED BY MALASPINA UNIVERSITY-COLLEGE

Canada's rural regions are in a time of transition. Many of these regions have started to incorporate service-based industries such as tourism into social and economic development goals. Communities are struggling in this transition for a number of reasons, including a lack of information and resources. While much information exists in businesses, communities, academic institutions, and government agencies much of it remains inaccessible to those who need it.

The Tourism Research and Innovation Project (TRIP) is the first of its kind to address the need for enhanced knowledge exchange in tourism development within rural areas in the province of British Columbia (B.C.). It is intended to act as a model for rural communities throughout Canada. The goal of TRIP is to locate and share resources that support tourism development in rural areas among community leaders, tourism entrepreneurs, government agencies, students and academic institutions.

8.2.1 Project Objectives

Figure 8-1 shows the intended outcomes. Specifically, the objectives are to:

- Synthesize and mobilize information and resources in tourism development within rural communities by engaging in innovative, field-based activities;

PROJECT OBJECTIVES

- Develop an understanding of the realities of rural tourism development by engaging in dialogue with community leaders and tourism entrepreneurs;
- Enhance community based tourism development by documenting case studies and innovative practices and sharing them throughout the province;
- Develop a cluster of expertise in rural tourism development in B.C. by linking academic and non-academic partners,
- Reshape policy and planning decisions and education programming in B.C. to reflect the needs of tourism development in rural areas.

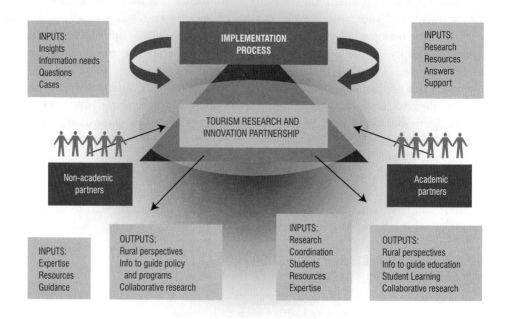

FIGURE 8-1: Intended outcomes and impacts.

8.2.2 Project Activities

The project is focused on mobilizing local knowledge, academic literature and government resources.

The program of activities is based on research about the needs of rural communities, and builds upon the current activities and expertise of the partners involved. The project is focused on mobilizing three types of knowledge including local knowledge, academic literature, and government resources. The team is implementing a variety of activities including: (1) an annual tourism research extension project, (2) placement of student interns to work in rural regions, (3) development of a series of "how to" manuals to respond to information needs, (4) responding to a series of questions about rural tourism in community newspapers, (5) design of a web portal linking available resources, and (6) hosting of a research forum.

The assembled team has a wide collective scope and reach to support rural tourism development within the province. Academic partners include Malaspina University-College as the lead institution, Thompson Rivers University, University of Northern British Columbia, College of the Rockies and the College of New Caledonia. Other partners include: Tourism British Columbia; B.C. Parks; the Ministry of Tourism, Sport and the Arts; the Ministry of Small Business and Economic Development; and the B.C. Centre for Tourism Leadership and Innovation. Each partner has a direct or indirect mandate to support tourism and economic development in B.C.

At the end of three years, it is expected that rural communities in B.C. will have developed greater capacity for tourism development and be in a strong position to welcome the world to the 2010 Olympic Games. A series of outreach initiatives conducted in each region of the province is enabling dialogue between partners and rural leaders. Those involved are developing a stronger perspective and understanding that is informing programs, policies and research projects. Partners have developed a coordinated system that consolidates and mobilizes knowledge and resources. These resources will live beyond the project and be made accessible to audiences within and beyond B.C., informing rural areas about the opportunities and risks to consider when embarking on tourism development and enabling smooth transitions into the industry.

At the end of three years, it is expected that rural communities in B.C. will have developed greater capacity for tourism development and be in a strong position to welcome the 2010 Olympic Games.

8.3 THE MANAGING KNOWLEDGE FOR SUSTAINABLE REGIONS IN NEWFOUNDLAND AND LABRADOR PROJECT LED BY MEMORIAL UNIVERSITY OF NEWFOUNDLAND

This project helps ensure that Newfoundlanders and Labradorians have access to quality social sciences and humanities research, enabling positive change in regional policy and development through evidence-based decision-making. The project is taking research at Memorial University and making it available to non-academic, community stakeholders. One principal stakeholder, the Rural Secretariat, has been established by the Government of Newfoundland and Labrador to focus on sustainable development in a regional context through the integration of social, economic, cultural and environmental aspects of regional development. This project assists the Rural Secretariat in developing regional visions by creating a knowledge mobilization process that connects research to the community. These visions then influence subsequent government funding and policy decisions.

One principal stakeholder is focused on achieving sustainable development in a regional context through the integration of social, economic, cultural and environment aspects of regional development.

8.3.1 Project Description

The project first identified research needs of the nine Regional Councils which comprise the Rural Secretariat. This process includes face-to-face regional meetings in each council area to catalogue regional research needs. Graduate students then compile research relevant to these needs by collecting lay summaries (which describe each individual activity) or by developing lay summaries where they do not already exist. Lay summaries are easy to understand summaries written in non-academic language for community users that are coded by key search words. Follow-up knowledge transfer sessions are held in each region to broker the utilization of existing research to address identified needs. Regional councils receive a presentation on the accumulated research relating to their needs, copies of relevant lay summaries, and, in some cases, an opportunity to seek clarification on research findings from the research author.

The lay summaries collected as part of the project will be used to help populate the Memorial University Regional Inventory (MURI), an online searchable database website. The MURI website will have the capacity for online search by region, sector and theme. One-page summaries describing any unmet regional research needs are also being carried on the database as "new opportunities." MURI will facilitate knowledge transfer on an ongoing basis after the project has ended.

8.3.2 Project Goals

- Developing a volume of lay summaries of research extending throughout the range of social sciences and humanities research areas.
- Identifying research needs for each of the nine Province's nine Regional Council areas
- Linking regional policy makers to researchers using easy to understand, non academic lay summaries.
- Creating linkages among university faculty, staff, students and community stakeholders
- Stimulating knowledge transfer between partners.
- Compiling a comprehensive inventory of research at Memorial which pertains to Newfoundland and Labrador.
- Making research available to community stakeholders (businesses, municipalities, community groups, individual residents, etc.) via the Internet.
- Developing a searchable on-line database to facilitate easy access to Memorial research (especially rural areas).
- Providing enriching work experiences for graduate students which facilitate community interaction as well as interdisciplinary learning.
- Determining effective methods for integrating knowledge mobilization practices into the research of graduate students.

8.3.3. Core Challenges

The project addresses several knowledge mobilization challenges, including:

8.3.3.1 Linking Policy Makers to Quality Research

The Rural Secretariat has identified nine regions which were selected based upon existing patterns of economic, social and community activity. These regional councils are mandated to develop a common, evidence-based understanding of the social, economic, environmental and cultural realities of a region. This KMb project links these regional policy groups to existing research and researchers at Memorial University through face-to-face meetings and knowledge transfer sessions.

8.3.3.2 Research Translation

University research is written in a formal, academic style which potential users may find confusing or intimidating. The project team is collecting and developing "lay summaries" written in an easy-to-understand fashion. Community users are then able to view these lay summaries and be able to determine if the research is applicable to their needs.

PROJECT GOALS

8.3.3.3 Access to Research

Newfoundland and Labrador consist of approximately 600 communities spread over 405,720 square kilometers. Approximately 20 of these communities do not have road linkages. By making the project outputs available through an online database, businesses, individuals, and community groups can access existing research at Memorial via the Internet with the click of a button.

8.3.3.4 Community Feedback

Memorial University is home to many excellent researchers pursuing interest-based scholarly research. However, the community often has no input into the direction or planning of this research, and researchers receive no feedback as to the applicability of their research. Workshops engaging community stakeholders with researchers are helping to identify collaborative opportunities while providing the researcher with valuable feedback.

8.3.3.5 Dissemination of Research through New Channels

Academic research is often communicated through academic conferences and publications. This project reaches beyond traditional audiences by bringing actual research (and the researchers who produced it) into communities where people can hear first-hand about the research and its value. It also makes lay descriptions of the research available via the Internet.

8.3.4. Partners

8.3.4.1 External Partners

- Department of Innovation, Trade and Rural Development: Contributing office space, meeting facilities, telephone, and fax services in-kind to project staff. They also provided one Seasonal student each summer to assist with the project.
- College of the North Atlantic: Provided support with stakeholder identification, facilitation of knowledge exchange meetings, and advice on steering committees.
- Newfoundland and Labrador Federation of Labour, Newfoundland and Labrador Federation of Municipalities, and Newfoundland and Labrador Regional Economic Development Association: Promotion of project using internal communication tools and advice on steering committees.
- Service Canada: A cash contribution to the development of the online Memorial University Regional Inventory database and travel support.
- The Rural Secretariat: Use of staff (Regional Planners) for the coordination of meeting logistics, and planning support.

8.3.4.2 Internal Partners

Within the university setting, the project also enjoys considerable support:

- Queen Elizabeth II Library: Advice on database construction and key word search criteria.
- Office of Research: Access to records, communication support, advice and guidance
- Marketing and Communications: Marketing and promotional support as well as access to an existing database of university experts.
- Deans and Directors: Mentorship for graduate students working on the project.
- Office of the Vice-President of Research: Cash contribution and communication support.
- School of Graduate Studies: Cash contribution and student recruitment support
- Harris Centre: Administrative support.
- Computing and Communications: Contract administration support and technical advice.

8.4 THE UNIVERSITY AS A CIVIC CHANGE AGENT: COMMUNITY-BASED KNOWLEDGE MOBILIZATION LED BY YORK UNIVERSITY

York's knowledge mobilization strategy is supported by two SSHRC grants: an Intellectual Property Mobilization (IPM) grant, and a KIS grant. The KMb Unit (York actually uses the abbreviation "KM" but for purposes of consistency KMb is used here) was formed within the division of the Vice President Research and Innovation to implement this strategy, and to provide services that connect researchers at the University with community stakeholders.

York University defines knowledge mobilization as the active, two-way exchange of information and expertise between knowledge creators and knowledge users.

York University defines knowledge mobilization as the active, two-way exchange of information and expertise between knowledge creators and knowledge users. In other words, York's KMb model views decision-makers—the users of knowledge—as active partners in the research cycle. York believes that knowledge has greater value when it is shared and that academic research projects are enriched by grounding them in the experience of practitioners, service providers, and policy-makers.

The KIS project at York experiments with a community-focused "input" model of KMb, which seeks to identify knowledge needs in the community and then focus university research expertise to help fill that need. (York's IPM project investigates the inverse model by locating new audiences for the "outputs" of social sciences and humanities research.) York has forged a dynamic partnership with the Human Services Planning Coalition of York Region (HSPC). Representing such sectors as education, immigration, and health services, HSPC is distinctive in Canadian municipalities for planning human services in a coordinated and integrated fashion. Through its sixteen sectors, HSPC serves as the University's gateway to both municipal departments and community service agencies. The KMb Unit works in the diverse communities of York Region (governments, non-profit organizations, service agencies, labor, business, and professional associations) to understand local knowledge needs and build sustainable research partnerships, ensuring research is better able to impact social programming, public policy, and professional practice.

The KMb Unit offers a full range of services to serve both York University and York Region. Enabled by the KIS grant, these services are built on three pillars: Creating Spaces, Building Capacity, and Supporting Partnerships.

8.4.1 Creating Spaces

York's KMb Unit is built on three pillars: CREATING SPACES, BUILDING CAPACITY and SUPPORTING PARTNERSHIPS.

The KIS grant creates spaces in which knowledge creators and knowledge users can interact face-to-face. For example, the KM Unit regularly hosts "KM in the AM" breakfasts where faculty members, graduate students and community stakeholders with a shared thematic interest (e.g. mental health) meet, discuss, and explore opportunities to exchange knowledge or work together. In the summer, York is also planning a Knowledge Expo, a larger-scale event designed around the same principles as the breakfasts.

8.4.2 Building Capacity

By providing training and education, York is building capacity for KMb both inside and outside the university. M.A. students can apply for internships at community agencies in an area relevant to their discipline of study. The KMb Unit has also established a Peer-to-Peer KMb Group, which is a forum for interns, mentors and community supervisors, as well as a KMb Seminar Series.

8.4.3 Supporting Partnerships

In partnership with the University of Victoria, York is building a national KMb infrastructure called ResearchIMPACT that includes a website and a shared database of research needs and research expertise. The KIS grant permits a scan of York Region to populate the research needs portion of the database. Through ResearchIMPACT, knowledge users and knowledge creators can find each other, work together, and share their results. KIS also enables modest financial support to encourage new partnerships, such as incentive grants to facilitate the development of joint research proposals. Faculty release time is available to allow York researchers to sit on community committees or otherwise share their expertise with a community group, or to conduct a systematic review in an area of critical need for a community agency. The KMb Unit further assists knowledge exchange and collaboration by "translating" research findings or research questions into appropriate formats for different audiences.

8.4.4 OTHER CHARACTERISTICS

KIS has allowed the KM Unit at York to develop a strong service orientation. Other important characteristics of York's KIS grant include:

- Service delivery through a local knowledge broker – the community has one point of contact for all knowledge needs.
- Service delivery in York Region – events are held primarily off-campus.
- Community input – services are planned with the guidance of a community advisory group, to ensure that community needs are heard and are met.

CHARACTERISTICS

155

- Ongoing evaluation – outputs, outcomes, and impacts of KMb activities are tracked over both the short and long term.

With one of the highest percentages of SSHRC-eligible faculty in Canada, and an institutional strategic plan that calls for outreach and collaboration with local communities, York University, is well poised to deliver KMb services to faculty and to the larger community of York Region. Through the KIS grant, the University will, over time, contribute to more responsive public policies, more effective social programs and an increased quality of life in one of Canada's fastest growing and culturally diverse regions. By responding to research needs in York Region and supporting evidence-based decision making, knowledge mobilization at York is turning research into action.

The three KMb projects presented above led by Malaspina University-College, Memorial University of Newfoundland and York University along with the other nine KIS projects represent a starting point for SSHRC. While these projects are specifically focused on developing knowledge mobilization approaches for using existing research in service of Canadian citizens, they also are breaking ground by developing and assessing KMb processes that can become a part of future research programs.

The second round of KIS funding began in 2007.

CHAPTER 9

POWERPLUS COMES OF AGE

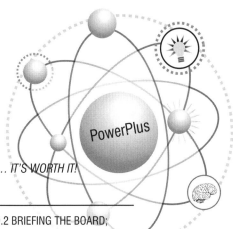

THIS CHAPTER IS NOT FOR THE FAINT OF HEART, BUT READ IT ANYWAY … IT'S WORTH IT!

THIS SECTION INCLUDES: 9.0 INTRODUCTION; 9.1 THE SITUATION; 9.2 BRIEFING THE BOARD; 9.3 UNDERSTANDING THE PROBLEM; 9.4 GETTING STARTED; 9.5 THE KMB STRATEGY; 9.6 BUILDING THE KMB TEAM; 9.7 STILL LEARNING; 9.8 DEVELOPING A STRATEGY; 9.9 A CRITICAL INSIGHT; 9.10 WHAT KNOWLEDGE DO WE NEED?; 9.11 MEASURING THE OUTCOME; 9.12 IMPLEMENTATION.

9.0 INTRODUCTION

This chapter considers a potential application of knowledge mobilization in an area outside of the social sciences to demonstrate the applicability of KMb in areas related to organizational development, and perhaps other complex situations. While much can be done to further develop the concepts and processes of KMb, there is no doubt that the product of knowledge mobilization, that is knowledge and its application, will play an increasingly important role in dealing with complex situations, or what Russel Ackoff calls "messes." (Ackoff, 1978) Some have called these "wicked problems," situations where one knows there is a problem but does not know exactly what the problem is or whether a good solution exists. (This idea was introduced in chapter 1).

Anyone can make a messy problem; only knowledge mobilization can clean one up.

　　When considering the application of KMb to a situation, it is best to remember that the heart of KMb is knowledge, not information. Although the KMb process extensively uses information and data, its focus and challenge is to *get the right knowledge to the right people* in a way that they can, and will, take effective actions that will help solve a problem or improve their world. The lens of perspective is knowledge and through knowledge-action. Knowledge (understanding, insight, meaning and comprehension) leads to prediction and anticipation, which in turn results in a higher probability of good decisions and effective actions. Knowledge surfaces through statements, questions, dialogue, intuition, judgment and behavior. Thus KMb centers around people, their interactions, perspectives, histories, competencies, frames of reference, limitations and strengths. With this quick review in mind, the following episode is provided.

9.1 THE SITUATION

PowerPlus is a public Utility with 800 employees governed by a Board of Directors composed of citizens elected by the two million member community. Many of its employees joined the organization in the 1970's when PowerPlus was expanding to meet the energy needs of the baby boomers. This group of workers, ranging from senior managers to foremen and senior technicians, now represents a major retiree exodus. PowerPlus' Chief Executive Officer John Marcus has been watching this trend for several years, and has now decided that something must be done. He sees two major issues: The first is the lost knowledge and experience from senior people who are retiring. Over the years these people have developed a *deep knowledge* of their work and a *strong understanding of the purpose* of PowerPlus and its contribution to the community. John believes that much of the performance of PowerPlus is due to the leadership and tacit knowledge of these senior people.

The second issue is with the difficulty his HR people are having hiring younger employees who are willing to work hard. Although these new employees are very bright, they seem to live in a different world. He has heard many comments from his foreman that these young people cannot stop asking questions and insist on understanding *why* things are done the way they are. His foreman finds trying to answer these questions very frustrating since the new hires have neither the experience nor the context in terms of language to *really understand what is going on*. In addition, these younger employees have a very high turnover rate. It is proving a real challenge to keep them in the organization! Although these two problems might appear not to be related, John felt that they probably were.

Before you simplify a problem, you had better understand its complexity.

9.2 BRIEFING THE BOARD

The CEO's first act was to brief his Board of Directors to bring them up to speed on how he saw the issues and their importance to PowerPlus. In particular, John wanted to make sure that they understood the downstream implications of not addressing these situations now. The briefing went well, and John hired an organizational development consultant with strong experience in the power industry to work with Nancy, his HR manager, to look into the situation and make recommendations on what needed to be done. It was also decided that the new entry turnover issue would be addressed first because of its cost and the concern over possible mistakes, accidents or loss of service. The consultant, Kerry Morris, was brought on board and met with John and Nancy to brainstorm possible causes of the turnover problem, and the extent of its potential consequences. John insisted that they not jump to solutions too quickly. Over the years he had seen too many quick reactions result in failed attempts to solve problems, reinforcing employee skepticism concerning management organizational projects.

9.3 UNDERSTANDING THE PROBLEM

After the meeting, Nancy set up a one-day exploratory workshop that included the majority of the supervisors working with the new employees. Throughout the day there were numerous views, ideas, and solutions expressed, and some participants left with hard feelings. Ideas ranged from bringing in foreign workers who would be willing to work hard, to raising the pay scale of new employees, to putting new employees on probation for six months. Several of the supervisors complained that they did not have time to answer all of the foolish questions that these new hires were asking. The supervisors were used to workers who just followed orders and did their jobs. By the end of the day one thing became clear: no one really understood the issues, much less the root causes, and it would be wrong to assume the problem was due to the only to the attitudes or laziness of the new hires.

As often happens in workshops, at one point Mike, a young foreman, told the group that at a recent conference he had heard a speaker talking about complex organizational problems. These kinds of problems required both a systems perspective and the recognition that the answer—whatever it ended up to be—would probably be found in knowledge and how knowledge is created and applied. Kerry jumped in to describe the importance of the perspectives, feelings, attitudes and goals of employees in a complex system, and how much they were willing—and allowed—to learn and apply that learning in their own areas of responsibility. Kerry suggested that the group look into what it might mean to consider PowerPlus as an organic system, and, building on their ongoing knowledge management efforts, look at the potential of knowledge mobilization for understanding and resolving their issues.

At the end of the workshop John authorized the creation of a team led by Nancy, Mike, the outside consultant Kerry, and other organizational representatives as needed to dig into these issues and find out more about what was going on. As this new team began their work, they realized that taking an organic perspective required shifting their own frames of reference. They began by thinking about PowerPlus as a complex adaptive system embedded in a community and world within which they continuously interacted, which they both influenced and were influenced by, and which was—at the same time—subjected to unpredictable forces and demands from governing bodies and external parties. This new frame of reference meant that they could no longer see the problem as *due only to the external source of workers*.

Everything is exactly as it should be, yet nothing is what it seems.

After talking to several people who had studied complexity, the team knew that the problem was indeed complex, that it would include their own people, and that the solution would not lie in any one specific action. They were also reminded of the old management adage: *if you are a manager and you're not getting what you want, the first thing that has to change is you*. They began to realize that they must look first within their own organization.

Nancy had heard about the KMb process from several employees who were working on small knowledge management projects in PowerPlus. She also recognized that knowledge was significantly different from information, and that knowledge was much, much harder to share among employees, yet it was the primary driving force for decision-making and taking effective action. Thinking outside the box, her team looked at the possibility of using the knowledge mobilization process to guide their understanding of the problem as well as to help generate and implement potential solutions.

9.4 GETTING STARTED

After reviewing the recommendations of the team, John, and Nancy briefed the Board of Directors and got approval to develop a strategy and a plan of action and a set of milestones for measuring progress. There was some discussion at the board meeting of the potential cost of the effort. John made it clear to the Directors that, while no one knew what the actual costs would be, it was not going to be cheap in terms of time or dollars. He pointed out that they were dealing with unknowns, the current cost of their turnover rate was quite expensive and, most importantly, performance was beginning to suffer. In his own mind, John intuitively felt there was a connection between the brain drain and the turnover problem. The common elements seemed to be culture, structure and how employees were viewed by management. In conversations with colleagues, John had heard about the need for organizations to change the way they dealt with knowledge workers, and the increasingly important role these workers played in organizational success. But he had never had the time to consider this deeply.

John began to think that PowerPlus might need to take a serious look at themselves in the mirror to see if they were keeping up with the future. He hoped this project would shed considerable light on the critical success factors that would propel PowerPlus to achieve high performance and, even more important, *sustainable high performance*. In fact, John had wanted to explore this area for a long time but felt too many of his senior managers were ingrained in their habits to change. The more he thought about it the surer John was that this problem with new hires was indirectly connected with the knowledge retention problem caused by senior people retiring. Complex systems seemed to have subtle and weird paths of influence.

Never ignore your intuition, gut feelings or hunches. They may be detecting patterns that your conscious mind isn't.

9.5 THE KMb STRATEGY

When Nancy got the go-ahead from John, she called Shelly, an organizational change agent who had developed several workshops on KMb. Following their initial meeting which included a quick overview of their situation, Nancy invited her to become part of the team. At the first meeting of the growing KMb team, Shelly explained what knowledge mobilization was about. In order for the team to get a handle on some of the key aspects of the KMb process, she suggested a seven step approach. As she presented the steps, she invited the team to jump in with their thoughts. She began:

KMb TEAM PREP APPROACH

1. *Identify and describe the situation as objectively as possible.* Everyone thought that this was a good starting point.
2. *Validate, to the best extent possible, that the situation and problem is as interpreted.* This made sense to the team.
3. *Analyze the knowledge areas needed to determine what expertise is necessary to bring into the KMb team.* Shelly suggested that as a minimum, they needed individuals with strong knowledge in theory, change management, organizational development and leadership.
4. *After filling all of the team's knowledge requirements, spend time building the group into an effective team.* Shelly pointed out that this step was often overlooked because it was assumed that senior professionals already know how to work effectively in teams. However, this was often not the case. It was suggested that one way to help the team get started was to set up a KMb workshop prior to commencing the project.

5. *Identify individuals with specialized knowledge who need to be available to the team on an on-call basis.* Mike wondered what specialized knowledge might be needed for this project. Shelly suggested that the KMb team itself would be in the best position to identify any gaps between their areas of expertise and what might be needed during the course of the KMb project. And, of course, along the way a need for knowledge in other areas might emerge. Nancy mentioned that a "Yellow Pages of Knowledge" had been developed of PowerPlus employees by the KM team, and they could connect to company knowledge resources as needed.

6. *Have the team review the situation to provide the basis for developing a strategy.* Nancy thought it would be useful to review the purpose, values, culture, structure, history and leadership of the organization. Reading policies, interviewing, reviewing past events, listening to stories and informally talking with all levels of employees could provide valuable insights and information. Observing the physical structure of offices, conference rooms and how people meet and talk to each other as they go down the hall would say much about the organizations identity and the feelings of its employees.

7. *Once the strategy is developed, a plan of action and milestones should be prepared.* It was agreed this would force all team members to look at and think about the anticipated schedule of the project. To identify the end goal, the differences between the current state and the desired state would need to be clearly understood. The POA&M would represent the actions needed to move the organization in the direction of the desired state. Shelly emphasized that since the situation was complex and adaptive, the team should not expect single actions to always achieve their anticipated results. It would be important to stay flexible as actions were taken and changes evolved. What Shelly proposed was an action-learning approach that would promote learning as they went.

At this point Shelly re-emphasized the importance of having the right people with the right expertise involved in the KMb process. Further, these needed to be people who would continuously communicate and collaborate with each other, and with other employees of PowerPlus. She described them as integrators with trusted networks. Some of these might be members of formal communities of practice or less formal communities of interest supported by PowerPlus. With these connections across the organization, the KMb team would be able to gain the respect and cooperation of other employees, and get the honest feedback needed to determine desired changes. Another critical factor in the solution process was to make sure everyone on the team understood what was going on and the impact their actions were having on the organization. To help ensure openness and objectivity, she suggested team members ask each other, and other employees throughout their individual relationship networks, a lot of questions. Then, through intense listening and keeping an open mind, team members could surface insights to guide the KMb process and create conversations that would help gain the employees' trust and

You don't know what you don't know, unless you ask questions and look for it!

confidence in the KMb process.

Shelly reminded the team that each discipline has its own ways of thinking, terms of art, and value judgments, and that these could be very confusing and intimidating to non-specialists. Because several disciplines were involved and specialized terms could be easily misunderstood, she cautioned her teammates to use plain language when discussing the KMb process. Finally, Shelly made the point that senior management needed to be kept informed of progress, and should be prepared to participate in the project as requested. John agreed to see that this would happen. They all realized that PowerPlus could not change unless their senior management was willing to change and demonstrated that willingness through active participation in the change process.

9.6 BUILDING THE KMb TEAM

After interviewing a number of new employees, their supervisors and coworkers, the team realized just *how much they did not know or understand about their organization.* One member of the team, a sociology professor who had done extensive research in organizational cultures, knew a graduate student who had just finished his thesis on the new generation worker. They quickly invited him to the next KMb team meeting. Together, the sociologist and graduate student provided the team with a sound theoretical basis for understanding the generational conflict between the younger employees and their supervisors. Indeed, these two groups lived in different worlds; they thought differently, and had different values and frames of reference.

Whether among nations or generations, there is a knowledge gap in translation and understanding.

As a general rule, long-time supervisors worked hard, were control oriented and did not like new technologies. They were comfortable with stability and repetition, and comfortable within their local milieu. Conversely, the younger people new to the organization loved technology, expected to be respected, and liked to ask questions and challenge everything they heard and saw, and were often driven by the desire to make it better. They did not understand their supervisors. In fact, they did not like them, and since they were networked, they knew that they could find a good job somewhere else. So they did. No wonder PowerPlus was having problems!

If you have been making decisions a certain way all during your career and you have become a senior manager, why should you change now? Clearly your past decisions have been the right ones.

The sociologist showed the team how a culture of control and knowledge privacy had prevented senior personnel from passing their knowledge down to the next level. This was not so much the intentional hoarding of knowledge, it was that senior leaders were very busy and didn't have the time or the incentive to teach others what they knew. These leaders had learned years ago that their knowledge (and hard work) was what moved them up the ladder, and this had led them to believe that every employee was expected to learn their own way on their own time. The organization did not have time to waste on learning because learning was lost work and therefore inefficient. People were focusing and working hard, as they had been doing in the past. The high output and cost had reinforced the senior managers' belief in this management policy. They saw no need to change. As the team listened, they could identify similar attitudes in a number of the senior leaders and mid-level managers. They realized that the mindset problem would not be easily solved. logic box of

success had trapped them.

A pragmatic knowledge of change management was provided by Shelly and Kerry, who specialized in organizational development. Nancy, together with several of PowerPlus' best supervisors, represented the pragmatic knowledge of implementation. As Shelly had suggested, when the team came together they took a look at what knowledge they felt would be needed to fully understand and resolve the emerging issues. Shelly further emphasized that the that the team needed to understand Kmeta or *knowledge about knowledge*: knowledge creation, attributes, flows and integration as it could be applied to their organization.

9.7 STILL LEARNING

After listening to the sociologist and the graduate student, the team realized that the issue was much broader and deeper than originally thought, and that it could not, and should not, be limited to the behavior of new hires. The more they dug into this situation, the more they became aware that the culture, perspectives and attitudes of current employees and their managers played a big role in the way the utility operated on a day-to-day basis. Nancy had always heard that neophytes spent more time solving problems than experts, but experts spent more time understanding problems than neophytes. While this was perhaps a generalization, the team recognized the importance of taking time to develop a good and cohesive understanding of the situation (see Figure 3-1).

The team suspected that the issue of the turnover of new hires and the knowledge retention of senior people retiring were *symptoms* and not *causes*. Even though the word from the CEO was to "get on with it," the team gave John a detailed briefing of their insights and approach and noted that in this case *slow may be fast*. The team now suspected that the real source of the issues lay in the identity, culture, structure and leadership of the organization. They realized that since this was sensitive territory, they needed to be sure of their facts. Politics, personal sensitivities and differences in perspectives would all come into play. Nevertheless, this was their job, and their responsibility.

9.8 DEVELOPING A STRATEGY

Nancy and her team felt it would take at least six months to develop a strategy, plan of action and a cone of possibilities before starting implementation (see Figure 1). They also felt that implementation might take two to three years to be successful. During their briefing to the Board of Directors, the team addressed the current situation, the anticipated future environment, and the complexity and challenges of PowerPlus, its community and the broader environment. They emphasized that the organization needed a major internal transformation to create a Utility with the capacity to handle current and future challenges. They also noted that the Utility had many good employees who were doing the best job they could by *working around the system*. But in many cases these long-term employees had become non-learners who did the same jobs every day and were not aware of the impact the external world was having on their Utility. While they talked about new technologies, terrorist threats, changing customer needs and the rising costs of power, they could not relate them to the work they did every day. It would be a challenge to change PowerPlus into the kind of intelligent complex adaptive system recent research had shown as necessary for a knowledge organization to survive and succeed in the present and future environment.

The team briefed the Board on what they envisioned the new PowerPlus might look like in order to achieve a sustainable high performance. They made it clear that this transformation was not guaranteed, and that there were risks. Further, there was only a good probability of success if, and only if, the CEO and Board actively backed the proposed changes and continued their support well into the future. The KMb team representatives spent three days with the Board in briefings and dialogue covering every part of the project, making sure that everyone understood the approach, and was behind this effort. The team invited challenges, questions and disagreements, treating everyone with respect and using appreciative inquiry to move the group toward a mutual understanding. At the end of this process, while there were still some members with misgivings, the Board approved the project, and even agreed to participate in parts of its implementation. Now the real challenge began; how to move an 800 employee organization into the 21st century.

9.9 A CRITICAL INSIGHT

A stable, control-oriented bureaucracy within an increasingly dynamic and complex environment must either shrink, change or disappear.

A critical insight that the team passed to the Board was that even though their Utility was a large plant with a lot of machinery, because of its complexity and the need for adaptation, it was rapidly becoming a knowledge organization. As technology continues to explode exponentially and take on more artificial intelligence, and as the customer base becomes better educated and more dynamic, PowerPlus must become more knowledge focused, with its employees using their understanding and intuition to solve technical and organizational problems, and respond to external demands. This meant that the challenge of leadership was to build, nurture and sustain organization-wide empowerment, collaboration, adaptability, innovation and continuous learning—quite a tall order!

During the workshop with the Board, Shelly realized that there were actually two knowledge mobilization processes to be considered. The first was the challenge of mobilizing knowledge for the team to effectively implement its strategy of creating the new PowerPlus. The second was designing the new PowerPlus so it could continuously mobilize its own knowledge when needed to adapt to changing external requirements and emergencies. Since one could not forecast the specific knowledge needed in the future, the new PowerPlus to have a built-in capacity to create, assimilate, leverage, mobilize, target and apply the right knowledge at the right time and place. This was a tall order and would be considered as the transformation unfolded. While the knowledge management team had begun to tackle elements by connecting specific knowledge and the target audience related to that knowledge, a KMb process could help ensure collaborative advantage. The relationship of the KMb process to knowledge management was beginning to surface. While knowledge management had been around in PowerPlus for a number of years—and projects such as the Yellow Pages were proving valuable—the field had been difficult to bring down to bite-size chunks. What it had done, however, was to spread an awareness of the value of knowledge, and since people were the source of knowledge, knowledge management had begun to seed ideas that would be supportive of using KMb processes in the transformation of PowerPlus.

9.10 WHAT KNOWLEDGE DO WE NEED?

After reflecting on the intensive three days with the Board of Directors, Nancy asked her team to identify any additional areas of theory and pragmatic knowledge they thought might be needed. Kerry, the organizational development specialist, suggested that theories of bureaucracy, hierarchy and complex adaptive organizations would be useful to the team. A number of theories related to individual and organizational change were also discussed. Since there was no single theory that exactly matched PowerPlus's structure, Kerry suggested several texts for team members to scan and look for ideas. These included: Kotter, 1996; Chawla & Renesch, 1994; Bennet & Bennet, 2004; Gilley & Maycunich, 2000; and Conger, et al. 1999. Kerry was adamant that real change must come from inside the organization, and from inside individual employees. The other team members nodded in agreement. They all understood that no one could successfully order change to happen, or even create rules and policies which would force people to change their behavior. In this day and age workers were smart enough—and independent enough—that they could and would decide for themselves how much they were willing to personally change.

You don't have to know everything. You just have to know where to find it—and you have to understand it when you find it.

Several techniques for creating environments for change, and motivating processes to encourage employees to change were discussed. For example, where individuals are concerned, the Bennet model posits that in order for people to willingly change the following should occur: they must be aware of the change, understand it, believe it, feel good about it, have ownership (responsibility) for it, feel empowered to execute it, and know how to do it. Similarly, where organizations are concerned, change from the inside will occur if employees feel ownership, understand the purpose and need for change, and feel that they will not be hurt by the change. Techniques such as social network analysis, specialized workgroups, event intermediation and small team task assignments have demonstrated their efficacy in specific applications.

Another area that was considered significant was learning. While there are numerous theories of learning, Mezirow's transformational learning, (Mezirow, 1991; Mezirow, 2000) and Tough's theory of self-directed learning seemed to be the most applicable (Tough, 1971). Others suggested were Kofman, et al., 1994 and Merriam, et al., 2006. In addition, Blooms taxonomy might be helpful in assessing learning levels and communicating effectively with various members of the workforce (Sousa, 2006). Kerry brought up his favorite topic of systems and complexity theory and suggested they would be quite useful in designing and understanding the new vision of PowerPlus. He recommended the following reading for team members: Garvin, D. 2000; Kelly & Allison, 1999; Weick & Sutcliffe, 2001; Bennet & Bennet, 2004; and Marion, 1999.

Last, but certainly not least, was a theory of leadership that would serve as a guide in describing and recommending roles, behaviors and responsibilities of the leadership in support of the transformation. While it was understood that there was no single type of leadership that would work in a dynamic, uncertain and complex environment, it was also agreed that it was useful and necessary to outline the basic ingredients needed to move the organization towards its goals. Several suggestions for references included: Hamel, 2000; Neo & Chen, 2007; Frick & Spears, 1996; and Tichy & Devanna, 1986. The team felt it would be best if the CEO would take an active role in developing and approving the leadership development needs of the organization. Not only was his involvement politically correct, but John was a critical thinker and closet academic who would jump at the opportunity to synergistically combine theory and praxis.

During the team discussions of relevant knowledge, the need for theories was questioned. One team member felt that action was what was needed to change the organization, and suggested that if the team knew the best actions to take, why worry about theory? After bouncing this idea around a few times, the team realized they and the organization were moving into uncharted territory. There would be many instances where decisions and directions would be unclear. During these times, theory would hopefully provide the background and understanding needed to guide the team's actions. From the change agent's perspective, theory would serve as an *evidence-based foundation* for what was being applied and as *guiding principles (offering limits and possibilities)* for its application. Of course, from the theoretician's perspective, pragmatic applications such as the PowerPlus situation would serve to validate, enhance or even negate theories. Nancy reminded the team that their approach was an action-learning process, and that every one of them would be expected to learn a great deal outside of their normal areas of competence.

Another topic of discussion was the concept of pragmatic knowledge, and how it could be used to support their KMb project. Specifically, the team developed a brief list of areas where pragmatic knowledge would be applicable. The following topics came to mind: communication via discourse and dialogue; values and their application throughout the organization; the application of KM strategies; the creation and implementation of teams; rewards and incentive structures; the informal networks operating throughout the organization; and leadership training and employee development. A final area considered highly pragmatic was when the organization implemented problem-solving or decision-making. The team agreed to stay sensitive to the need to stress action and application that yielded results in these areas, and not to spend time talking to employees about theory unless requested. However, the team needed to *understand why* their actions and decisions would lead to the desired outcome, and that would come likely from theory.

Recall the seven areas of knowledge:

Kmeta

Kpraxis

Kaction

Kdescription

Kresearch

Ktheory

Kpragmatic

In addition to theoretical and pragmatic knowledge, the team also looked at the seven categories of knowledge to determine which areas they needed to understand and apply. For example, what kind of descriptive information would they need, and where should it come from to enable them to understand the current situation. The team would also have to decide which individuals could best implement the decisions and actions decided upon. For example, in understanding the culture and structure of the Utility, they planned to review the policies, the way the work gets done, the expectations of the employees, and how well they worked together. Who would be the best individuals to gather, understand and interpret this pragmatic knowledge? They knew that Klearning would become important because of the changing environment needed to keep up with new technology and a changing workforce. The challenge related to Kresearch was to find the best evidence-based theory and research with the principles and guidelines that would support PowerPlus' transformation.

Since each of these knowledge categories carries its own subtle nuances of language, interpretation, meaning and ways of perceiving issues, Nancy made sure that the team members understood the different perspectives of each category. This led to a discussion of the power of different frames of reference and the importance of each member being able to shift their individual frames of reference so that they could critically evaluate their personal beliefs, assumptions and habits of the mind. During these discussions it became clear that these same challenges would be faced by the organization's employees. While this was insightful, by far the most valuable result of these discussions was the recognition of the significant role that information and knowledge played in understanding a situation, developing an effective strategy, and implementing the changes necessary to create the PowerPlus of the future. After all of this preparation, the team had finally realized that the solution to their task would come from the quality of (1) relationships among all of their employees, (2) employee knowledge, and (3) employee actions.

9.11 MEASURING THE OUTCOME

A final of concern was how to measure the outcome of the project and how to monitor progress during implementation. The team knew there were some easy numbers to measure, such as employee turnover rate, number of accidents per year, power outages, etc. But even though these might be useful, they did not seem to represent the full spectrum of the organization's performance. While the performance of PowerPlus was determined by the actions of every employee every day, it was not possible—nor desirable—to monitor these actions. But, *the quality of their actions* did depend on the information and knowledge of each employee, their willingness to use their competence to support the purpose and mission of PowerPlus, and the amount of collaboration and support they gave each other. This led the team to think about, and look for, answers to questions such as: How effective were PowerPlus teams? Could they engage in creative dialogues? Were they willing to innovate and take risks? Did employees feel they were growing and developing both personally and professionally? Were employees proud to work at PowerPlus? Did they believe they were contributing to a higher purpose than a salary or a job?

The KMb team believed that the answers to these questions would be strong indicators of project success. They also knew there was no perfect way to assess a project such as this. However, after the KMb project was finished, everyone would be able to recognize the differences and observe the results. Nancy laughingly noted that the organization would never really be finished, because in a changing world successful organizations had to continuously learn, adapt and remake themselves. The only real question became how often?

Focusing back on the task at hand, the team identified specific items that would provide some measure of *progress toward the goal*. They felt that the best technique for assessment was simply to talk with, and listen to, those employees who were directly involved in implementing the project. It was the employees and their managers who could, and would, feel the difference and appreciate the changes that the team was orchestrating. The team realized that they themselves could not possibly change PowerPlus, but that they could act as catalysts, guides, and mentors as PowerPlus changed from within.

9.12 IMPLEMENTATION

The KMb team decided not to visibly approach their task as a major reorganization. All too often management projects start with a big bang and end up gradually fading away, causing employees to become skeptical and thinking, "OK, here we go again" or "I wonder how long this one will last?" So, instead of making a big deal of the KMb project the team initiated a number of local actions at several levels, even though they knew this multiple approach to change was counter to most proven management approaches. Simultaneous multiple changes do not provide good cause-and-effect tracking, and somehow control is often lost when too many changes happen at once. That was just the point. Complexity theory indicated that causal tracking was not possible anyway, and that the intersection of multiple changes had a good chance of synergistically moving the organization forward. The catch was that while they knew the direction these changes would take, they could not be sure exactly where the changes would end up. Changes that take hold do so because the organization is comfortable with them, and these changes have a good chance of lasting and expanding their influence. Some people call this change strategy "seeding."

During implementation the team observed a variety of responses from the managers, and eventually about 50 percent of the senior managers left the organization. Nonetheless, because of the CEO's personal interest, all of the managers cooperated, and many became actively involved in reviewing, assessing and objectively studying their departments from the viewpoint of the KMb program. This included a close look at how well the departments were cooperating and supporting each other. This was the shift in perspective that broke down the silos that had maintained a local control mentality for many years.

If you want to change employee behaviour, get them involved in organizational change, give them direction, and get out of their way!

As the KMb approach was implemented, one progressive department manager became frustrated at not being able to get his workers to suggest ideas for better ways of doing their work. He found a simple but elegant solution. After talking to his division managers about how important it was to rethink their operations and the need for innovation, he told all of his people that he wanted them to think out of the box and come up with new ideas and new ways of getting the job done. He then emphasized that "he was the only person in the department who could say 'no' to any idea they proposed". He was amazed at the number of ideas that were generated. Instead of having a chain of people who could stop an initiative before it was ever fully voiced, there was a single point: him.

To get all levels of the workforce involved, Nancy asked John to let her charter 15 teams, each comprised of seven to nine volunteers from different levels and departments of the organization. Each team would select one task from a proposed list, with each task representing an aspect of the desired future PowerPlus. These tasks were the ones that had been determined by the KMb team to be the significant issues, concerns and opportunities. For example, one task was to research and prepare a briefing on what new technologies the Utility would need during the next 15 years. Another team was tasked to identify 10 ways that the organization could better communicate and collaborate internally among divisions and departments. A third task entailed developing specific actions and processes that would ensure that PowerPlus became a learning organization. Another team's task was to review and make recommendations on employee career growth and human resource development.

To help the teams get started, Nancy set up a three-day workshop to introduce knowledge and knowledge mobilization (see appendix F for the workshop agenda). The workshop would help them understand the overall strategy for change, and allow them to begin thinking about the role of knowledge and its importance in building the PowerPlus of the future. When they were ready to start their task, each team was given authority to talk with anyone inside or outside the organization as they felt necessary. They were assured they would have the full cooperation of all employees. The KMb team would serve as a knowledge resource on the KMb process and coordinate resources, information, and lessons learned across the teams. They would also jump in as needed when any issues emerged that the team felt required additional clarification. A directive was issued to all employees to ensure support of these teams. At their first meetings, the teams were to self organize, selecting their own leaders and, guided by the KMb process, plan their approach. They were expected to complete their work in six months, and were asked to make recommendations for actions and brief the CEO and Board of Directors on their results. Following that briefing each team would be scheduled to provide briefings to representative groups from across the PowerPlus organization.

The task-team approach got the employees directly involved, provided them ownership of solutions, and give them an opportunity to contribute to the future success of the Utility. Further, since the people who volunteered for these teams were typically go-getters who were most interested in improving the organization, they were influential and, in talking with their coworkers over the life of the task team, the entire organization would become aware of the KMb project from the inside out. Learning about the project from their colleagues, rather than their bosses, gave the project much more credibility and support. This approach provided a second advantage because the employees knew the internal workings of their organization and had a stake in its success.

During implementation of their team assignment, each team member gained a broader perspective on his/her work and an appreciation for the importance of coordinating and communicating with other departments. In addition to the KMb workshop, at the kickoff of each team, the KMb team spent time discussing the overarching objectives and providing training on systems and complexity thinking as it applied to PowerPlus. They also provided information and knowledge on how to improve performance and create a collaborative, empowering, flexible and learning environment.

The most challenging and exciting part of KMb is the implementation. There will be surprises, uncertainties, ambiguities, and roadblocks that will challenge everyone's patience, intuition, confidence and judgment. Welcome to the new world of complexity!

During the implementation process the KMb team worked with many managers and supervisors to get their views and assistance in trying out new ideas and relationships, passing information on to the task teams if it was related to their area of focus. The KMb team's philosophy was to let everyone know that they did not have all of the answers but that everyone working together could figure out what made sense for PowerPlus. There was very little information withheld from anyone, and the KMb team worked hard to develop trust and openness in all of their communication and actions. They set up an Intranet to support the KMb team and the task teams, and provided regular updates on progress. The Intranet also made research material available to all of the teams—and other interested employees. It also provided a mechanism for feedback and new ideas. A blog was added to allow employees to ask questions and provide comments on the process or any issues they felt needed to be addressed. The KMb team and task teams rotated managing the Intranet in order to keep all the teams actively aware of the transformation to a learning organization and a complex adaptive knowledge-centric utility.

PowerPlus

REFLECTIVE THOUGHTS

In the KMb implementation process at PowerPlus, there was a clear focus on how people could work together and what the best actions were to meet the organization's goals and objectives, with the continual questioning: Why are we doing it this way? There were many tough questions from the workforce that had to be answered honestly and openly. This was, of course, not without challenges, difficulties, misunderstandings and some setbacks. However, the KMb approach, using appreciative inquiry and action-learning, led to creation of a common vision and collective understanding of—and appreciation for—the mission of PowerPlus, something that had not previously occurred. This served to bring people into closer working relationships. Organizations do not change quickly. As in the story above, *slow can be fast*; patience and perseverance do pay off. Knowledge has to be nurtured, shared, reflected upon, allowed to simmer, and *sometimes even discarded*. But when *knowledge is mobilized* it becomes one of the most powerful assets of the organization.

Those teams, organizations, and leaders who can envision, feel, create and apply the *power of knowledge* are the true leaders of tomorrow. By learning to mobilize knowledge, a synergy and focus is created that brings forth the best of actions *and* values. When knowledge is mobilized and used for the greater good, humanity will have left the information age and entered the age of knowledge, ultimately leading to compassion and—hopefully—wisdom.

EVENTS

Advisory Board. Provides review process, expands the sphere of interest, and offers the opportunity to have expertise readily available as needed. Serves to keep advocates involved in the research process. Periodic meetings. (Also included in Appendix D, Sustainability.)

Book Launch/Signing. May be held separately or in concert with another event. Specifically takes advantage of researchers, advocates, community members, etc. who have written on a subject closely related to research or application area. Offers potential for increased visibility and shared understanding of the importance of research.

Colloquium. Mix of formal/informal interactions encouraging conversation, discussion, elaboration, dialogue and questions. Presentation of papers by researchers and/or research interns. All stakeholders are invited. Focus on practical ramifications of research and gaps that need to be addressed.

> **Student Colloquium.** Provides students an opportunity to showcase their initiatives, both processes and outputs, e.g., findings. Also provides an opportunity for peer-to-peer dialogue among students, and for the development of peer knowledge networks.
>
> **Stakeholder Colloquium.** Brings together research papers developed by stakeholders, who present their own observations. (see Papers, below). Researchers, policy-makers, advocates and practitioners invited to attend presentations and engage in dialogue on issues presented.

Community Meeting. Another form of town hall (see Town Hall below), with formal invitations to community leaders and key opinion leaders, those individuals connected to service clubs and associations, religious organizations, and small businesses central to the community. Focus is on engagement, making connections, and open information flows.

Consortium. Brings together assortment of groups (partners and stakeholders) who have agreed to work together toward a common goal.

> **Local Knowledge Consortium.** Interface between researchers and community, with support materials provided that facilitate self-reflection and the mobilization of insights from this self-reflection. The focus is on developing an understanding of assumptions and values underlying ongoing research from varied stakeholder frames of reference.

Conference. Formal meeting for presentation, consultation and discussion. Brings all geographically-dispersed participants together to share knowledge, assess and evaluate their experiences and dialogue among stakeholders about what they are learning. Presentation of research findings, implementation approaches and results, and shared insights. Recognized national leaders and experts may be invited to speak about innovative responses to issues. Can be an annual event with geographical location rotation. May be tied to significant policy actions.

International Conference. Platform for widely sharing newly discovered knowledge. Provides opportunity to inculcate valuable insights from researchers, policy makers and community members around the world working on similar issues. May be a single or periodic event.

Contest. A process for promoting participation in specific areas of research. For example, teenagers may be asked to write a poem or short story about drug and alcohol abuse in their community, an awareness-raising exercise that may simultaneously serve as an indicator of the level of effectiveness within this community of related research implementation projects. Conversely, adults in a stakeholder population might be asked to submit their ideas for sharing specific research findings. Contests are self-selective by their nature, involving individuals through the possibility of personal reward and/or recognition who might otherwise not engage.

Demonstration. A practical application of something by example. Generally complements some other scheduled event, taking advantage of a gathering of stakeholders. Can be used to teach or inform or convince.

Exhibit. A show or display held separately or in conjunction with another event at a point in time that makes available for public enjoyment or consideration a group of objects or products related to the area of research or with a demonstrated relationship to the community's need for this research. For example, if research was focused on demonstrating the different values emerging in elementary-age children on the one hand who have no parental restrictions and continuous access to media and on the other hand those who have parental restrictions and limited access, an exhibit of art and poetry over a specified period of time from both control groups might be appropriate. As a second example, there might be a group of paintings and poems generated during the two-week period following release of a high-visibility, emotionally-charged movie that represent the theme of the movie. In other words, dependent on the research content, exhibits offer the rare opportunity for researchers to demonstrate their findings.

Art Exhibit. Highly engaging and often emotive way of communicating meaning.
Floating Exhibit. The movement of a pertinent show from one region to the next. Particularly effective approach to a cultural-based exhibit that has relevance to large or geographically dispersed stakeholder communities.
Photograph Exhibit. May be particularly poignant to illustrate need and/or the effectiveness of social science research application (while taking care to preserve individual rights).

Festival. A high-energy, joyful (festive) approach to knowledge sharing. Might include musical or theatrical performances, food booths, games and exhibits. Effective when held in conjunction with a special day or celebration pertinent to the research area or target community. Opportunity for creative avenues of expression. See Knowledge Fair.

Focus Group. A planned coming together of a small number of stakeholders to dialogue on a specific area or subject related to the KMb process or the content of research findings.

Forum. Periodical meeting or gathering for purposes of discussion, dialogue or debate. Means of sharing information, knowledge and research while focusing on common interests and challenges.

TOOL: **DIALOGUE**

Dialogue is a process for the respectful exchange of different views, perspectives and opinions providing the opportunity for the formation of, reflection on, and alteration of opinions and understanding. As forwarded by David Bohm (1992), dialogue describes a situation by which group participants as co-equals inquire and learn about some specific topic to create a common understanding and shred perception of a given situation. It can be considered as a collaborative sharing and development of understanding. Participants must suspend judgment and not seek specific outcomes and answers. The process stresses the examining of underlying assumptions, beliefs and listening deeply to the self and others with the goal of developing a collective meaning.

Knowledge mobilization utilizes structured dialogue among key stakeholders. An ongoing dialogue among researchers and stakeholders helps keep research relevant, accessible and responsive and practitioners and communities receptive and continuously learning.

Community Forum. Provides networking opportunities and increased visibility of research process and work underway. Opportunity for partners to highlight specific findings and experiences.

Forum Series. Brings policy-makers together with practitioners, advocates and consumers with the opportunity over time of involving geographically dispersed stakeholders.

Knowledge Exchange Forum. Planned process, specifically: (1) the group meets to review objectives and establish ground rules; (2) breaks out into domain specific discussion groups to share practices and experiences; (3) reconvenes to discuss commonalities and differences; and (4) works together to create an action plan for improved collaboration and knowledge exchange between key stakeholders.

Public Forums. Research area driven. (1) Sponsoring an event open to all interested citizens providing the opportunity for dissemination of research findings and application results supported by a question and answer sessions. (2) Participation of stakeholders in externally-sponsored (but related) local and national public forums and government meetings to better discern challenges and issues.

Special Forums between policy makers and academic researchers. Defined topics. Inclusive of larger stakeholder input and participation as appropriate.

Informal Events. This may take the form of walks, lunches, fireside chats or various social events. Networking and the sharing of ideas taking place outside normal everyday activities can result in new undertakings, new insights, and new collaborations (Bergeron and McHargue, 2002; McDonald and Klein, 2003).

Knowledge Exchange Panel. Small group of stakeholders pulled together for specific exchange (or as part of an inquiry, advisory board, conference, etc.) Creates an opportunity for focused, extended dialogue on common issues of concern and interest among specific stakeholders. Recurrent (perhaps annual or semi-annual). Builds community capacity while informing researchers.

Knowledge Fair. A large intermediation event focused on knowledge sharing. Exhibits, briefings and demonstrations highlight a full-day event. The knowledge fair is designed as a "fair" in terms of high energy, entertainment and amusement, but the buying and selling aspect is that of knowledge broker and seeker, with a wide and deep level of knowledge resources provided. This would include speakers and panels, exhibits and displays. Could be coupled with a ribbon-cutting, release of a new movie, action demonstrations and an awards ceremony, all focused on the KMb project. Booths and separate segments of the overall fair could be self-organized by community stakeholders, with a plethora of hand-outs and take-home information and tools. A follow-on virtual reference tool would include video clips from each exhibit coupled with text and graphic presentations, and would include candid remarks by senior policy-makers and experts who attend. As a follow-up to the event, this tool would be widely distributed to stakeholders.

Media Panel. A media event including a group of people selected to discuss a specific issue.

Meetings. The formal, planned assembly of a group of people, generally limited to those specifically invited.

> **Gap Meeting.** Pulls together a specific group of representative stakeholders to brainstorm gaps in research.
>
> **Samplings.** Short meetings between researchers and practitioners to sample ideas and experiment with new strategies. Opportunity to explore questions from current and past participatory action research.

Performance. Provides opportunity to personally experience information, theatre, art and music, thus making more lasting impressions on audiences. Simultaneously, the actors and performers embed the subject information within themselves, becoming catalysts for the focused material delivered. A performance may be in concert with an over-arching event, or planned and executed for a specific target audience.

> **Live Theatre.** When appropriate an effective vehicle in terms of both development and performance.
>
> **Musical Rendering.** Adds the additional element of music and rhythm.

Professional Associations. Local, provincial and national associations that meet regularly and offer a platform for the sharing of information and knowledge (might also be called a knowledge network, a community of practice or a community of interest). This linking offers feedback opportunities and the potential for developing advocates.

Professional Development Day. Similar to special days allocated in educational systems, only geared toward community members. The focus is on skill sets that will help practitioners and stakeholder leaders implement research findings. Regularly scheduled and structured to provide continuing education units for participating professionals.

Retreat. An emersion process where stakeholders commit to learning, sharing and social interaction focused on key challenges, questions, and emergent findings. Uses dialogue to strengthen relationships, develop shared understanding and meaning, and facilitate mutual support. Can be used to jumpstart development of a learning community or community of practice.

Round Table. Small group discussion format where all participants have equal voice. Large stakeholder groups would be segmented and round tables held in different locations (as appropriate to accommodate participation). Serves as a venue to clarify and share academic research and promote dialogue among stakeholders.

Seminars. A short, intensive course focused on a specific topic or area of research.

> **Brown Bag Seminars.** Scheduled during a meal period (for example, lunch) with participants invited to bring and eat their meal during the seminar. Informal structure with a planned speaker followed by open discussion.

Speaker Series. Formal talks by an expert, advocate or stakeholder, followed by a question and answer session. Vehicle for debating local and provincial issues of concern. Builds good will and expands community support. Community plays an active role; for example, through suggesting lecture topics. Series would be open to the public and could be streamed live via the Internet, then archived online and accessible free of charge.

Stand-down. The stand-down is based on a military approach used to support a specific behavior change. In the KMb setting this would be a one-day stop-work community event focused on conveying focused information and skill sets necessary for KMb implementation. During this event, researchers and their partners might participate with community stakeholders to explore new avenues of implementation as well as support of that implementation. This event would demand hands-on stakeholder participation, and include the sharing of stories.

Strategy Session. High-level meeting specifically focused on planning and direction toward a desired end state. Generally limited to researchers and practitioners and representatives of stakeholder groups, often self-selected.

> **Advocacy Strategy Session.** Special meeting called to address specific issue or to garner advocacy support and energy toward a specific KMb goal.

Symposium. Brings researchers and practitioners involved in a specific interest area or project together to share opinions, philosophies and conversation. Approaches: (1) Annual activity open to all interested individuals with new themes each year. Provides theoretical knowledge to practitioner while simultaneously providing researchers with practical insights into the application of research findings and ideas for future research. (2) Major event on mutually agreed-upon topic. For example, a full-day workshop designed by and for multiple stakeholders. (3) Small group (10-15), week-long interdisciplinary activity to build shared understanding across diversity of populations and learners, interpret intellectual contexts shaping research questions, explicate differences between theoretical research and applied research, and brainstorm potential solutions.

TOOL: **STORYTELLING**

Anecdotes and the construction of fictional examples to illustrate a point can be used to effectively transfer knowledge. A variety of story forms exist naturally throughout organizations and communities, including scenarios—the articulation of possible future states, constructed within the imaginative limits of the author, and anecdotes—brief sequences captured in the field or arising from brainstorming sessions. Scenarios provide awareness of alternatives and are often used as planning tools for possible future situations. Success stories can prove catching.

The capture and distribution of anecdotes across stakeholders carries high value. Once a critical number of anecdotes are captured from a community, the value set or rules underlying the behavior of that community can be determined (Snowden, 1999). The dissemination of true anecdotes that embody the value of research findings or research underway reinforces shared understanding. Anecdotes can be inserted in events, publications, and available through sustainability tools.

Pairing Symposia. Provides opportunity for researchers and larger stakeholder group to come together at a location within the stakeholder community. Event jointly planned by researchers and practitioners. Structured presentation by researcher in plain language of the results of research and potential uses. Practitioner would then relate research results to policy debates, and present approaches for addressing policy-makers. Summaries by researchers and practitioners would be disseminated along with ideas for future actions.

Public Sector Symposia. Partnering between non-government organizations and the public sector to dialogue on cutting-edge research. Focus on techniques for enhancing the relevance of research to policy-makers.

Tours. Physical and mental sharing of spaces and places. (1) From the researcher perspective, this might entail exploring the spaces and places related to KMb implementation. (2) From the community perspective, this might mean exploring the academic setting and gaining an understanding of the theory grounding specific research.

Field Trip. A visit by selected stakeholder groups to any site that has significance to, and will build understanding of, research or research implementation.

Site Visit is a variation of the tour approach with a specific agenda.

Speaking Tour. Repeated use of presentations geared toward delivering a bounded message to specific stakeholder audiences. Provides person-to-person exchange and offers opportunity for question and answer sessions.

Town Hall. Formal interactive public gathering based on a discussion framework, and promoting dialogue among partners and stakeholders. Information on all aspects of project would be widely available to stakeholders, and open discussion on all issues encouraged. Annual event held in cultural tradition of knowledge beneficiaries; for example, the Blackfoot tradition of the communal meal and the telling of stories.

Training. Providing or receiving instruction for a specific skill or skill set related to the process of research, implementation of research findings, or other related skills.

> **Partner Counselor Training**. A mechanism to bring new partners up to speed as they are recruited. Provided in local setting with researcher and community involvement. Provides first interactions with committed community representatives. Planned as needed.
>
> **Training Packets.** (1) Collection of support materials and resources related to specific training. (2) Packets that themselves become training instruments, often tied to CD or Internet-based interactive training.

Training Literacy. Specific training sessions that facilitate the learning of meta-skill sets called integrative competencies. (See chapter 3.)

> **Information Literacy.** Approach to working with broad array of stakeholders to facilitate critical thinking and processes to access, value and validate Internet-based information related to research project.
>
> **Media Literacy.** Focused on developing an informed and critical understanding of the nature of mass media, and the techniques and impact of techniques used by the media (Duncan, et al., 2000). Specific focus is on how the media contributes to meaning and the construction of reality. This requires a hands-on and experiential approach to learning. A media workshop might also build an understanding of the power of the visual image through hands-on exploration of computer animation and video production techniques.
>
> **Research Literacy.** Approach to working with decision-makers and non-academic stakeholders to expand their understanding of the research process in order to help understand the meaning of research findings and to nurture knowledgeable participation. Topics might include writing grant proposals, introduction to community-based research, research designs, research ethics, and participatory approaches to program evaluation. Would address core issues such as multi-university collaboration and commercialization of research results.
>
> **Systems and Complexity Thinking.** Approach to working with leaders in all stakeholder sectors to facilitate understanding of the interconnectedness of a wide array of activity underway, the difficulty of tracking cause-and-effect relationships, the power of emergence, and paths for facilitating and nurturing change.

Workshops. Workshops are content-rich delivery systems revolving around discussion, study and experimentation. They provide the opportunity for one-on-one and group interactions. Since content may significantly differ for specific stakeholder groups, attendance may be focused and segmented.

Capacity BuildingWorkshop. (1) From the perspective of researchers, participation in workshops with community members and non-research stakeholders helps to build a shared understanding of research processes, knowledge mobilization, and evaluation techniques. (2) From the perspective of non-community members, participation in workshops with all stakeholders contributes to a better understanding of larger, inter-related community issues. This could include considering the potential entanglement of implementing research findings in terms of culture, resistance to change, as well as political and economic ramifications.

Community Leaders Workshop. Focused on sharing ideas and learning from one-another.

Educators Workshop. Provides platform for embedding research approaches and findings into the educational system at all levels (as appropriate). Attendees could be school teachers and administrators (local or national, dependent on research) or university representatives and representatives from the larger stakeholder group.

Knowledge Transfer Workshop. Focus on two-way, hands-on knowledge exchange between research group and community. Similar to knowledge exchange panel only held in a workshop format.

Mini-KMb Workshop. A specially designed workshop to share understanding about knowledge mobilization approaches and techniques. This meta-workshop (which could also be considered a meta-tool) is an essential part of a KMb project or program, since designing the KMb approach must be exemplary of the process of research application.

Multiple Solutions Workshops. Audience is similar to educators workshop only designed as half-day workshops tied into professional development days for teachers in order for researchers and educators to work together to explore solutions that could be applied to their common field of interest. Content focus is driven by the questions and concerns of teachers, educators and administrators rather than the researchers.

Professional Development Workshop. Specifically focused on identified areas of professional specialty that, when improved, could support successful understanding and implementation of research findings. Connected with continuing education units or university credit to facilitate ease and reward of attendance.

Professionals Workshop. Creates dialogue in order to grapple with issues of content and perceptions versus intent of research and programs as understood by the professionals implementing the research. Focus is on underlying values, beliefs and assumptions. Attendees are those directly related to implementation and representatives of the perceived beneficiaries of that implementation.

Workshop Series. Can be focused on all stakeholders or specific sets of stakeholders or any of the workshops above. Appropriate for (1) repeating the same workshop across different segments of the stakeholder population; or (2) running a series of workshops focused on different themes involved in the research issue and application.

APPENDIX B
PUBLICATIONS

Background Papers. These can focus on the research approach, research content, or community history and culture. They would provide pertinent background material in plain language to raise the awareness and understanding of current research directions and implementation issues. These should, if possible, be made accessible to all stakeholders.

Bibliography. While usually providing sources for a particular work, bibliographies can also be a collection of suggested readings, or sources of additional depth for stakeholders interested in more information about an area of research.

Book Review. Opinion piece on written or literary work related to the area of research or KMb process. Could be made available on-line.

Brief. Similar to a presentation, but less formal. A brief is often extracted from academic papers to make research more accessible and understandable to a wider audience. It can be presented in oral or written format.

> **Issues Brief.** A short paper describing issues (background, content and context) and framing questions around those issues. Written in non-technical language for accessibility by all stakeholders.

Brochures. A pamphlet or short printed work that has been stitched, stapled or folded, usually supporting high-level information focused on positive aspects. Could be used to share information and contact points about a project, the content of a website, or location of resources around specific research. Brochures are generally used in combination with other media or events.

Case Study. A detailed analysis or study of a group, event or unit. Generally used as a model or guide for learning.

Editorial. Article that expresses personal opinion, specifically that of the editor.

Editorial Board. A group of individuals providing review services for materials being prepared for KMb.

Fact Sheet. A means of providing factual material to a broad array of stakeholders. Generally one page focused on a single issue with relevant facts presented in clear language. Would be provided free of charge and placed in locations that are easily accessible by stakeholders. Could also be made available on a web site.

Flyers. A short form of the flysheet or flyleaf (the leaves at the beginning and end of a book that carry short overviews, quotes from advocates, and/or short author biographies). Flyers are similar to handbills, a quick form—generally one page—of disseminating information about an event or publication.

Guidelines. A book of instruction on a specific subject. A document providing directions, but softer directions than laws, rules or policies. While moving toward standardization, guidelines embed a level of meaning and understanding, combining "why" as well as "why not."

> **Road Map Guidelines.** Specific step-by-step mapping of actions used for specific processes (such as incubators).

Handbook. See manual below.
Ice Breaker. Game or exercise at the beginning of an event that helps relax participants and provide an atmosphere conducive to information exchange and learning.

Information Packets. These are collections of pertinent printed and CD-based materials provided to specific stakeholders. For example, the target stakeholders may be schools and parent groups, or doctor's offices and rehab clinics, etc.

Interpretative Materials. Materials that provide background and context to areas of focus. This might include historical relevance, economic significance, or future value. Generally developed and delivered in support of events or other publications.

Manuals. A manual is a handbook or a book of instruction (about a specific subject matter) which serves as a learning tool. Pragmatic in nature, it provides a methodology for use or application. After release, a stakeholder workshop could be held on the use of the manual.

> **Community Manual.** Guidance on how to form and support a community of interest, community of learning, or community of practice and the subtle differences among these various communities. Specific focus is on the support and application of research. This manual might cover start-up, processes and practices, tools, and evaluation approaches.

One-Pager. Collaboration piece or lay summary that provides the main points of a specific topic.

Policy Updates. Social science research may offer the potential to impact policy. Since advocacy is participative, these one-page updates of research underway keep policy makers interested and the KMb project in their conscious awareness.

> **Policy Advisory Report.** A report that is formally issued that summarizes findings and recommendations.

Posters. Large sheets of paper or placards sharing ideas. Prepared such that they catch attention and quickly convey core ideas.

Presentations. The act of presenting or demonstrating, generally connected with visuals and models such as PowerPoint slides.

> **Cartooning.** Animation and humor. A powerful form of communicating a concept in a surreal manner with underlying meaning. Offers the opportunity to deal with difficult, emotional issues from an external frame of reference.

Presentation Handout. Take-home slides or support materials.

Press Release. Formal and official statement offered to the general public via publication in public media. Usually connected with an event or point in time, i.e., approval of a research grant, unique and powerful findings, successful implementation results.

Public Service Announcements. Formal statement provided for community or stakeholder welfare, usually under the direction of policy-makers or community officials. May or may not be time dependent.

Publishing Program. Publication of materials in support of research, and subsequently the results of research implementation. Specific titles related to area of project. Impact can be increased by linking publications to public events, panels and conference themes related to publications.

> **Community Experiences.** Stories about the community, its implementation of specific research, and follow-on effects from research implementation. May be written as non-fiction, or as pseudo-fiction.
>
> **Fiction.** Used as a tool to accelerate understanding and relevance of research findings. Provides opportunity to create a picture of the effect of research results in a way that can be understood by a large groups of stakeholders. Could be stakeholder-focused and self-published,or published through formal processes by larger interest groups with specific issues of interest.
>
> **Magazine.** A formal serial publication for general reading that may contain both fiction and nonfiction articles by a collection of authors as well as photographs, illustrations, poetry, etc. Generally designed around a specific theme for a specific target audience. For example, this might take the form of a periodic release on research progress written in plain language with photos and stories from partners and community representatives. Excellent vehicle for connecting pertinent ideas to wide audiences. Potential for high community focus and participation.
>
> **Memoir.** A story about the activities of the researcher or practitioners implementing research findings. Biographical or autobiographical in nature. Tells the human side of the research or implementation process, thereby offering a unique viewpoint to share background and meaning. May be used as a learning tool in a university setting, or in a broader fashion across the stakeholder community.

Op-Ed. The term used to describe the page in a newspaper that is across from the editorial page. Historically, this is a place where opinions are expressed freely, perhaps including such things as letters to the editor or reader voice.

Poetry. Word images which may be streams of thought expressions or expressed in metrical (or musical) form that create imaginative impressions in the reader or listener. A vehicle for the sharing of ideas and meaning tied to emotion.

Popular Press Books. Used as a tool to increase access to sometimes difficult-to-explain concepts involved with on-going research and application of research findings. Co-authored by expert and practitioner. Could be stakeholder focused and self-published or for pertinent issues with larger interest groups published through formal press mechanisms.

Quizzes. Short set of questions to test an individual's knowledge. Can be developed in the form of a game.

TOOL: **MODELS**

Models are simplistic representations (pictures) of some part of reality created to aid stakeholders in understanding and dealing with some area/situation or objective. While all models are by nature artificial constructions, they serve to limit an area of focus, providing the opportunity to create new knowledge within the boundary of the model and to test new ideas. Models also provide a way of sharing new learnings.

Research Papers. Traditional academic vehicle.

Formal research paper. Findings submitted through scholarly medium, including refereed journals, refereed conference presentations, and proceedings.

Co-Authoring. Brings together research and results of research in an appropriate peer-reviewed professional journal. Conversely, could be jointly written for and published in a community magazine.

Research paper by stakeholder. Describes results of implementation and explores potential implications of these results.

Popularized version of research paper distributed to stakeholders. (See translation under the chapter on meta-tools.)

Resource Toolkit. A collection of simple tools (print and web-based), available for wide distribution. Includes resource locator, presentation materials supporting project themes, and promotional materials.

Synthesis Paper. Synthesis of all key issues in a project used to clarify objectives of the research program. Includes pertinent information presented logically. Identifies what is known and where gaps need additional research. Synthesis topics would be mutually agreed-upon by stakeholders.

APPENDIX C

META TOOLS

GENERIC META-TOOLS

Academic Research Papers. Meta-research on effective KMb, addressing the ways, means, challenges and impacts of KMb. Opportunity to engage approaches best suited to the implementation of specific research findings. Charts the approach from the framework in which research was executed.

Environmental Scan. A broad scan to determine current trends in a community to identify opportunities for, and barriers to, KMb approaches related to research implementation. This is most effective when performed by a joint researcher-community team.

Journaling. A reflective process for students (of all ages) providing the opportunity to relate the new to what is known, making comparisons and expressing opinions and judgments side-by-side with events. Journaling helps the individual interpret activities and feelings, a precursor to sense-making and learning.

Knowledge Mobilization Handbook. Guidance for implementation intended for scholars, researchers, practitioners and other stakeholders involved in a KMb program, project or process. Would include the underlying theory and value of investing time and energy in the KMb plan and process, a guide for translation of research to plain language, etc. The focus would be on moving beyond traditional academic dissemination activities to engagement, full partnering and participation with stakeholder communities. Might include a best practices inventory.

Needs Assessment Studies. Focused on KMb strategies tailored to identifying the needs, preferences and goals of researchers and community partners, and providing KMb strategies tailored to address those needs.

Synthesis. The research synthesis creation process is itself a form of translating research findings into a shorter, more-easily-consumed form while maintaining meaning. The difference is, of course, that thoughts, not language, are the focus of the synthesis. A synthesis would include research knowledge pulled from a specific area or concerning a specific issue.

Template. A guide or pattern. In KMb, this might be a template for articulating key insights, or developing summaries, or translating research findings into plain language (see below).

EXPLORING AND GETTING STARTED

Design Experiments. Exploration and testing of theoretical ideas in an authentic setting to understand how learning occurs. Brown calls this learning in situ, assessing the change resulting from a number of interactive factors in the authentic environment (Brown, 1996).

Experimental Projects. Multidimensional and multidisciplinary in nature. Represents the exploration of non-traditional research and different KMb approaches, and tests adaptations of traditional research and KMb projects. May cross traditional research areas and cultural, ethnic, and geographical boundaries.

Incubator. An artificial environment set up to nurture the start-up of a KMb program. This would be a formal, controlled experiment over a specified period of time.

Matchmaking. Marketplace for research. (1) A process to connect individuals and organizations with others who have related research aims. (2) A process to connect researchers with potential research topics.

Pilots. Small experimental tests executed prior to a larger-scale undertaking. In this instance, a pilot would mean starting the KMb implementation within a small group of the larger stakeholder group. The process and results would then be assessed and modified before starting larger implementation.

DEVELOPING REFERENCE MATERIALS

Acronym List. Abbreviations or words formed with representative letters of other words. Short forms that are usually related to the process of research, the functional area of focus, or the forms and activities of stakeholders.

Bibliography. An annotated presentation of existing resources to facilitate easy access to research information to all stakeholders. Arranged alphabetically, chronologically and/or in classifications related to research. Usually updated annually.

Catalogue. List of available materials in support of specific research. Arranged in a definite order and descriptive in nature. Vehicle for organizing related research. Includes abstracts written in a non-technical language. Uses key words as locators.

Glossary. An alphabetical listing of selected words relative to project research. Includes definitions, pronunciation, origin, and usage examples (as appropriate) related to research underway.

Lexicon. A dictionary that focuses on the specific language (vocabulary) related to an area of concern or practice. (1) A lexicon of local dialects and acronyms related to the community in which research is being implemented. (2) A lexicon of research terms available to stakeholders to build familiarity with terminology.

Thesaurus. A collection of concepts and terms designed to facilitate interdisciplinary dialogue. It also functions as a vocabulary for database searches to aid in connecting researchers to resources. Includes subject access.

Value Chain. A meta-tool to assist stakeholders in appraising value of research and benchmarks to community needs. Also available for use by decision-makers.

CONSULTING APPROACHES

Community Consultation. Wide scale consulting approach to establish common goals and priorities within research area. Community serves as consultants. Repeated annually or semi-annually to revisit question and reframe research in response to experiences in projects.

Consultations. Small formal or informal meetings, often one-on-one, to address specific process issues involving a knowledge provider and a knowledge seeker among stakeholders. Often a two-way flow of information.

Consulting Network. A network of professional and practitioner experts that can bring theoretical and practical knowledge to bear on challenges and solutions in research implementation.

Related and Specialized Expertise. Experts as consultants. There are a number of closely-related areas of expertise that apply to most research efforts, yet are not necessarily included as part of university classes or community adult learning; for example, start-up of a company to commercialize research results, advice on multi-community or multi-university partnering, or ownership and boundaries of intellectual property. Since expertise for these types of issues may be outside the scope of involved stakeholders—yet pertinent and relevant to promulgating personal and community welfare—it may be necessary to draw in experts from other disciplines as needed. This specialty consulting might be provided to specific individuals or a group of stakeholders with special interests.

MEDIA PRODUCTIONS

Documentary. A fact-based film.

DVD. A format for delivering audio and high definition video recordings. Can provide face-to-face presence across large stakeholder population, and offers the opportunity to provide resources and specialized tools for research implementation and share a story in creative form. For example, a DVD might be used to capture life stories and community history.

Film Festival. Opportunity to combine film media with focused areas of research. Can build a groundswell of support through encouraging networking and advocacy. See the entry for festival in the chapter or point events.

Graphics. Use of models that can exploit the knowledge introduced in a specific research project. Another vehicle for communicating information to stakeholder audiences.

Movie. An individual film that presents moving images usually accompanied by speech and sound. Can entertain, educate, inform, enlighten, and inspire. Visual elements require little, if any, explanation making them highly accessible, and easily understood by many different viewers. Movies are also cultural artifacts, in that they are created by a specific culture, reflect that culture, and in turn affect that culture.

Radio Program. The transmission of information through electromagnetic waves such that it can be picked up by receivers. Widely available to the general public.

Story Pitches. Short human-interest media pitches that focus on unique and high-interest postings about the researcher and the story behind the research. Help build visibility of the research findings while serving as a reward mechanism for the researcher. Can also be focused on individuals implementing research findings.

Television Show. A designed, time-driven event for television broadcast specifically focused on communicating a specific message. Video broadcasts and streaming through the Internet are rapidly replacing television as the medium of choice because of time access and cost benefits. Supports specific programming.

Theatre. Portrayal of stories in front of an audience using multiple elements of the performing arts, e.g., speech, music, dance, gesture. Theatre is a collaborative art form since it involves the participation and skills of many different contributors, not just the performers.

> **Drama.** Theatre in which speech is paramount. Based on written texts or thematic improvisation.

Training Videos. (1) Support material for training sessions. (2) Self-contained training sessions for self-learning. Could be used on-line or down-loadable for just-in-time training. Offers opportunity to demonstrate concepts through visual scenarios.

Video Series. Recording and distribution of visual images, usually inclusive of sound track. Formerly related specifically to tape reproduction, but the term often refers to reproduction on DVD as well. Opportunity to shape opinion and expand understanding and commitment through a series of directly-pertinent learning tools. May be distributed on-line or via DVD or video tape.

> **Practitioners Guide.** Would focus on process but in the community setting, with historical and contemporary information. Provides foundation for and implications of research.

> **Voice Series.** Opportunity to provide specific target groups with their own voice. For example, this could include group discussion by young people on research-related contemporary issues.

SUSTAINABILITY

THE LIVING NETWORK

Advisory Board. Provides review process, expands the sphere of interest, and offers the opportunity to have expertise readily available as needed. Serves to keep advocates involved in the research process. Periodic meetings. (Also included in Appendix A, Events.)

Champion Network. A network (primarily virtual) providing connection to and dialogue space with national and international key stakeholders who are long-term advocates of research in a specific area. These individuals will sustain interest beyond the term of specific research implementation projects, and therefore offer the opportunity for sustainability and increased impact on future efforts.

Communication Forum. A periodic virtual forum or gathering for purposes of discussion and debate.

Community Maps. Interactive mechanism for connecting locations and people. Shows the relationships among stakeholders and areas of research implementation.

Conferences (Web-Based). While they lack the face-to-face interaction, web-based conferences provide greater access in terms of embedded translation mechanisms (multi-lingual and from technical to plain language) and linking of context. The entire conference process can be performed via the web, including soliciting and adjudicating papers, creating and publishing schedules, and publishing and disseminating the proceedings.

Content Management System. A system for ensuring relevant and current content that covers the sphere of a research area and connects to related topics. Includes semantic interpretation and linking of content.

Databases. Collections of data around specific areas of focus. A data warehouse would combine many different databases across an organization or enterprise and would usually include search and retrieval systems.

Decision Support System. A system that provides the tools and capabilities needed by researchers and practitioners in their implementation of research findings. While a specific software decision tool might be employed, the decision support system also includes connectivity to the information needs of decision-making stakeholders.

Directory. A list, contact points, and focus of interest for researchers and service providers linked to other state, national and international contacts. Serves as a resource and tool for researchers and service providers.

Discussion Forum. Enables scheduled sharing on specific topics. Brings together those who have knowledge and those who seek knowledge, those who have experience and those who seek experience. As with any interactive virtual forum, inclusion of an expert adds value and involvement of a champion keeps up interest, and association with an on-going community of interest, learning or practice supports larger participation.

> **Problem of the week.** A participatory methodology for building relationships and increasing involvement of stakeholders. Real issues handled in real time.

Discovery Tools. Various software tools that expand search capabilities to include visual and audio elements tied into educational materials. Would include interactive formats.

Distance Learning Studio. A facility that supports development of distance learning, a method of structured learning conducted without physically meeting a teacher in a classroom.

Expert Network. A network of professional and practitioner experts who are available for consultation. (See all consultation in the chapter on point events.) This network would be made up of individuals who bring theoretical and practical knowledge regarding specific areas of research. Research and practitioner partners mutually take the responsibility to identify and recruit potentially valuable experts to the network.

Gaming. Used in the positive sense of playing games of chance which simultaneously entertain and provide learning experiences.

Global Dialogue. As the space among countries of the world collides on the Internet, it offers the potential to develop multiple frames of reference focused around areas of research. Intense connections in terms of open and high-volume exchange of related information will promote the emergence of patterns.

Hot Links. In this usage, application-defined sequence that switches from one application to another, from one information sources to another. Similar to hyperlinks, only the focus here is on moving from one application to another, while the focus in hyperlinks is connecting to supporting text.

Hyperlinks. Specific text within larger documents that contains automatic links to other parts of the document or to other documents. Single words or phrases are linked directly to related information that helps the user understand or clarify, or provides more depth.

Intranet. An internal network sharing information management systems that acts as a small, contained Internet (where sensitive discussion forums and list serves might reside).

Knowledge Networks. Similar to COPs. Act as critical conduits for innovative thinking and facilitate knowledge generation, dissemination and use. On-line discussion forums; on-going communication focused around relevant issues, both domain-specific and cross-domain

knowledge. Identification of gaps in research. Platform for relationship building and partnering. Open to broader membership beyond direct stakeholders. Incorporates point action groups.

Archives. A place or space where old records and reports are stored. While today much of this is virtual, there is still tremendous validation in the printed word. However, archival material is only as effective as its accessibility, which the living network supports as easily as material that is more current. With this "gift" comes the responsibility for a higher level of context embedding so that archived thought is tied to its place and time and situation.

Calendar. Includes descriptions of upcoming related activities and reports on past activities, including summaries from symposia, etc.

Expertise Locator. An early knowledge management tool in terms of developing information not only about people (name, address, job, etc.) but also about developing context (what they are passionate about, values, dreams, learning approaches and focuses, roles they would like to play in implementing research, etc.). In other words, potential future expertise can be as important as current expertise. Providing an opportunity for a stakeholder to learn, acquire new capabilities, or move forward in their area of passion can build strong partnering relationships and advocacy.

Interactive multidimensional data tables. Provide relational analysis capabilities.

Learning Trajectory. Pathways for learning. A connected flow of links that provides stakeholders the ability to follow themes through web-based materials, and by doing so, expand their learning in a given domain of knowledge.

Linking. As used here, linking refers to a path for communication. For example, a portal might build linkages and connections to international knowledge brokering initiatives or request links from policy-maker websites such as that for the Ministries of Education.

Marketing Platform. A self-managed bulletin board or similar virtual approach where researchers have the option of freely sharing or selling their work.

Portal. A website that serves as a gateway or door to the Internet. This could serve at a very high level, crossing areas of research and providing a wide range of connectivity, or at a specialty level focused around a specific research project, but connecting to related areas and serving stakeholder interests. Learning and tangible resources from events become sustainability factors in on-going activities such as a web-based portal.

Reading Tools. Aids to understanding specific documents; for example, an outline of important points, a vocabulary aid, or a context field or paper. When implementing research, this might also mean connecting implementation ideas directly to research findings.

Server. A specific computer that connects to other computers to serve information. In this usage specifically a web-server that would host applications and files that would be accessible to other specified stakeholders via the Internet.

Simulations. An imitation of a system's behavior, what is commonly called a flight simulator. Can be used as a prediction or learning tool.

User Accounts. An account set up by username, the identification of a specific stakeholder, User accounts provide the opportunity for stakeholders to create personal spaces and customize the portal to their needs.

Virtual Learning Commons. An interactive meeting place where participants engage in discourse focused on a specific area of research. Connected to living network and repositories.

LIVING REPOSITORIES

Annals. Record of recorded events (history of project). Chronological.

Art Gallery On-Line. Made up of visual art created by community participants that have been scanned and posted with accompanying thoughts and discussion about artistic and cultural implications, and related in some way to research findings. Would include digital photographs as appropriate.

Bulletin Boards. A general message center where shareholders can leave and retrieve messages. Messages can be read by all stakeholders.

Clearinghouse. A large collection of related materials that includes context pieces such as surveys, statistics and research data. Serves as a data archive and is easily accessible.

Compendium. A collection of research summaries in plain language and a glossary of short articles about related events, people, places and concepts which has search capabilities and links to additional resources.

Events On-Line. A virtual form of events listed in the chapter on point events. May be real-time, interactive, and link to applicable resource materials. Opportunity here to also stream speakers and dialogue sessions, providing a rich context to other materials.

Exhibits. For research that is connected to media itself, the Internet offers an increased opportunity for demonstrating and sharing research findings. The virtual exhibit embraces media forms based on sound such as musical renditions (for example, rap) as well as visual demonstrations (such as a painting), or both (in a short documentary or movie or a story read by the author).

Interactive Q&A. A program where questions can be submitted and experts will either be scheduled live on-line or have published periodic response opportunities. Both questions and answers are retained on the site for the broader audience. A more private format where questions are submitted and responses are not broadcast may also be available.

Library. Organized collection of materials and media administrated formally. The virtual library contains meta-tools (acronym list, bibliography, catalogue, glossary, thesaurus, etc.) and virtual copies of available and pertinent print materials. This would include, but is not limited to, papers (including citations to papers and links to relevant theoretical and empirical works), presentations, accumulated methodologies, analytical findings, context and interpretation analyses, and references (both academic and key reports, government documents, workshop materials, etc.). Includes both historic research findings and descriptions of and links to research underway. As appropriate, context is built into all materials in terms of use, outcomes, and contact points for additional information.

TOOL: CYBERCARTOGRAPHY

In a networked age, as we embrace increasing complexity and uncertainty coupled with information abundance, the concept of mapping is becoming multidimensional. Cybercartography not only provides live feeds and interactive connectivity across various types of media, but it does so providing a multi-sensory experience, using the map as a way of organizing, understanding and presenting large amounts of data and information to decision-makers. This tool also provides multiple points of view and the opportunity for translating the language and representations of specific content into an information package accessible (in terms of available for use) and Accessible (in terms of understanding leading to use) to those without specific expertise.

What is mapped is not the product of a single individual or group in isolation, but the result of experts collaborating across disciplines and business sectors around the world! (Taylor, 1997; Taylor, 2003). They become living documents built by a living network of experts and users. For example, Cybercartographic atlases combine data and information from remote information sources to render maps, charts and tables in real time, and—based on an open systems approach—data and information relationships and metadata are simultaneously generated, i.e., the system and sources are interactively re-creating themselves every time a decision-maker seeks an answer.

Literature Reviews. In areas of focus, includes systematically updated literature reviews and reviews of significant material as available.

Ontology. Conceptual framework expressed in a classification scheme. What has been called the mental models of a specific area of concern or a body of related research. May inherently have connections to many other concepts with different strengths of relationships and often have coordinating themes.

Taxonomy. Structured set of names and descriptions used to organize a domain or set of domains. While typically using a logical arrangement, a knowledge taxonomy is focused on enabling efficient and interoperable retrieval and sharing of knowledge, information and data by building in natural workflow and knowledge needs in an intuitive structure.

Publications On-Line. A virtual form of publications listed in the chapter on point events. Would become part of the on-line library resources.

Preservation Systems. Embedded processes or systems to ensure long-term availability of materials. Popular approaches include the use of PDF file formats (documents are viewed and down-loaded as documents) and file back-up systems.

Project Journal On-Line. Focuses on research and application of research, but presented in plain language. Follows "journaling" approach, i.e., a diary or record of events and thoughts about events presented in chronological order. Representatives from each sector volunteer to input updates from their area of concern. Volunteers are rotated periodically to facilitate stakeholder awareness of progress and issues.

Research Inventory. A repository of research findings, case studies and other reports and materials on specific research topics. Particular focus on availability and accessibility for policy makers and decision-makers. Feedback mechanisms for policy-makers on implications of research findings. Also tied to "push" mechanisms to keep policy-makers informed.

Web Page. A location (home address) on the World Wide Web that is identified by its URL (uniform resource locator). It can contain software tools, text, images, sound and links to other web pages.

Virtual Resource Room. Similar to a portal, with availability or links to research, but with a focus on additional resources, to include: other web sites, policy-makers and decision-makers, other stakeholders, events, advocates, areas of funding, available researchers and students, and listings and links to any other available resources. Similar to the front section of a telephone directory, the virtual resource room would offer connection to emergency and potentially needed resources connected to specific research implementation.

Web Site. While this could be considered the central repository of project knowledge, it also offers the capacity for interactivity and can provide the architecture necessary to link to other relevant sites and connect users and researchers.

MEDIA AND WEB COMMUNICATIONS

Blog (or Weblog). An open forum for the community at large to discuss personal experiences related to their work as well as professional issues or concerns.

Chat Rooms. A program that provides a platform for real-time Internet conversation with another individual or group of individuals. Can be open access or by invitation. Once logged in, visitors can type in text that will be simultaneously viewed by other visitors. Can support virtual meetings.

Commentary. An explanatory or interpretative series of thoughts about something that is meant to aid in understanding. For example, commentary can be used to help explain the intent of creative art, help clarify the meaning of a technical speaker, or to explain the philosophy underpinning an activity captured in a video.

Community Bulletins. Highlights and synthesizes research in progress. Issued at regular intervals. Short and concise. Offers opportunities for community collaboration.

Distribution List. Some media communications utilize electronic distribution lists; for example, a group of e-Mail names and Internet addresses (handled as a group) used in connection with on-going research and research projects. While these may enable a fast "push" of information to interested stakeholders, various software programs providing this service are often considered generators of "spam" and emails are therefore not accepted.

e-Mail. Messages sent via the Internet between and among users of computers. While e-mail has largely replaced the telephone in many organizations, effectiveness is dependent on user attention. Can become permanent records.

e-Newsletter. Highlights upcoming events, new findings, collaborative opportunities. Jointly developed by partners, and includes short articles by collaborators and community members. Letters from stakeholders welcomed.

Knowledge Streaming. Proactive use of communications software to push on-going research findings directly to stakeholders. Generally focused on information impacting day-to-day life and services.

Knowledge Transfer Rounds. Use web-streaming to connect multiple stakeholders for periodically scheduled interactions. Provides opportunity for implementers to report experiences and achievements, which are in turn added to the web-based information bank. Simultaneously, provides researchers the opportunity to solicit feedback on recent findings or explore collaborative opportunities.

Newsletter Summaries. Brief statement (limited in size to the order of 150-200 words and one image) that contain essential ideas of larger research or reports.

Pod-Casts. A fast-growing and significant technology, pod-casts are Internet-based radio programs (media files) that can be downloaded onto an iPod. These programs are subscribed to and delivered via the Internet. Pod-casts could be developed on key issues for wide dissemination across stakeholder audiences.

Public Service Announcements. Short spots developed in television and radio formats highlighting research value-added. Time-framed multiple showings.

Question and Answer Initiative. Series of question and answer sessions hosted through web portal and released for inclusion in community-based newspapers. Both academic and community partners contribute to responses.

Research Progress Report. Activity record available to all stakeholders. May be distributed with e-Newsletter.

Streaming. Live or recorded audio and video offerings via the web.

Telecommuting. An approach to working via telecommunications outside the normal office location. Enabler for field researchers and practitioners.

Teleconferencing. Computer-based system enabling connections across geographical locations—but not necessarily simultaneous—joint conferencing. May use audio and video equipment.

Video Conferencing. A virtual meeting supported by video connectivity. Each participant would have a video camera and speakers attached to a computer, allowing audio and video data to be transmitted over the Internet. Alternately, a virtual conference room may be used. Provides face-to-face and voice-to-voice benefits across geographically-dispersed stakeholders.

Web-casting. The term used to define broadcasting across the World Wide Web. This medium can provide the live streaming of events.

Web Magazine. Designed on a query system, offers information in plain language about on-going research with key concepts and easy-to-read commentaries written by scholars.

Wikipedia Functionality. Similar to the Wikipedia model, an interactive system that allows stakeholders to add their own information in individualized subject modules. While Wikipedia is open worldwide, this functionality would be with a smaller and more controlled community of contributors or stakeholder groups who have interest and knowledge in the area of focus.

You-Tube Uploads. Short, free video clips available on the web that capture the imagination while making critical points. Can be uploaded by the general public.

KMb AND LEARNERS

FORMAL EDUCATIONAL OPPORTUNITIES

Adult Education Sessions. Special sessions focused on specific areas of research held for practitioners. These might offer Continuing Education Units. Could also be opened to community leaders and other stakeholders. Might include skills that would further policy development and advocacy.

Camp Assistants. Students from the university serve as camp assistants, assisting in both the planning and coordinating of activities built around implementation of research findings. They might also engage in story-telling.

Coaching. Personal training or tutoring generally focused on a specific area or task.

Collaborative Exploratory Events. Events that bring together researchers, practitioners and community leaders to (1) identify potential research needs of stakeholder communities in a specific area of interest; (2) explore the potential of implementing specific research findings in a local community; or (3) explore partnering opportunities within a community or across communities.

Distance Learning. Method of structured learning conducted without physically meeting a teacher in a classroom setting. Distance learning requires, on the part of the student(s), self-discipline, and well-developed reading, writing and analytical skills. On the part of the sponsoring institution, provision must be made for clear presentation of curriculum materials, a means of evaluation, and vehicles and processes for communication between the instructor and students.

Interpretative Center. A virtual or physical place accessible to the local community that serves to translate research, research findings and support materials into various levels of accessibility. Should be somewhat conversational in nature, with scheduled discussion groups.

Job Shadowing. A mentoring relationship between a doer and learner to provide the learner with a glimpse of the real-life experience of the doer. Typically, a day or week in length, where the learner silently observes and takes notes while accompanying the doer throughout the work-day. While there may be dialogue and interaction between the doer and learner on and off throughout the day, the intent is for the doer to continue normal work while being observed by the learner. Excellent opportunity for students to follow in the footsteps of researchers, practitioners. policy-makers and community leaders.

While historically used for university students to shadow practitioners, in their area of study, could be expanded to include practitioners and community leaders shadowing researchers. Collectively these approaches would add considerably to the understanding of researchers and practitioners, and support development of deep collaboration opportunities.

Mentoring. The process of personal counseling and teaching. Usually long-term built on a trusted relationship.

On-the-Job Training. Learning while working (learning while doing).

Practice Fellowship. Full-time placement of researchers or research students with practitioners in related areas of study for a bounded period of time.

TOOL: BEST PRACTICES AND LESSONS LEARNED

Best practices (or promising practices) are knowledge, situation dependent and context sensitive, which makes them extremely difficult to replicate. Best practice information can take the form of processes, studies, surveys, benchmarking, or research. The concept is to identify exemplars with evidence-based outcomes that make sense and try to replicate them.

Lessons learned are innovative solutions to common problems that arise from experience; for example, a specific approach to implementation of research findings concerning elementary school approaches to diversity in a small, bounded ethnic community.

A best practice and lessons learned database would not only include catalogues of services and resources available and widely distributed, but would build in "effectiveness" summaries (context). Another approach is to develop a best practices inventory, offering the opportunity to contrast and compare related practices in specific situations.

In relatively stable environments with repetitive processes, best practices, where they can be transferred successfully, may well work and significantly improve performance. However, since best practices are focused on action, they frequently omit the level of belief and understanding of how things actually work and are often difficult to transfer or ineffective in differing situations and context. (Brown and Duguid, 2000) Concurrently, while best practices are indications of past needs and capabilities that worked, they are typically not designed for adaptability. Given this short discussion, with the decision to apply best practices comes the responsibility to understand to the fullest extent possible the situations and contexts within which the practice was successful and within which it is to be applied.

Professional Development. (1) Stakeholders participating in web-based distance learning. Could be tied to the areas of research, integrative competencies, or KMb itself. This technology-supported approach maximizes opportunities for learning and accessing resources. Also supports collaborative decision-making, problem solving and innovating among professionals. Could include events such as pod-casts and two-way interactive video (ITV). (2) Stakeholders helping develop and facilitate professional development for practitioners and community leaders in the areas of research and/or integrative competencies.

Student Field Testing. Use of students related to a specific group within a community to field test implementation of research findings.

Train-the-Trainer Packet. This would be a packet of virtual materials provided to organizations and community groups to aid in specific training. Materials would be designed to be easily transferable across a diverse community of learners. These materials could then be printed and distributed to support local workshops and training sessions.

Training Partner. Linking knowledgeable partners and practitioners to new practitioners and community leaders for the purpose of providing enriching learning experiences.

Web Courses. Collectively developed by researchers, practitioners and community leaders to provide broad learning opportunities to the larger stakeholder group. Self-directed, but supported by interactive forums and informal blogs.

IN THE UNIVERSITY SETTING

Accreditation Self-Study. A virtual approach to working toward a certificate connected with KMb.

Co-op Arrangements.

> **With Community College and Business Schools.** Agreements with local colleges to simultaneously fulfill "field learning" requirements while providing assistance to the KMb process.
>
> **For University PR Students.** Builds a cohort of KMb trained professionals. From the beginning of the KMb project, pulling public relations students into the hands-on work of implementation. Building this relationship between public relations and the implementation of social sciences and humanities research as part of the curricula provides specialized training and experience that will integrate social marketing into the work place. This will help identify KMb as a significant and valued activity for the community and provide expanded future community capacity.

Certification Programs Any program offering a certificate at completion. In a university setting, this would be a formal program combining specific courses culminating in a specified number of credit hours.

Curriculum Addition. The addition of a KMb course to those undergraduate and graduate programs including individuals who as professionals would be involved in community research programs. Cross-disciplinary in nature. Would demonstrate the day-to-day impact of research findings and stress the significance of collaborative implementation of these findings. Course would include elements of community service-learning.

Graduate Program in KMb. University certificate program set up for participation from cross disciplines. Would include all aspects of KMb (see integrative competencies in chapter 3) to include training in public program delivery. Open to practitioners and community leaders who have an undergraduate degree. Could also be provided as a non-credit certificate program and a professional certificate program according to community needs.

Graduate Research Forum. A forum dedicated to presentation of original research by graduate students. Project partners and community members would be invited to attend. This forum provides the opportunity for graduate students to develop the leadership and research skills they need as future scholars and KMb leaders.

Internships. Intense hands-on learning and training over a period of time, providing the opportunity for both variety and depth of learning. Could be a series of overlapping interns to promote the shared learning.

Lunch and Learns. Programs designed for youth combining learning experiences with the mid-day meal.

Peer Review. An experienced person reviews and evaluates the written work of a student. Develops critical thinking and prepares students for future publishing of their own work.

Practicum for Language Students. Brings researchers, research students and language students together to dialogue, debate and discover common translation patterns between the translation of research to plain language and the translation of research from one language to another. Would address the specific research areas pertinent to participating researchers.

Practitioner on Campus. The concept here is to bring practitioners directly into research efforts on campus though a program similar to the visiting scholar arrangement. As appropriate, each research group would host a visiting scholar for a term. Practitioner would have full access to university student facilities, including the library. Courses would be audited.

Research Mentor. A university representative who works with the practitioner on campus or resident fellow to plan studies and other learning opportunities.

Research Mobilization Symposium. Intensive one-week interdisciplinary study on the intellectual contexts that shape research questions: (1) relevance of research; (2) differences in the laboratory and classroom (theoretical and applied) approaches; (3) building and sustaining relationships and collaboration among researchers, practitioners and the community; (4) research translation approaches; (5) the knowledge mobilization program; (6) challenges of, and opportunities offered by, knowledge mobilization; and (7) assessment and evaluation. Would also cover current research KMb trends and controversies. The end product would be to formulate a research area, simulate results, and design an approach to mobilize research findings. This takes an active engagement approach that would include reflection, debate, and hands-on application.

Residence Fellowship. Opportunity for a senior community leader, stakeholder or practitioner to take a sabbatical from their professional duties and spend a year in studies related to a particular area of research. Practitioner would have full access to university student facilities, including the library. Depending on the individuals, courses could be either for credit or audited.

KMb FOR YOUTH

Art Production Contests for material suitable for publication (music, videos, posters).

Children and Youth Certificate/Diploma. As appropriate, expansion of the area of research to include programs that provide extra-credit opportunities for school-age children. Held in conjunction with schools or community groups. Could work in combination with the General Education Diploma for those who have dropped out of school.

Essay. The essay format offers the opportunity for an individual to express personal views around a specific topic. In this sense, it is a valuable tool in the classroom for students to use to construct their learning, serving as both a mechanism for critical thinking and as a template for developing information-based products. Information-based products such as proposals, reports and letters form the connective tissue for the knowledge worker. The social science essay starts with a thesis or argument that is generated by—and therefore important to—the student. The structure of the essay is driven by the thesis, since the student must now find evidence (facts, figures and supporting statements) to support the thesis. In the KMb approach essays would combine both research concepts and their application and be written following exposure to and involvement with project stakeholders. While generally in written format, this could also be set up as a photo essay experience.

> **Concept Map Visualization.** The process of mapping the argument made in the essay and relating concept terms. This mapping serves as a reinforcement of concepts and their relationships.

Role Playing. An approach to shifting frames of reference. Generally used in conjunction with other learning approaches.

Summer Camps. Would address both social and science dimensions, providing discovery experiences related to all aspects of the research. Week long, offering interactive and educational activities.

Summer School for High School Students. Hands-on learning intensive for high-school students to explore specific research findings, the ramifications of those findings, and approaches to community change. Also, opportunity to teach methodologies used in social sciences research.

Three-Dimensional Virtual Reality. Interactive and challenging approach for youth that is set up to move participants through learning experiences that are also entertaining, fun and memorable.

Video Series for Youth. Professional video with the script created by an interdisciplinary group of graduate students. Story would include animation, music, with youth participation (school class, community group, etc.)

Web Quests. Specific Internet journeys prepared for youth accompanied by discovery tools that assist in finding materials suitable for a successful journey. These would relate to research implementation either in terms of expanding related skill sets or content exploration.

Youth Mentoring. Youth mentoring youth, offering the opportunity for reinforcement and peer reflection. Could be used in conjunction with other methods of teaching and in a group setting.

Youth Newsletter. Created by youths for youths, with youths designing and developing materials around the central research theme, posting and virtually distributing materials, hosting question and answer sessions, and analyzing feedback. Could be tied to a school class, or a group project related to a segment of the population.

WORKSHOP AGENDA

This is the agenda for the KMb three - day workshop provided to PowerPlus employees as part of their organizational transformation program. (See chapter 9.)

INTRODUCTION TO KNOWLEDGE MOBILIZATION
(A PROCESS FOR EFFECTING CHANGE)

Day One

08:00 - 08:30	Welcome, Administrative remarks, Participant introductions, Expectations
08:30 - 09:15	Why KMb?— Problems, Situations, Messes and the New Environment - CUCA
09:15 - 10:15	Overview of the Knowledge Mobilization Process
10:15 - 10:30	*Break*
10:30 - 12:00	Learning How You Learn—How do we know what we know?
12:00 - 13:00	*Lunch*
13:00 - 14:45	Knowledge, Its Creation, Assimilation, Leveraging and Application
14:45 - 15:00	*Break*
15:00 - 16:15	The Intelligent Complex Adaptive KMb Team
16:15 - 16:30	Actions for Tonight, Questions for Tomorrow

Day Two

08:00 - 08:45	Review & Discussion
08:45 - 10:15	Complex Organizations & Change
10:15 - 10:30	*Break*
10:30 - 12:00	Situational Assessment & Problem Solving
12:00 - 13:00	*Lunch*
13:00 - 14:45	Decision - Making & Implementation
14:45 - 15:00	*Break*
15:00 - 16:15	Action Learning & Competency Development
16:15 - 16:30	Actions for Tonight, Questions for Tomorrow

Day Three

08:00 - 08:30	Review & Discussion: Actions & Questions
08:30 - 10:15	Putting It All Together—The KMb Process Returns
10:15 - 10:30	*Break*
10:30 - 11:15	Case Study 1 - Small group exercises
11:15 - 12:00	Small groups report out
12:00 - 13:00	*Lunch*
13:00 - 13:45	Individual Case Studies - Small groups
13:45 - 14:30	Small groups report out
14:30 - 14:45	*Break*
14:45 - 15:30	Deep Dive into selected topics.
15:30 - 16:00	Group Discussion of KMb Process - PMI Analysis
16:00 - 16:30	Monday Morning Actions, PMI, and Wrap - up

REFERENCES

Ackoff, R. L. (1978). *The Art of Problem Solving: Accompanied by Ackpff's Fables.*
New York: John Wiley & Sons.

Allee, V. (2000). "Knowledge Networks and Communities of Practice," in *OD Practitioner: Journal of the Organization Development Network*, Vol. 32 (4). Retrieved on September 2, 2006 from: http://www.odnetwork.org/odponline/vol32n4/knowledgenets.html. *American Heritage Dictionary of the English Language* (3rd ed.) (1992). Boston: Houghton Mifflin Company.

Andreasen, A. R. (1995). *Marketing Social Change: Changing Behavior to Promote Health, Social Development, and the Environment.* San Francisco, CA: Jossey-Bass.

APQC (2000). *Report on Knowledge Management.* Houston, TX: APQC.

Argyris, C. (1993). *Knowledge for Action.* San Francisco, CA: Jossey Bass.

Argyris, C. and D.A. Schon. (1978). *Organizational Learning: A Theory of Action Perspective.* Philippines: Addison Wesley Publishing Co.

Ashby, W. R. (1964). *An Introduction to Cybernetics.* London: Methuen.

Astin, A. W. and L. J. Sax (1998). "How undergraduates are affected by service participation," in Bergeron and McHargue (2002); *Journal of College Student Development*, 39(3), 251-263.

Atwater, F.H. (2004). *The Hemi-Sync Process.* Faber, VA: The Monroe Institute.

Baker, C. L. (1989). *English Syntax.* Cambridge, MA: The MIT Press.

Bargh, J. A. (2004). "Bypassing the Will: Toward Demystifying the Nonconscious Control of Social Behavior," in Hassin, R.R., J.S. Uleman, and J.A. Bargh, (Eds.) *The New Unconscious.* New York: Oxford University Press, pp. 37-60.

Battram, A. (1996) Navigating Complexity: *The Essential Guide to Complexity Theory in Business and Management.* Sterling, VA: The Industrial Society.

Bennet, A. (2006). "Hierarchy as a Learning Platform," in VINE: *The Journal of Information and Knowledge Management Systems*, Volume 36, Number 3. United Kingdom: Emerald Publishing, pp. 255-260.

Bennet, A. (2005). *Exploring Aspects of Knowledge Management that Contribute to the Passion Expressed by its Thought Leaders.* Frost, WV: Self Published. Available at www.mountainquestinstitute.com

Bennet, A. and D. Bennet (2007a). "CONTEXT: The Shared Knowledge Enigma," in VINE: *The Journal of Information and Knowledge Management Systems*, Volume 37, Number 1.

Bennet, A. and D. Bennet (2007b). "The Decision-Making Process for Complex Situations in a Complex Environment," in Holsapple, C. W. and F. Burstein (Eds.) *Handbook on Decision Support Systems.* New York: Springer-Verlag.

Bennet, A. and D. Bennet (2006). "Learning as Associative Patterning," in VINE: *The Journal of Information and Knowledge Management Systems*, Volume 36, Number 4.

Bennet, A. and D. Bennet (2004). *Organizational Survival in the New World: The Intelligent Complex Adaptive System.* Boston: Elsevier.

Bennet, D. (2006). "Expanding The Knowledge Paradigm" in *VINE, The Journal of Information and Knowledge Management Systems*, Vol 36 No 2, 175-181.

Bennet, D. (1996). *IPT Learning Campus: Gaining Acquisition Results through IPT's.* Alexandria, VA: Bellwether Learning Center.

Bergeron, P. and M. McHargue (2002). "Recent Advances in Retreats: Adapting the Great Teachers Model to Serve an Entire College," in *New Directions for Community Colleges* 120, 75-84.

Berry, J. (2000) "Bridge all the digital divides." *Library Journal*, 125, pp. 9-10.

Beyer, J.M. and H.M. Trice (1982). "The Utilization Process: A Conceptual Framework and Synthesis of Empirical Findings," in *Administrative Science Quarterly*, 27, 591-622.

Blackmore, S. (1999). *The Meme Machine*. Oxford: Oxford University Press.

Bohm, D. (1992). *Thought as a System*. New York: Routledge.

Bossidy, L. and R. Charan (2002). *Execution: The Discipline of Getting Things Done*. New York: Crown Business.

Brown, J.S. and P. Duguid (2000). *The Social Life of Information*. Boston: Harvard Business School Press.

Brown, J.T. (1996). "Crossing Boundaries: Knowledge, Disciplinaries, and Interdisciplinarities." Charlottesville, VA: University Press of Virginia.

Buchanan, M. (2004). "Power Laws & the New Science of Complexity Management" In *Strategy + Business*, Issue 34, Spring 2004, Canada, pp. 70-79.

CIHR, Canadian Institutes of Health Research, *Knowledge Translation*. Retrieved August 31, 2006, from *http://www.healthinfonet.ecu.edu.au/html/html_home/home_kt.htm*

Carrillo, F. J. (Ed.) (2006). *Knowledge Cities: Approaches, Experiences, and Perspectives*. Oxford: Butterworth Heinemann Elsevier.

Cassady, M. (1990) *Storytelling: Step by Step*. San Jose, CA: Resource Publications, Inc.

Castells, M. (1996). "The Information Age: Economy, Society and Culture" in Vol. 1. *The rise of the network society*. Malden, MA: Blackwell.

Chawla, S. and J. Renesch (Eds.) (1994). *Learning Organization: Developing Cultures For Tomorrow's Workplace*. Portland, OR: Productivity Press.

Choi, Y., S. Gray, M. Heather and N. Ambady (2004) "The Glimpsed World: Unintended Communication and Unintended Perception," in Hassin, R. R., J. Uleman, and J.A. Bargh (Eds.). *The New Unconscious*. New York: Oxford University Press, pp. 309-333.

Conger, J., G. M. Spreitzer, and E. E. Lawler III (1999). *The Leader's Change Handbook: An Essential Guide to Setting Direction and Taking Action*. San Francisco, CA: Jossey Bass Publishing.

Clark, G. and L. Kelly (2005). *New Directions for Knowledge Transfer and Knowledge Brokerage in Scotland*. Scottish Executive Social Research, Edinburgh, Scotland.

Cross, R.and L. Prusack (2002) "The People That Make Organizations Stop-or Go," in *Harvard Business Review*, 80, No. 6, pp. 104-112.

Cross, R., S. Borgatti, and A. Parker (2002). "Making Invisible Work Visible: Using Social Network Analysis to Support Human Networks," in *California Management Review*, 44, No. 2, pp. 25-46.

Crossan, M. M., Lane, H. W., and White, R. E. (1999). "An Organizational Learning Framework: From Intuition to Institution," in *Academy of Management Review*, 24 (3), pp. 522-537.

Davis, D., M. Evans, A. Jada, L. Perrier, D. Ryan, G. Sibbald, S. Straus, S. Rappolt, M. Wowk, and M. Zwarenstein (2002). "The Case for Knowledge Translation: Shortening the Journey from Evidence to Effect," in *British Medical Journal*, Vol. 327 (July), p. 33-35.

De Furia, G. *Interpersonal Trust Surveys*. San Francisco: Jossey-Bass, 1997.

DeGaetano, G. (2004). *Parenting Well in a Media Age: Keeping Our Kids Human*. Fawnshire, CA: Personhood Press.

Delmonte, M. M. (1984). "Electrocortical Activity and Related Phenomena Associated with Meditation Practice: A Literature Review." In *International Journal of Neuroscience*, 24, pp. 217-231.

Devlin, K. (1999). INFOSENSE: *Turning Information into Knowledge*. New York, NY: W. H. Freeman and Company.

Dijksterhuis, A., H. Aarts and P. K. Smith (2004) "The Power of the Subliminal: On Subliminal Persuasion and Other Potential Applications," in R.R. Hassin, J.S. Uleman, and J.A. Bargh (Eds.) *The New Unconscious*. New York: Oxford University Press, 309-333.

Dijksterhuis, A., and J. A. Bargh (2001). "The Perception-Behavior Expressway: Automatic Effects of Social Perception on Social Behavior," in Zanna, M.P. (Ed.). *Advances in Experimental Social Psychology* (Vol. 33, pp. 1-40). San Diego: Academic Press.

DON (2001). *Metric Guide for Knowledge Management Initiatives*. Washington, D.C.: Department of the Navy Chief Information Officer.

Doyle, Sir A. C. (1994). *Memoirs of Sherlock Holmes*. New York: Book of the Month Club.

Driscoll, A., B. Holland, S. Gelmon and S. Kerrigan (1996). "An Assessment Model for Service-Learning: Comprehensive Case Studies of Impact on Faculty, Students, Com-munity, and Institutions," in *Michigan Journal of Community Service Learning*, 3, 66-71.

Dufour S. and C. Cumberland (2003). *The Effectiveness of Child Welfare Interventions: A Systematic Review*. Montreal, QC: Centre of Excellence for Child Welfare.

Duncan, B., S.J. Pungente, and R. Shepherd (2000). "Media Education in Canada," in Goldstein, T. and D. Selby (Eds.), *Weaving Connections: Educating for Peace, Social and Environmental Justice*, pp. 323-341. Toronto: Sumach Press.

Dvir, R. (2006). "Knowledge City, Seen as a Collage of Human Knowledge Moments," in Carrillo, F. J. (Ed.) *Knowledge Cities: Approaches, Experiences, and Perspectives*. Oxford: Butterworth Heinemann Elsevier.

Edelman, G. and G. Tononi (2000). *A Universe of Consciousness: How Matter Becomes Imagination*. New York: Basic Books.

Eich, E., J. F. Kihlstrom, G. H. Bower, J. P. Forgas, and P. M. Niedenthal (2000). *Cognition and Emotion*. Oxford: Oxfort University Press.

Fischer, R. (1971). "Cartography of Ecstatic and Meditative States," in *Science*, 174 (12), pp. 897-904.

Flach, F. (1988). *Resilience: Discovering a New Strength at Times of Stress*. New York, NY: Fawcett Columbine.

Freire, P. (1982). "Creating Alternative Research Methods: Learning to Do It by Doing It," in Hall, B., Gillette, A. and Tandon, R. (Eds.). *Creating Knowledge: A monopoly? Participatory research in development*. New Delhi: Society for Participatory Research in Asia.

Frick, D. and L. Spears (1996). *On Becoming a Servant Leader*. San Francisco, CA: Jossey Bass Publishers.

Frith, C. D., S.J. Blakemore, and D.M. Wolpert (2000). "Abnormalities in the Awareness and Control of Action," in *Philosophical Transactions of the Royal Society of London*, 355, pp. 1771-1788.

Gardner, H. (1993). *Frames of Mind: The Theory of Multiple Intelligences* (10th Anniversary Ed.). New York: Basic Books.

Garvin, D. (2000). *Learning in Action: A Guide to Putting the Learning Organization To Work*. Boston, MA: Harvard Business School Press.

Gell-Mann, M. (1994). T*he Quark and the Jaguar: Adventures in the Simple and the Complex*. New York: Abacus.

Gilley, J. and A. Maycunich (2000). *Organizational Learning Performance and Change: An Introduction to Strategic Human Resource Development*. Cambridge, MA: Perseus Publishers.

Gladwell, M. (2000). *The Tipping Point: How Little Things Can Make a Big Difference*. Boston: Little, Brown and Company.

Goleman, G. M. (1988). *Meditative Mind: the Varieties of Meditative Experience*. New York: G. P. Putnam.

Gordon, W. T. (1997). *Marshall McLuhan: Escape into Understanding*. New York: Basic Books.

Gray, J. I., & J.E. Egbert (1993). "Using the Volunteer Experience to Strengthen the Professional Classroom Curriculum," in *Journal of Excellence in College Teaching*, 4, 105-117.

Gray, M. J., E.H. Ondaatje, R. Fricker, S. Geschwind, C.A. Goldman, T. Kaganoff, A. Robyn, M. Sundt, L. Vogelgesand, and S.P. Klein (1998). *Coupling Service and Learning in Higher Education: The Final Report of the Evaluation of the Learn and Save America*, Higher Education Program, The RAND Corporation.

Hamel, G. (2000). *Leading the Revolution*. Boston, MA: Harvard Business School Press.

Hammond, S. A. and J. Hall (1996). (Cited 9/2006 from www.thinbook.com).

Hanks, W. F. (1996). *Language & Communicative Practices*. Boulder, CO: WestviewPress.

Harris, T. L. and R.E. Hodges (Eds.) (1981). *A Dictionary of Reading and Related terms*. Newark, DE: International Reading Association.

Hawkins, J. and S. Blakeslee,.(2004). *Intelligence: How a New Understanding of the Brain Will Lead to the Creation of Truly Intelligent Machines*. New York, NY: Henry Holt and Company.

Hink, R.F., K. Kodera, O. Yamada, K. Kaga, and J.Suzuki (1980). "Binaural Interaction of a Beating Frequency Following Response," in *Audiology*, 19, pp. 36-43.

Ho, K., S. Jarvis-Selinger, M. Fedeles, C. Steele, E. Robertson, and A. Gunasingam, (2003). *Knowledge Translation and Learning Technologies: Perspectives, Considerations and Essential Approaches*. Downloaded September 2006 from:www.msfhr.org/sub-whats-resource.htm

Holmes, D., S.J. Murray, A. Peon, and G. Rail (2006). "Deconstructing the Evidence-Based Discourse in Health Sciences: Trust, Power and Fascism," in *International Journal of Evidence Based Healthcare*, 4: 180-186.

Horvath, J., L. Sasson, J. Sharon, A. Parker (2000). White Paper. *Intermediaries: A Study of Knowledge Roles in Connected Organizations*. Cambridge, MA: Institute for Knowledge Management.

Huseman, R. C. and J. P. Goodman. (1999). *Leading with Knowledge: The Nature of Competition in the 21ˢᵗ Century*. London, UK: SAGE Publications.

Illingworth, D.J. (2001). *The Facts on File Dictionary of Computer Science*. New York: Market House Books, Ltd.

Jacobsen, N., D. Butterill, and P. Goering (2003). "Development of a Framework for Knowledge Translation: Understanding the User Context," in *Journal of Health Services Research & Policy*, Vol. 8, No. 2, pp. 94-99.

Jevning, R., R.K. Wallace, and M. Beidenbach (1992). "The Physiology of Meditation: A Review," in *Neuroscience and Behavioral Reviews*, 16, pp. 415-424.

Kanter, R. M. (2005). "Execution: The Un-Idea," in *Strategy + Business*, Issue 41, Winter. Booz Allen Hamilton, p. 39.

Karadimos, M. (2006). "Action Research: A Formal Social Movement Strategy." Retrieved on September 1, 2006 from http://www.mathguide.com/research/ActionResearch.doc

Katzenbach, J. R. and D.K. Smith (1993). *The Wisdom of Teams: Creating the High-Performance Organization*. Boston: Harvard Business School Press.

Kawachi, I., D. Kim, A. Coutts, and S. Subramanian (2004). "Commentary: Reconciling the Three Accounts of Social Capital," in *Internal Journal of Epidemiology*, 33: pp. 682-690.

Kehoe, J. and N. Fische (2002). *Mind Power for Children*. Vancouver, BC: Zoetic, Inc.

Kleiner, K. (2005). "Carving Up the Rainbow," in Science NOW 23 May: 2, p. 16.

Kelly, S. and M. Allison (1999). *The Complexity Advantage: How the Sciences of Complexity Can Help Your Business Achieve Peak Performance*. New York, NY: McGraw Hill.

Knowles, M.S., E.F. Holton, and R.A. Swanson (1998). *The Adult Learner: The Definitive Classic in Adult Education and Human Resource Development*. Houston, TX: Gulf Publishing Company.

Knuf, L., G. Aschersleben and W. Prinz (2001). "An Analysis of Ideomotor Action," in *Journal of Experimental Psychology*: General, 130, pp. 779-798.

Kolb, D. A. (1984). *Experiential Learning: Experience as the Source of Learning and Development*. New Jersey: Prentice-Hall.

Kotler, P. and W. Roberto (1989). *Social Marketing: Strategies for Changing Public Behavior*. New York, NY: The Free Press.

Kotler, P. N. Roberto and N. Lee (2002). *Social Marketing: Improving the Quality of Life*. New York, NY: SAGE.

Kotter, (1996). *Leading Change*. Boston, MA: Harvard Business School Press.

Kuntz, P. G. (1968). *The Concept of Order*, University of Washington Press, Seattle, WA.

Landry, R., N. Amara and M. Lamari (2001). "Utilization of Social Science Knowledge in Canada," in *Research Policy 2001*; 30, pp. 333-349.

Lavis, J., D. Robertson, J. Woodside, C. McLeod, and J. Abelson (2003). "How Can Research Organization More Effectively Transfer Research Knowledge to Decision Makers?" in *The Milbank Quarterly*, 81 (92), pp. 221-248.

Lee, R. G., and T. Garvin (2003). "Moving from Information Transfer to Information Exchange in Health and Health Care," in *Social Science & Medicine*, 56:449-464.

Lennick, D. and F. Kiel (2005). *Moral Intelligence: Enhancing Business Performance & Leadership Success*. Upper Saddle River, NJ: Wharton School Publishing.

Leonard, D., and W. Swap. (2004). *Deep Smarts: How to Cultivate and Transfer Enduring Business Wisdom*. Boston, MA: Harvard Business School Press.

Leonard-Barton, D. (1995). *Wellsprings of Knowledge: Building and Sustaining the Sources of Innovation*. Boston, MA: Harvard Business School Press.

Lerner, J. (2004). *Learning disabilities*. Boston: Houghton Mifflin.

Marion, R. (1999). *The Edge of Organization: Chaos and Complexity Theories of Formal Social Systems*. Thousand Oaks, CA: SAGE Publications Ltd.

Marquardt, M. J. (1999). Action Learning in Action: *Transforming Problems and People for World-Class Organizational Learning*. Palo Alto, CA: Davies-Black Publishing.

Marquardt, M. and A. Reynolds (1994). *The Global Learning Organization*. Burr Ridge, IL: Irwin.

Marsh, J. T., W.S. Brown and J.C. Smith (1975). "Far-Field Recorded Frequency-Following Responses: Correlates of Low Pitch Auditory Perception in Humans." in *Electroencephalography and Clinical Neurophysiology*, 38, pp. 113-119.

Mavromatis, A. (1991). *Hypnagogia*. New York: Routledge.

McDonald, J. and E. Klein (2003). "Networking for Teacher Learning: Toward a Theory of Effective Design," in *Teachers College* Record Volume 105, Number 8, pp. 1606-1621.

McLuhan, M. (1964). *Understanding Media*: The Extensions of Man. New York: McGraw-Hill.

Merriam, S. B. and R.S. Caffarella (1999). *Learning in Adulthood: A Comprehensive Guide*. (2nd ed.) San Francisco: Jossey-Bass Publishers.

Mezirow, J. (2000). *Learning as Transformation: Critical Perspectives on a Theory in Progress*. San Francisco: Jossey-Bass.

Mezirow, J., and Associates (1990). *Fostering Critical Reflection in Adulthood*. San Francisco: Jossey-Bass.

Mezirow, J. (1992). *Transformative Dimensions of Adult Learning*. San Francisco: Jossey-Bass Publishers.

Newman, J. (2000). "Action Research: A Brief Overview; Forum; Qualitative Social Research." Retrieved on September 2, 2006 from http//qualitative-research.net/fqs-texte/1-00/1-00newman-e.html

Neo, B. and G. Chen (2007). *Dynamic Governance: Embedding Culture, Capabilities And Change in Singapore*. New Jersey: World Scientific.

Nikolova Eddins, S. and D. Williams (1997). "Strategies for Sustainable Integration of Research Activities with Established Curriculum," in *Journal on Excellence in College Teaching* 8 (3), pp. 95-108.

Nisbett, R. & L. Ross (1980). *Human Inference: Strategies and Shortcomings of Social Judgment*. Englewood Cliffs, NJ: Prentice-Hall.

Norton, B.L., K.R. McLeroy, J.N. Burdine, M.R.J. Felix, and A.M. Dorsey (2002). "Community Capacity: Concept, Theory and Methods," in DiClemente, R.J., R.A. Crosby, and M.C. Kegler (Eds.). *Emerging Theories in Health Promotion Practice and Research: Strategies for Improving Public Health*. San Francisco: Josey-Bass, 194-227.)

O'Dell, C. (2001). *Stages of Implementation: A Guide for Your Journey to Knowledge Management Best Practices*. Houston, TX: APQC.

Ontario Ministry of Education (1986). Media Literacy Resource Guide. Ontario: Ministry of Education.

Oster, G. (1973). "Auditory Beats in the Brain," in *Scientific American*, 229, pp. 94-102.

Park, P. (2001). "Knowledge and participatory research," in Reason, P. and H. Bradbury (Eds.), *Handbook of Action Research: Participative Inquiry and Practice* (pp. 81-90). Thousand Oaks: Sage.

Pawson, R., T. Greenhalgh, G. Harvey, and K. Walshe (2005). "Realist Review—A New Method of Sysematic Review Designed for Complex Policy Interventions," in *Journal of Health Services Research Policy* 10(1), pp. S21-34.

Pinker, S. (2007). "The Mystery of Consciousness," in *Time*, January 29, 2007, pp. 59-65.

Polyani, M. (1958). *Personal Knowledge: Towards a Post-Critical Philosophy*. Chicago: The University of Chicago Press.

Porter, D., A. Bennet, R. Turner, and D. Wennergren (2002). *The Power of Team: The Making of a CIO*. Washington DC: Department of Navy Chief Information Officer.

Potthoff, D. E., Dinsmore, J., Eifler, K., Stirtz, G., Walsh, T., and Ziebarth, J. (2000). "Preparing for Democracy and diversity: The impact of a Community-Based Field Experience on Pre-Service Teachers' Knowledge, Skills and Attitudes," in *Action in Teacher Education*, 22(1), pp. 79-92.

Putnam, R. D. (2000). *Bowling Alone: The Collapse and Revival of American community*. New York: Simon and Shuster.

Reason, P. (2000). *Handbook of Qualitative Research: Three Approaches to Participatory Inquiry*. Thousand Oaks, CA:Sage.

Revans, R. (1998). In Marquardt, M. (1999). *Action Learning in Action: Transforming Problems and People for World-Class Organizational Learning*. Palo Alto, CA: Davies-Black Publishing.

Revans, R. (1971). *Developing Effective Managers: A New Approach to Business Education*. Westport,CT: Praeger Publishers.

Richardson, G. E. (2002). "The Metatheory of Resilience and Resiliency," in Journal of *Clinical Psychology*, 58(3), pp. 307-321.

Ritchey, D. (2003). The H.I.S.S. of the A.S.P.: *Understanding the Anomalously Sensitive Person*. Terra Alta: Headline Books, Inc.

Robson, C. (1993). *Real World Research: A Resource for Social Scientists and Practitioner-Researchers*. Oxford: Blackwell.

Rogers, E. M. (1995). *Diffusion of Innovations* (4ᵗʰ ed.). New York: The Free Press.

Rogers, W. T. (1978). "The Contribution of Kinesic Illustrators toward the Comprehension of Verbal Behavior within Utterances," in *Human Communication Research*, 5, pp. 54-62.

Rose, C. and M.J. Nicholl (1997). *Accelerated Learning for the 21ˢᵗ century*. New York: Delacorte Press.

Ross, P. E. (August, 2006). "The Expert Mind," in *Scientific American*, 64-71.

Schank, R. E. (1990). *Tell Me a Story: Narrative and Intelligence*. Evanston, IL: Northwestern University Press.

Senge, P. (1990). *The Fifth Discipline*. New York: Doubleday.

Senge, P., C.O. Scharmer, J. Jaworski, and B.S. Flowers (2004). *Presence: Human Purpose and the Field of the Future*. Cambridge, MA: The Society for Organizational Learning.

Shapiro, B. (2004). "Government and Universities: Challenges in the Formation of Public Policy." The 2004 David C. Smith Lecture, October 14.

Sharp, C. (2005). "The Improvement of Public Sector Delivery: Supporting Evidence Based Practice through Action Research," in *Scottish Executive Social Research*, Edinburgh, Scotland. *Shorter Oxford English Dictionary* (5ᵗʰ Ed.) (2002). Oxford: Oxford University Press.

Simmons, A. (2001). *The Story Factor: Inspiration, Influence, and Persuasion through The Art of Storytelling*. Cambridge, MA: Perseus Publishing.

Slocum, T. A. and S. L. Egbert (1991). Cartographic Data Display," in Taylor, D.R.F. (Ed.). *Geographic Information Systems: the Microcomputer and Modern Cartography*. Oxford: Pergamon, pp. 167-200.

Smith, J.C., J.T. Marsh, S. Greenberg, and W.S. Brown (1978). "Human Auditory Frequency-Following Responses to a Missing Fundamental," in *Science*, 201, pp. 639-641.

Snowden, D. (1999). "The Paradox of Story: Simplicity and Complexity in Strategy," in *Journal of Strategy and Scenario Planning*. November.

Sousa, D. A. (2006). *How the Brain Learns*. Thousand Oaks, CA: Corwin Press.

Srivastva, S. and D.L. Cooperrider (Eds.). (1990). *Appreciative Management and Leadership*. San Francisco: Jossey-Bass.

SSHRC (2005a). Knowledge Impact on Society (KIS) Program Description. Canada.

Sternberg, R. J. (2003). *Wisdom, Intelligence and Creativity Synthesized*. Cambridge, UK: Cambridge University Press.

Stonier, T. (1997). *Information and Meaning*: An Evolutionary Perspective. New York, NY: Springer.

Stonier, T. (1992). *Beyond Information: The Natural History of Intelligence*. New York, NY: Springer-Verlag.

Sveiby, K. E. (1997). *The New Organizational Wealth: Managing & Measuring Knowledge-Based Assets*. San Francisco, CA: Berrett-Koehler Publishers, Inc.

Swann, R., S. Bosanko, R. Cohen, R. Midgley and K.M. Seed (1982). *The Brain—A User's Manual*. New York: G. P. Putnam & Sons.

Szreter, S. and M. Woolcock (2004). "Health by Association? Social Capital, Social Theory, and the Political Economy of Public Health," in *International Journal of Epidemiology*, 33: pp. 650-667.

Taylor, D.R.F. (1997). "Maps and Mapping in the Information Era," in *ICC Proceedings*, Vol. 1. Stockholm: Swedish Cartographic Society, pp. 1-10.

Taylor, D.R.F. (2003). *The Concept of Cybercartography. Maps and the Internet*. Cambridge: Elsevier.

Tesch, R. (1990). *Qualitative Research: Analysis Types and Software Tools*. New York: The Falmer Press.

Tichy, N. and M. Devanna (1986). *The Transformational Leader*. New York, NY: John Wiley & Sons.

Tinto, V. (1998). "Colleges as Communities: Taking Research on Student Persistence Seriously," in *The Review of Higher Education*. 21:2, p. 171.

Tomblin, M. S. (2007). "Group and Organizational Learning Effects from Multiparticipant DSS Usage" in Holsapple, C. W. and Burstein, F. (Eds.). *Handbook on Decision Support Systems*. New York: Springer-Verlag.

Tough, A. (1971). *The Adult's Learning Projects: A Fresh Approach to Theory and Practice in Adult Learning*. Toronto: Ontario Institute for Studies in Education.

von Krogh, G. & J. Roos, (1995). *Organizational Epistemology*. New York, NY:MACMILLAN PRESS LTD.

Webster's New World Dictionary of Computer Terms (5th Ed) (1994). New York: Macmillan.

Weick, K. and K. Sutcliffe (2001). *Managing the Unexpected*. Boston, MA: Jossey Bass Publishers.

Wenger, E. (1998). "Communities of Practice: Learning as a Social System," in *Systems Thinking*, June 1998, pp. 1-10.

West, M.A. 91980). "Meditation and the EEG," in *Psychological Medicine*, 10, pp. 369-375.

West, P. (2004). *Applied Health Research: A Briefing Paper on Knowledge Transfer, Dissemination and Utilization*. Downloaded September 2006 from www.continuousinnovation.ca

White, G. W., M. Suchowierska, and M. Campbell (2004). "Developing and Systematically Implementing Participatory Action Research," in *Archives of Physical Medical Rehabilitation*, 85, 2, pp. S3-S12.

Wiig, K. (2004). *People-Focused Knowledge Management: How Effective Decision Making Leads to Corporate Success*. New York, NY: Elsevier.

Wilson, E. O. (1998). *Consilience: The Unity of Knowledge*. New York: Alfred A. Knopf.

ABOUT THE AUTHORS AND CONTRIBUTORS

Alex and David Bennet

Alex and David Bennet are co-founders of the Mountain Quest Institute, a research and retreat center nestled in the Allegheny Mountains focused on achieving growth and understanding through quests for knowledge, consciousness and meaning. See *www.mountainquestinstitute.com*. The Institute's aggressive research agenda is focused on knowledge mobilization, decision-making in complex adaptive situations; developing a new theory of adult learning; individual and organizational learning; and consciousness studies, including new ways of perceiving, thinking and knowing.

The Institute is the home of the Intelligent Complex Adaptive System model for organizations. This ground-breaking work on developing a new theory of the firm was brought to maturity with the publication of Organizational Survival in the New World: the Intelligent Complex Adaptive System (ICAS) in 2004 (Elsevier). The ICAS concept enables organizations to react more quickly and fluidly to today's fast-changing, dynamic business environment. ICAS, based on research in complexity and neuroscience—and incorporating networking theory, knowledge management and organizational learning—turns the living system metaphor into a reality for organizations. Organizational Survival in the New World combines theory and practice in a new vision of the organization—all embedded within a thorough description in terms of structure, culture, strategy, leadership, knowledge workers and integrative competencies.

Alex, internationally recognized as an expert in knowledge management and an agent for organizational change, served as the Chief Knowledge Officer and Deputy Chief Information Officer for Enterprise Integration for the Department of the Navy, and was co-chair of the Federal Knowledge Management Working Group. Among her many awards and honors, Dr. Bennet is the recipient of the Department of the Navy Distinguished and Superior Public Service Awards, the National Performance Review Hammer Award from the Vice President, and the National Knowledge and Intellectual Property Management Task Force Award for distinguished service and exemplary leadership. Dr. Bennet is a Delta Epsilon Sigma and a Golden Key National Honor Society graduate. She has a Ph.D. in Human and Organizational Systems and holds degrees and certificates in Management for Organizational Effectiveness, Human Development, English, Marketing, Total Quality Management, System Dynamics and Defense Acquisition Management. She may be reached at *alex@mountainquestinstitute.com*

Dave Bennet's experience spans many years of service in the Military, Civil Service and Private Industry, including fundamental research in underwater acoustics and nuclear physics, frequent design and facilitation of organizational interventions, and serving as technical director and program manager of a major DOD acquisition program. Most recently, Dave was CEO, then Chairman of the Board and Chief Knowledge Officer for Dynamic Systems, Inc., a professional services firm located in Alexandria, Virginia. Dave is a Phi Beta Kappa, Sigma Pi Sigma, and Suma Cum

Laude graduate of the University of Texas. He holds degrees in Mathematics, Physics, Nuclear Physics, Liberal Arts, and Human and Organizational Development. He may be reached at *dbennet@mountainquestinstitute.com*

Katherine M. Fafard

Katherine is a private consultant based in Ottawa, Canada. Her consulting practice, Basswood Associates, helps organizations find solutions by linking the practical knowledge that exists within the organization to external research and theoretical considerations for the purposes of improving policy and program responses in real time, in other words mobilizing knowledge to create value in a public sector context. Clients include Canadian universities, departments and agencies of the Canadian federal government, the Government of Saskatchewan, and municipal organizations.

Katherine's work in knowledge mobilization follows a number of years spent as a public sector manager specializing in intergovernmental relations, labour market and immigration policies where research and theory were frequently used to inform practice. In the university sector, Katherine has chosen to focus her attention on extending the engagement of academic research institutes in knowledge transfer activities related to public policy. For example, Katherine was responsible for creating and implementing the first professional outreach program and the first research agenda of the Saskatchewan Institute of Public Policy *(www.uregina.ca/sipp/)* conceived as an innovative university-government partnership linking the research community with policy practitioners.

A graduate of Trinity College, University of Toronto (B.A., History Specialist, English Minor), and Carleton University, Ottawa (M.S., Public Administration), Katherine's on-going research interests include knowledge mobilization, research use in the public sector, public policy design, and Canadian intellectual history.

Katherine can be reached at *kfafard@basswood.ca* or at 613-830-5302.

Marc Fonda

Marc Fonda received a doctorate in humanities from the University of Ottawa in 1995 after defending his work on the emergence of a new concept of selfhood in contemporary western society (see www.magma.ca/~mfonda). Since then he has worked as a freelance writer and editor, researcher and applied ethicist while publishing on occasion.

In 1998, he entered employment with the Social Sciences and Humanities Research Council of Canada (SSHRC). Dr. Fonda who has been responsible for developing and managing a suite of programs dealing with social policy research (such as the PRI-SSHRC Policy Research Roundtable Series, the Policy, Family and Work Research networks and symposia), was a member of the Social Cohesion Research Network, helped either develop, support or renew the Research Date Centres Network, the Metropolis Project, the Social Economy Suite, the Oceans Management Research Network, and the Knowledge Impacts in Society program, as well as the Homelessness and Diversity Issues in Canada and the Multiculturalism Issues in Canada programs.

Since October 2005, Dr. Fonda has been the acting Director of Strategic Programs and Joint Initiatives at SSHRC, managing a portfolio of 25 programs and partnerships, many of which emphasize knowledge mobilization in order to facilitate the uptake of research results in Canadian Federal policy and program development. Marc may be reached at *marc.fonda@sshrc.ca*

Ted Lomond

Ted is a project manager with the Leslie Harris Centre of *Regional* Policy and Development at *Memorial* University of Newfoundland and a facilitator of management training with the Lifelong Learning *Division* of Memorial University. He also develops and delivers training with the Community Capacity Building Program, which provides leadership and management training to not-for-profit organizations.

Prior to joining the university, Ted worked as a business/economic development consultant providing services such as feasibility analysis, community economic development, strategic planning, business counseling and business plan development. His clients comprised such public and private businesses and not-for-profit groups as the Atlantic Canada Opportunities Agency, Memorial University, Newfoundland and Labrador Federation of Cooperatives, Newfoundland and Labrador Women's Institute, Marnier Resource Opportunities Network, Inc.

Ted has held senior positions with the Government of Newfoundland and Labrador including: Executive Director, Federal/Provincial Agreements, Department of Industry, Trade and Rural Development; Executive Director Regional Development and Economic Programs, Intergovernmental Affairs Secretariat, Executive Council; and Special Projects Manager, Department of Development and Rural Renewal.

Ted has completed Memorial University's Executive Development Program and Public Sector Leadership and Management Development Program. He holds a Masters in Business Administration from Heriot-Watt University and a Masters Certificate in Project Management from York University. He holds a Project Management Professional certification from the Project Management Institute, certified Small Business Counsellor certification from the Canadian Institute of Small Business Counselors, and an Advanced Diploma in Credit Management from Dunn & Bradstreet Canada. He may be reached at *lomond@mun.ca*

Laurent Messier

Laurent, a Senior Program Officer, Strategic and Joint Initiatives Division, with the Social Sciences and Humanities Research Council, is responsible for the development and implementation of new strategic programs of which the Knowledge Impact in Society is one. Prior to this position he has served as a Program Officer and Training Coordinator and a Program Officer on the History Committee. He also spent 8 years as a Heritage Program Consultant for the City of Ottawa, promoting, researching and teaching local history.

Laurent holds a Masters Degree in Canadian History from the University of Ottawa. His many qualifications and certifications cover the sphere from volunteer

215

service to professional expertise including group dynamics, human resources management, performance coaching and evaluation classification systems. He has authored or co-authored multiple articles on history and entrepreneurship. He may be reached at *laurent.messier@sshrc.ca*

Nicole Vaugeois

Nicole is a Professor at Malaspina University-College in the Department of Recreation and Tourism Management where she has been teaching since 1995. Nicole holds a Ph.D. from Michigan State University and an MA in International Leisure Studies from the World Leisure International Centre of Excellence in the Netherlands.

Nicole's research interests are in rural community economic development, primarily through amenity based industries like recreation and tourism. She has conducted numerous community-based research projects with rural communities throughout British Columbia. She believes strongly in engaging undergraduate students in research projects and has developed models that result in win-win scenarios for learners and external partners.

Together with a number of other academic and non academic partners, Nicole is leading an initiative called the Tourism Research Innovation Project to link those developing tourism in rural areas of British Columbia to the knowledge assets they need. Combining a host of outreach-based knowledge mobilization techniques, the TRIP project is the first of its kind to link tourism research to in rural areas. She may be reached at *vaugeois@mala.be.ca*

Fleur Flohil

Inkfish is a design company based in Porto/Portugal with a large experience in graphic and layout design for books and magazines. Fleur Flohil, co-founder and managing director of the company, holds a Bachelors degree in Fine Arts and Design from the Art and Design Academy of St. Joost in Breda/the Netherlands. Fleur has more than 12 years experience in design, having managed several large design projects for publishers and magazines. She may be reached at *fleur@inkfish-design.com*

INDEX

The Mountain Quest Institute

MQI is a research, retreat and learning center dedicated to helping individuals achieve personal and professional growth and organizations create and sustain high performance in a rapidly changing, uncertain, and increasingly complex world.

Current research is focused on Human and Organizational Development, Knowledge Management and KMb, Values, Complexity, Neuroscience and Adult Learning. MQI's goal is to build a long-term, not-for-profit research center with a small cadre of dedicated researchers doing full-time research, creating leading-edge ideas and programs that will contribute to the understanding, improvement and survival of life on the planet. MQI has three quests: The Quest for Knowledge, The Quest for Consciousness; and The Question for Meaning. MQI is scientific, humanistic and spiritual and finds no contradiction in this combination.

MQI is the birthplace of *Organizational Survival in the New World: The Intelligent Complex Adaptive System* (Elsevier, 2004), a new theory of the firm that turns the living system metaphor into a reality for organizations. Based on research in complexity and neuroscience—and incorporating networking theory and knowledge management—this book is filled with new ideas married to practical advice, all embedded within a thorough description of the new organization in terms of structure, culture, strategy, leadership, knowledge workers and integrative competencies.

Mountain Quest Institute, situated four hours from Washington, D.C. in the Monongahela Forest of the Allegheny Mountains, is part of the Mountain

Quest complex which includes a Retreat Center, Inn, and the old Farm House and Outbuildings. The Retreat Center is designed to provide full learning experiences, including hosting training, workshops, retreats and business meetings for professional and executive groups of 25 people or less. The Center includes a 20,000 volume research library, a conference room, community center, computer room, 12 themed bedrooms, a workout and Jacuzzi room, and a four-story tower with a glass ceiling for enjoying the magnificent view of the valley during the day and the stars at night. Situated on a 450 acres farm, there is a labyrinth, creeks, four miles of mountain trails, and horses, Long Horn cattle, Llamas and a myriad of wild neighbors. Other neighbors include the Snowshoe Ski Resort, the National Radio Astronomy Observatory and the CASS Railroad.

www.mountainquestinstitute.com
www.mountainquestinn.com

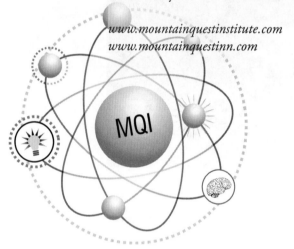